SURVIVOR'S GUIDE TO

TECHNICAL WRITING

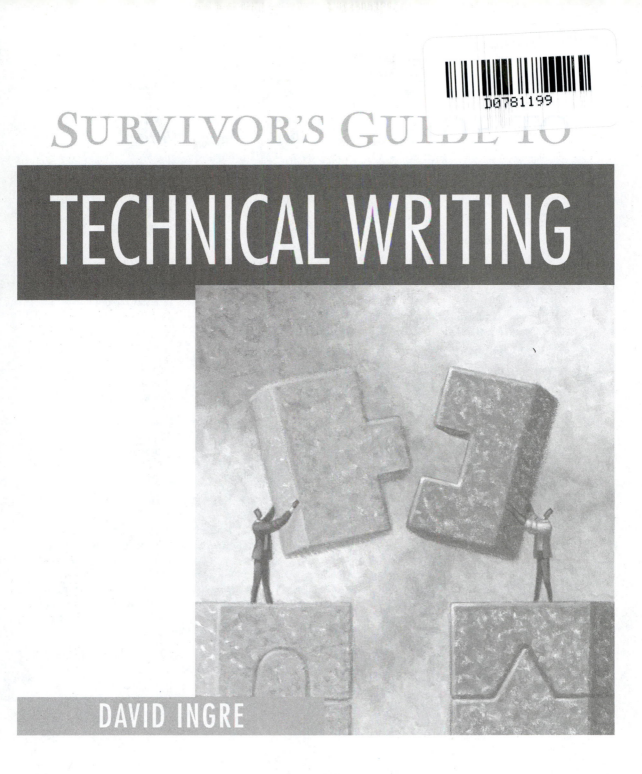

DAVID INGRE

SOUTH-WESTERN™

THOMSON LEARNING

Australia • Canada • Mexico • Singapore • Spain • United Kingdom • United States

SOUTH-WESTERN
THOMSON LEARNING™

Survivor's Guide to Technical Writing
by David Ingre

Editor-in-Chief
Jack Calhoun

Vice President/Executive Publisher
Dave Shaut

Team Leader
Karen Schmohe

Acquisitions Editor
Joseph Vocca

Project Manager
Penny Shank

Contributing Writer
Susan Carson, LastWord

Editorial Consultants
Sheridan Publication Services, Marianne Miller, and Vandalay Group Inc.

Production Manager
Tricia Matthews Boies

Production Editor
Tim Bailey

Executive Marketing Manager
Carol Volz

Channel Manager
Chris McNamee

Marketing Coordinator
Lori Pegg

Art and Design Coordinator
Tippy McIntosh

Manufacturing Coordinator
Kevin Kluck

Editorial Assistant
Stephanie L. White

Production Assistant
Nancy Stamper

Cover Design
Paul Neff Design

Cover Illustration
Rob Colvin/Artville

Internal Design and Composition
settingPace
Cincinnati, Ohio

Printer
Von Hoffmann Graphics
Eldridge, Iowa

Photo Credits
All photos © copyright
PhotoDisc, Inc. 1997-2001

YOUR COURSE PLANNING JUST GOT EASIER!

The *Survivor's Guide to Technical Writing* is a text like no other! Designed for professionals and managers who need to know the basics, this text will guide you through the world of technical writing. Using a conversational style, *Survivor's Guide to Technical Writing* is a comprehensive, easy-to-use guide for key workplace communication skills. Integrating the most current technology, this book reflects the most current topics and issues in technical communication.

Looking for other career-enhancement titles for today's professional? Explore these additional Survivor's Guides from South-Western!

Survivor's Guide to Finance
by Bergeron

Finance is the universal language of business! *Survivor's Guide to Finance* makes financial decision making clear and concise to managers of all levels. Users with no formal training in accounting or finance will find this book a solid source of financial understanding.

Text/CD Package   0-538-72517-6

Survivor's Guide to the Legal Environment
by Adamson

Success in the workplace often depends on your ability to understand the basics of contracts, business organizations, and other day-to-day legal issues. Join us as we guide you in exploring the essentials and foundations of the law.

Text/CD Package   0-538-72523-0

Survivor's Guide to Small Business
by Townsley

Designed for the entrepreneur, *Survivor's Guide to Small Business* emphasizes practical and useful information for starting a business. The content is comprehensive and universal and features the most current technology resources.

Text/CD Package   0-538-72573-7

SOUTH-WESTERN
★
THOMSON LEARNING ™

Join us on the Internet at www.swep.com

HOW TO USE THIS BOOK

Survivor's Guide to Technical Writing is designed to focus on the most important elements of contemporary technical communication. It presents the essentials of communication based on a unique and dynamic model that integrates context, message, audience, purpose, and product (CMAPP). This CMAPP model provides a consistent tool and strategy that can be applied in every communication situation. It is an excellent foundation for all communicators, regardless of their level of experience.

Survivor's Guide to Technical Writing focuses on the essentials of technical writing and communication. It covers the basics of technical communication—writing process, document and visual design, letters, memos, e-mail, reports, proposals, presentations, and employment communication. Because of the increasing importance of electronic communication and the Internet, they receive particular attention. Within chapter content and in chapter activities, the text also highlights contemporary issues such as ethics, critical thinking, and teams.

CMAPP MODEL Using *Survivor's Guide to Technical Writing,* you can master material by seeing an example, examining the theory behind it, and practicing its application in ways that are relevant and useful. At the text's core is the CMAPP analytical model for technical communication, built around five related elements:

- ◆ **Context:** the overall situation, relevant relationships, circumstances, and so on
- ◆ **Message:** the relevant main points and significant details
- ◆ **Audience:** the person or people to whom the communication is addressed—explicitly and/or indirectly
- ◆ **Purpose:** the originator's reason or reasons for communicating—explicit and/or indirect—and expectations with regard to the audience
- ◆ **Product:** the "shape" of the communication (e.g., a letter or an oral presentation) or its function (e.g., a proposal)

The text stresses the nonlinear, dynamic relationships of these components and consistently emphasizes the critical importance to effective technical communication of an analysis of their interaction.

TEXT FEATURES Take advantage of the many teaching and learning aids offered with *Survivor's Guide to Technical Writing.* These include:

- ◆ Numerous **checklists, summaries,** and **lists** designed to highlight the essentials of key technical communication skills.
- ◆ A **Grammar and Style Guide,** which reviews the key elements of grammar, punctuation, and style essential to good writing.
- ◆ A variety of end-of-chapter activities and cases, including:
  - ◆ **Critical Thinking Activities,** which are short-answer questions based on the ideas presented in the chapter.
  - ◆ **Skills Applications,** which allow students to apply the skills they have learned in the chapter.
  - ◆ **Contemporary Issues Cases,** which ask students to analyze a current issue and answer questions about it.

- ◆ **Case Studies,** which are built around four fictitious companies and require higher-level thinking skills, writing, and integration of text concepts.
- ◆ **TechLink** Internet resources listed in the margins for quick reference and links to real-time resources.
- ◆ **Document illustrations** throughout the text.

SUPPORT MATERIALS *Survivor's Guide to Technical Writing* is accompanied by the following materials designed to extend and enhance learning:

Instructor's Resource CD (**ISBN: 0-538-72580-X**)   For each chapter, the Instructor's Resource CD includes the following:

- ◆ Lecture Outline
- ◆ Contemporary Issues Case
- ◆ Reinforcement Activities
- ◆ Career Activities
- ◆ Lecture Extension
- ◆ Communication Clips (for the *Workplace Communication in Action* video cases)
- ◆ TechLinks (related web sites)
- ◆ Document Samples
- ◆ Sample Solutions for text and CD activities and cases
- ◆ PowerPoint presentation

Additionally, the Instructor's Resource CD contains an extensive bank of proof-reading and editing activities with solutions.

For each chapter, the Instructor's Resource CD contains Contemporary Issue and Lecture Extension features designed to extend course content beyond the essentials. Pick and choose from these learning modules to enrich basic course coverage.

CHAPTER	CONTENT
Chapter One	14 Diversity Tips
	Listening
Chapter Two	New Work Environment
	Nonverbal Communication
Chapter Three	Critical Thinking and Problem Solving
	Webbing and Clustering Techniques
Chapter Four	Media Literacy and Bias
	Guidelines for Conducting a Survey
Chapter Five	Culturally Correct Presentations
	Web Design Guidelines
Chapter Six	Ethics of Persuasion
	Training Manuals
	Logical Fallacies
Chapter Seven	Customer Service
	Goodwill Letters
Chapter Eight	Finding Information on the Web
	Specialized Reports
Chapter Nine	Team Development
	Leading Meetings
Chapter Ten	PowerPoint Guidelines
	Participating in Meetings
Chapter Eleven	Negotiation and Conflict Resolution
	Application Forms

Student Data CD (ISBN: 0-538-97029-4) For each chapter, the Student Data CD packaged with your text includes the following:

- Contemporary Issues Case
- Reinforcement Activities
- Career Activities
- TechLinks (related web sites)
- Document Samples
- PowerPoint presentation

The Student Data CD also contains an extensive bank of proofreading and editing activities.

For each chapter, the Student Data CD contains Contemporary Issue and Lecture Extension features designed to extend course content beyond the essentials. Pick and choose from these learning modules to enrich basic course coverage.

words@work (ISBN: 0-538-69049-6) This CD provides interactive exercises to develop grammar, punctuation, editing, and workplace communication skills.

WebGuide: Your Online Career Search (ISBN: 0-538-72204-5) With this CD, users can search for up-to-date career information, resume and job search strategies, and job opportunities on the Internet.

ELECTRONIC TEST BANK The *ExamView Pro*® electronic test bank (ISBN: 0-538-72579-6) provides 385 multiple choice, true/false, and short answer questions designed to assess student learning. We suggest that objective tests be used to measure students' understanding of the fundamental concepts of technical writing. While some questions will measure a student's ability to apply a technical communication concept, most will simply measure understanding of concepts.

VIDEO CASES Each text chapter is correlated to the *Workplace Communication in Action Video and Casebook Package* (ISBN: 0-538-97703-5). The video cases are accompanied by a casebook and can be used as an additional case study for students.

REVIEWERS

Dr. Linda Ginter Brown
University of Cincinnati
Cincinnati, Ohio

Stephen Kaczmarek
Columbus State Community College
Columbus, Ohio

Patricia Kato
Chattanooga State Technical Community College
Chattanooga, Tennessee

Katherine Ploeger
California State University Stanislaus
Turlock, California

Marilyn E. Price
Kirkwood Community College
Cedar Rapids, Iowa

TABLE OF CONTENTS

CHAPTER 1

Building a Foundation

Your success in every phase of your life will depend in part on how effectively you communicate, both orally and in writing. Technical communication has become an increasingly important area of communication in general. This chapter provides an overview of technical communication—its relevance and characteristics, the importance of ethical communication, the ways in which different cultures affect how you communicate, and effective communication in a team environment.

The Relevance of Technical Communication

You might think that a book about technical communication only applies to someone who intends to write a manual or sell a product. But did you know that the field includes the following types of communication?

- Letters or memos to, from, or between people who work in any kind of company, organization, or association, from multinational conglomerates to home-based businesses, and from professional or trade associations to charities such as the American Cancer Society.
- Advertising and promotional material, from magazine advertisements to business cards.
- A host of other documents, from the annual report of a firm such as General Motors to your own income tax return and from the operating and repair manuals for specialized equipment such as CAT scanners to the last parking ticket you received.

- Oral communication, from formally presenting a new product line to a large group of prospective clients to informally explaining your opinion at a small meeting.

You'll use technical communication throughout your professional and personal life. And the more effectively you communicate, the greater your likelihood of success. Suppose that you and your friend both study hard in a particular course and have some valuable ideas to contribute. If you have learned to express your ideas precisely and effectively but your friend hasn't, which of you is likely to get better grades? Similarly, if you are an employer deciding between two applicants with roughly equivalent qualifications and experience and only one demonstrates communication skills that will represent your organization well, which applicant will you hire?

As you read this book, think of it as a set of practical guidelines that can boost your chances of success in a wide range of areas.

Characteristics of Technical Communication

In recent years, the field of technical communication has been developing a style of its own. This is particularly true of written material. We can clarify some of the distinctions between technical communication and what I will loosely label "traditional prose" by examining five salient features of technical communication:

- Necessity for a specific audience
- Integration of visual elements
- Ease of selective access
- Timeliness
- Structure

Necessity for a Specific Audience

Much traditional prose is what we might term author-driven. Someone makes a discovery, has a revelation, develops a theory, wants to share feelings with others, wishes to entertain, or simply believes that a particular story will generate profit by appealing to a large number of anonymous readers. And so the person begins to write, believing that there will be "an audience out there" who will want to read what he or she has written. But no one gets up one morning and says, "I want to write the definitive business letter" or "Today I'll fulfill my dream of writing a lengthy report."

Technical communication is **audience-driven.** People create it to respond to a specific audience's need for information. Whether you are writing a letter, a memo, a report, or an e-mail, you always tailor it to a specific audience. In fact, if you don't already know exactly who your audience is, you don't really have

Tech Link

Visit the following two sites to learn more about the field of technical communication: *www.stc.org/* The Society for Technical Communication and *www.techcommonline.org* Journal of the Society for Technical Communication anything to say. The better you know your audience, the more effectively you'll be able to communicate. This principle also applies to oral technical communication.

Integration of Visual Elements

Great literature would be just as great if it were handwritten on loose-leaf pages rather than printed in a book. By contrast, the effectiveness of advertising or promotional material (such as a brochure, a flyer, or a sales presentation) relies at least as much on presentation as on content. The term *visual elements* refers to everything from illustrations, such as diagrams or charts, to headings and type. Careful integration of ideas and presentation is essential to effective technical communication.

Ease of Selective Access

Literary authors normally expect you to read every word, rather than to skim quickly, looking for the main points. They assume that you, as a reader, are willing to devote your full attention to the writing from start to finish. At the same time, you recognize that your understanding of the text is likely conditional on your having read all of it. By contrast, technical writers assume that readers will have other demands on their time and, as a result, may want to quickly identify only the principal points, perhaps returning later for a more careful reading.

If you are checking your office e-mail, for example, you're likely first to glance quickly at the header to see who sent the message and what it's about. In checking your advertising mail, you'll tend to scan for headings or other prominent words or phrases and, based on what you find, either delete the item or put it aside for later review. Effective technical communication allows the reader to make the choice without penalty. And it does so, in large part, through the judicious integration of visual elements.

Timeliness

The world's great books are supposed to be timeless, whereas the technicians' manuals for the Apple II or the IBM PCJr are well past their expiration dates. Last year's Land's End catalog is of little use to consumers. By the middle of January, the newspaper advertisement for a Memorial Day sale has no practical value. And after you have received your merchandise, the online purchase order you filled out at Amazon.com has been reduced to bits and bytes of electronic rubbish. Almost without exception, the useful life of technical communication is relatively short. It is usually over as soon as the reality it addresses changes.

Structure

You might have been taught that a paragraph must have a topic sentence, one or more supporting sentences, and a concluding sentence. You might also have been told never to begin a sentence with *and* or *but*. In contemporary technical communication, these rules don't apply. If you can express the idea of a paragraph in just one sentence, you should do so. Also, in the interest of brevity and ease of your audience quickly acquiring the information, you may replace topic sentences with headings or subheadings. And most business and technical writers accept the practice of beginning some sentences with *and* or *but*. They also vary sentence length and structure to avoid monotony of style.

Ethics

What do we mean by ethics? **Ethics** can be defined as "the rules or standards of conduct that are believed to be right and moral for individuals, organizations, or societies." Unfortunately, though, there is no consensus as to the meaning and implications of conduct that is "right and moral." Do you and your family and friends always agree on what is "right"? Does *moral* mean the same thing to every individual, organization, and society?

Over the centuries, philosophers have wrestled with questions about morality and conduct and with the meaning of ethics. More recent attention has been focused on the development and meaning of medical ethics, professional ethics, journalistic ethics, business ethics (which some people facetiously consider an oxymoron), and so on. Can we derive from a confusing but important maze of ideas any practical guidance for those who engage in technical communication?

Ethical Communication

However we define ethics, most of us have a sense of what we consider right and wrong, and most of us would agree that most of the time we should try to apply the injunction "Do unto others as you would have them do unto you." Most successful people believe that treating others as justly as possible is one of the cornerstones of their success. How might this approach be reflected in technical communication? Here are a few examples.

Honesty.   Many of us know someone who lied on a résumé and got the job because of the lie. We often forget that, in most cases, the lie is eventually discovered and the person loses not only the job but also his or her reputation. Telling someone that "the check is in the mail" when it isn't may bring short-term benefits. But if you persist in this kind of deception, you'll soon be thought of as dishonest. Being dishonest in dealing with others is illegal in some cases; for most people, it is always unethical.

Accuracy.   An important criterion for technical communicators is accuracy of information. If your document or presentation contains inaccuracies and if someone in your audience notices the errors, your entire message—and likely any future ones—is compromised. Whenever you communicate, your credibility is on the line. Regaining lost credibility is very difficult indeed. If the lack of accuracy in what you communicate is intentional, the issue becomes one of honesty and, thus, of ethics.

Exaggeration. Whether you're trying to sell a product or express an opinion, you should certainly try to present your information in the best possible light. You might do this, for example, by accentuating the advantages of your brand and glossing over its weaknesses. Similarly, in describing your preferred option, you might use more forceful vocabulary than you use in describing the alternatives. Here the question of ethics tends to be one of degree. Only a technical audience is likely to be swayed by neutral facts alone. Consequently, when you wish to persuade—and technical communication certainly involves persuasion— you must in some sense exaggerate.

Communication that exaggerates beyond what is reasonable, however, may be scorned. Of course, deciding what is "reasonable" can be difficult. Think of the difference between what you would consider "reasonable exaggeration" in a loan application and what you accept (despite the apparent absurdity of the claims) in advertisements for cars or toothpaste. For the sake of both expediency and your reputation, adopt an ethical approach at all times.

Creating Impressions. Whenever it conveys information, language also creates impressions. Consciously or unconsciously, audiences respond to the emotional effect of language (its connotation) as well as to its objective meaning (its denotation). Thus, the way you phrase a communication will influence how your audience responds to it. (Think of the importance of spin doctors in political circles.) Suppose that you are a manager in a company and your record shows that three-quarters of your decisions have proved to be good ones. To describe your success rate, we could say that you are right 75 percent of the time or we could say that you are wrong 25 percent of the time. Which description would you prefer to see in your personnel file?

As in the case of exaggeration, the ethical path may be indistinct. In most cases, technical communication requires you to be as objective as possible even though the nature of language itself makes it all but impossible to present communications that are entirely free of connotation.

Codes of Ethics

The importance of ethical conduct in business and in technological fields is broadly accepted. In fact, organizations ranging from businesses to self-regulating professional associations publish codes of ethical conduct. A group of international business leaders, primarily from Europe, Japan, and the United States, have developed what they called the Caux Round Table Principles for Business. Effectively a code of ethics, it states that

> While accepting the legitimacy of trade secrets, businesses should recognize that sincerity, candor, truthfulness, the keeping of promises, and transparency contribute not only to their own credibility and stability but also to the smoothness and efficiency of business transactions, particularly on the international level.

Tech Link

Visit *www.cauxroundtable.org/ english.htm* to see the complete Caux Round Table Principles for Business.

The Society for Technical Communication makes the following statement in its Code for Communicators:

My commitment to professional excellence and ethical behavior means that I will:

- Use language and visuals with precision.
- Prefer simple, direct expression of ideas.
- Satisfy the audience's need for information, not my own need for self-expression.
- Hold myself responsible for how well my audience understands my message.
- Respect the work of colleagues, knowing that a communication problem may have more than one solution.
- Strive continually to improve my professional competence.
- Promote a climate that encourages the exercise of professional judgment and that attracts talented individuals to careers in technical communication.

Conclusions

As an ethical communicator, you have to be willing to put the needs of your audience before your own interests. Twisting language to camouflage an unsavory truth may produce the results you want, but you should not ignore the potential repercussions. Rarely are ethical people comfortable with the rationalization that the end justifies the means.

To determine whether or not you are communicating ethically, try asking yourself how you would react if you were the audience. Would you think you were being treated fairly and respectfully? If you can't honestly answer yes, then it's likely that you haven't given sufficient thought to the ethical aspects of your communication.

Diversity

The United States is a society characterized by **diversity**—a society made up of people characterized by a variety of cultures, age groups, interests, and physical abilities. With at least 300 different cultures in the United States, you can be certain that the American workforce of the twenty-first century will be more diverse than at any other time in history.

In addition, the continuing increase in international trade and global markets will require many American workers to communicate effectively with people around the world. To work effectively with people from different backgrounds and experiences, you must learn to recognize, understand, and respect differences.

Cultural Referents

People, ideas, and things that form part of the popular culture and become ingrained in our thinking and in our language are referred to as **cultural referents.** As a technical communicator, you must consider whether your audience will understand the cultural referents that you take for granted. For example, an audience that has not been exposed to the Grade 1 primers common in the 1950s and 1960s would probably not know that a "Dick and Jane approach" is one that is overly simplistic.

The multicultural nature of our society means that you must pay attention to the cultural referents you use and consider whether they are relevant to your intended audience. If your audience doesn't relate to them as you do, you will not communicate effectively.

Cultural Preferences

Just as people respond differently to cultural referents, groups tend to react differently to certain types of behavior. People of different cultures tend to have different preferences for the way they interact in business and social situations. Knowledge of your audience and their preferences will help you develop worthwhile professional relationships.

Formality.   The use of first names in newly established business relationships is very common in the United States. Presumably, this behavior is designed to promote an impression of friendliness and conviviality. It is not, however, universally accepted. Many cultures believe that business relationships should be more formal, and that the appropriate form of address—even among people who know each other quite well—is a last name preceded by an honorific such as *Ms.* or *Mr.* Unless you know your audience's preferences, you run the risk of being thought impolite if you use first names in business relationships.

Directness.   Another characteristic of American business dealings is the value placed on directness. Thus, brevity and conciseness are seen as desirable qualities in letters and memos. In some other cultures, these same qualities would be regarded as brusque, curt, or abrasive. In Japan, for example, tradition dictates a much more roundabout approach in which ideas are conveyed through implication rather than stated explicitly.

Language.   As a technical communicator, you need to consider language in your communications. For example, although English is the language of the United States, Canada, and England, some words are spelled differently. When writing to a Canadian business, which should you use—Canadian or American spelling? Again, consider both your audience and your purpose. You should also be aware of differences in vocabulary. For example, if you are writing to someone in England, you will be better understood if you use the words *lift, boot,* and *biscuit,* rather than *elevator, trunk* (of a car), and *cookie,* respectively. Nor should you be shocked if someone from England offers to "knock you up" at 7 A.M. It's

Tech Link

The University of Maryland's Diversity Database is a comprehensive index of multicultural and diversity resources. Visit *www.inform.umd.edu/ EdRes/Topic/Diversity* simply that person's way of proposing a wake-up call. Another language consideration involves communication with people who speak English as a second language. In this situation, you should be careful not to use slang or jargon that might not be understood.

Humor. Because humor plays at best a minor role in technical communication, you should exercise care in its use. The same caution applies to references to religion and politics. North Americans tend to approach such references with what, for some cultures, is inappropriate familiarity. Unless you are certain of your audience's reaction, you should avoid potentially offensive references in your communications—in other words, stick to the facts.

Personal Space. The term *personal space* is often used to refer to the physical distance we like to maintain between ourselves and those with whom we are speaking. Different cultures have different norms. Many Europeans and South Americans, for example, prefer much less personal space than most North Americans find comfortable. When you see two people from different cultures talking, you might observe one advancing to decrease the personal space and the other backing up in an effort to increase it. Although the issue of personal space does not have a direct bearing on written technical communication, it is a good idea to be aware of the cultural differences involved.

Eye Contact. A related issue is eye contact. Most North Americans believe that looking someone in the eye while conversing is an indication of honesty and forthrightness. In some other cultures, however, such behavior can be viewed as rude or presumptuous. Although you should make eye contact with your audience during a presentation, you should not assume that your audience's failure to reciprocate implies shiftiness or deceit.

Teams and Collaboration

In today's workplace, as much as 75 percent of your time may be spent working in a group. Today teams are a common way of doing business. You may be asked to cooperate with a coworker to write a report, to solve a problem, or to make a presentation. When workers cooperate in completing a project, it is called **collaboration.** Collaboration, or teamwork, offers the following advantages:

- *Shared expertise.* People in a group complement each other by providing different proficiency levels, knowledge, and skills.
- *Shared responsibility.* Team members share the credit or blame for the outcome of their work, resulting in a high degree of accountability.
- *Varied perspectives on a problem.* Different viewpoints come together to offer a variety of perspectives and solutions.
- *Flexibility.* After a problem is solved or a project is completed, a team can be disbanded and reassigned as needed.

Characteristics of Teams

A group of people put together to complete a given task do not automatically work as a team. A group must learn to become a team. A successful team is composed of members who give mutual support to each other. When you become a member of a team, you can do several things to help the group function effectively. The Checklist below provides guidelines for working in a team.

 Checklist

Effective Teamwork

✓ Work cooperatively.

✓ Channel conflict constructively.

✓ Be supportive of the team's purpose.

✓ Work toward the team's common goals.

✓ State your opinions with sensitivity for other team members.

✓ Be a good listener.

✓ Share your knowledge and skills.

✓ Keep an open mind.

✓ Come to team meetings prepared.

✓ Maintain a positive attitude.

Collaborative Problem Solving and Writing

Often teams are made up of people from various departments in an organization and are set up to solve a specific problem. After the team has analyzed the problem and is ready to propose a solution, team members usually work collaboratively to prepare a written report and/or oral presentation for management. To successfully solve a problem, a team needs to:

- Define the problem.
- Research and analyze the problem.
- Brainstorm alternatives.
- Evaluate the advantages and disadvantages of alternatives.
- Make a final recommendation.
- Create an action plan to implement the recommendations.

Coworkers may also be called on to write together. Teams who work together to create a written product use a process called **collaborative writing.** Reports, brochures, and presentations are just a few examples of the documents you may create collaboratively. Typically, teams work together first to brainstorm and discuss the content, purpose, audience, and organization of their document. Then each team member may be assigned a specific section to write or task to complete.

After individual tasks are complete, the team may regroup to edit and revise each other's work. This process is known as **peer editing.** Finally, one or more individuals are assigned to prepare the final document.

Virtual Teams

In today's workplace, teams do not necessarily have face-to-face group meetings. Instead, teams use various types of technology to discuss a problem or collaborate on a project. **Virtual teams** communicate and complete their work using a combination of technology tools, or **groupware.** Commonly used tools include **teleconferencing** and **videoconferencing, e-mail,** networked **electronic meeting software,** and **collaborative writing software** (CWS). CWS allows two or more team members to work on a document at the same time.

One of the greatest challenges to virtual teams is keeping track of schedules, documents, and lines of communication. To help manage the process and work flow, teams can establish virtual office space on the Web. A number of commercial sites allow subscribers to pay a monthly fee to share office space. Features include shared file and storage space, discussion groups, calendars, synchronized chats in private conference rooms, and bulletin boards.

Chapter Review

CHAPTER SUMMARY

Technical communication includes many different types of written documents, (such as letters, memos, advertising and promotional material, and manuals) and various types of oral communication. Technical communication has five salient features: necessity for a specific audience, integration of visual elements, ease of selective access, timeliness, and structure.

Many organizations have codes of ethics, and technical communicators should practice ethical conduct in their messages. Communications should be honest and accurate and should put the needs of the audience first.

The diversity of the U.S. workforce and the increase in international trade will require American workers to communicate effectively with people from different backgrounds and experiences. As a technical communicator, you must be sure that your audience understands your cultural referents and that you are aware of cultural preferences. People of different cultures have different attitudes toward formality, directness, language, humor, personal space, and eye contact.

Working in teams is common in today's workplace. Advantages to teamwork, or collaboration, include shared expertise, shared responsibility, varied perspectives on a problem, and flexibility. A team needs to define the problem, research and analyze the problem, brainstorm alternatives, evaluate alternatives, make a final recommendation, and create an action plan to implement the recommendation. Virtual teams collaborate on projects using various types of technology.

KEY TERMS

Audience-driven

Collaboration

Collaborative writing

Collaborative writing software

Cultural referents

Diversity

Electronic meeting software

E-mail

Ethics

Groupware

Peer editing

Teleconferencing

Videoconferencing

Virtual teams

CRITICAL THINKING ACTIVITIES

1. Give four or more examples of what could be classified as technical communication.
2. Describe at least one real-world situation in which technical communication skills would serve you well.

3. Briefly explain the significance of the following characteristics of effective technical communication: (a) necessity for a specific audience, (b) integration of visual elements, (c) ease of selective access, (d) timeliness, and (e) structure.

4. Briefly discuss the importance of ethics in technical communication, referring specifically to the issues of honesty, accuracy, exaggeration, and the creation of impressions.

5. Discuss how ethics played a role in a situation from your own experience.

6. Give two or more examples of cultural referents that you take for granted, and suggest alternatives for an audience that might not understand them.

7. Reflect on an experience you've had as part of a team. What were the strengths and weaknesses of your team? What characteristics of effective teams did you experience?

SKILLS APPLICATIONS

1. Talk to someone in business or government who is involved in hiring new employees, and report back to your class on what that person thinks are the most important ethical issues in his or her workplace.

2. Visit *http://csep.iit.edu/codes/codes.html* (the Illinois Institute of Technology's Center for Study of Ethics in the Professions) and *www.ethics.ubc.ca/resources/professional/codes.html* (the Centre for Applied Ethics). View at least ten codes of ethics from various professions. Then write your own personal code of ethics for the workplace.

3. You have just been informed that the empty cubicle next to you will soon be occupied by a new employee from your company's international headquarters. Create a fictitious person and assign this person a name and nationality. Conduct research to discover the cultural differences you should expect. Assume this person has a working knowledge of English but no real day-to-day experience with the language or with American culture. What will you do to simplify communication between the two of you? Summarize your findings in an e-mail to your supervisor.

CONTEMPORARY ISSUES CASE

Dealing with Differences.   During a crowded cocktail party in Mexico, Elaine noticed her business client waving to her from across the room. Talking with someone else, she saw the wave and thought "How friendly!" and waved back. A little later he waved again—more adamantly and vigorously. She waved back more enthusiastically this time. In the days that followed, her client wouldn't return phone calls and canceled appointments with her. Why do you think the client became cool to her?

CASE STUDIES

In the subsequent chapters of this book, you will look at examples of technical communication involving one or more of four organizations based on real companies and institutions. Each case study presents examples of flawed communication produced by people within the organizations under consideration. The section entitled "Issues to Think About" presents questions raised by the examples. The following paragraphs provide profiles of the four organizations.

Grandstone Technical Institute (GTI)

GTI offers one- and two-year certificates or diplomas in such fields as management information systems and engineering technology as well as internship programs in such areas as automotive mechanics, electronics, and welding. GTI's reputation for excellence is such that its graduates are often welcomed by companies across the country.

Ann Arbor University (AAU)

AAU offers both undergraduate and graduate degrees, principally in arts, law, and engineering. One result of the university's successful fund-raising campaigns was the construction of a new Student Association Building. The Ann Arbor University Student Association Executive (AAUSAEx) remains very active in promoting cooperation among student associations across the country.

Accelerated Enterprises Ltd. (AEL)

In 1980, two young engineers, Sarah Cohen and Frank Nabata, opened a small consulting practice optimistically named Accelerated Enterprises Ltd. Over the next two decades, business prospered. Cohen and Nabata (now married) took in a number of associates and opened three branches. With the expansion came broadened expertise, and AEL is now involved in chemical, civil, and geological engineering as well as software design and development. While the original partners still oversee the firm's overall strategy, they believe in allowing their branch associates significant latitude in running the local operations. As well, AEL tries to maintain good working relationships with several postsecondary institutions, viewing them as important contributors to the country's economic growth and as likely sources for future AEL consultants and employees.

Radisson Automobiles Inc. (RAI)

RAI is a highly successful automobile dealership chain. Over the years, RAI has prospered, and in 1990, Maurice Radisson turned the stewardship of the business over to his eldest son, Griffin, who holds an automotive mechanics diploma from GTI and an MBA from AAU. As president and chief executive officer, Griffin built his father's dealership into a wealthy and respected cross-country network. To strengthen RAI's image as a good corporate citizen, he favors establishing relationships with postsecondary institutions.

CHAPTER 2

Communication Models and the CMAPP Analysis

I f you want to find out the effect on Vancouver of a two-foot rise in sea level, you wouldn't try to melt the polar ice cap and then visit Canada. You'd try to find a computer model that would predict the likely consequences. Similarly, when we study technical communication, we use a model.

Transactional Communication Models

Various communication models have been developed over the years. **Figure 2.1** on the next page shows a simple **transactional model,** so called to reflect the two-way nature of communication. The model, which in principle works for all types of oral and written communication, has the following characteristics:

1. The originator of the communication (the **sender**) conveys (transmits) it to someone else (the **receiver**).
2. The **transmission vehicle** might be face-to-face speech, correspondence, telephone, fax, or e-mail.
3. The receiver's reaction (e.g., body language, verbal or written response)—the **feedback**—can have an effect on the sender, who may then modify any further communication accordingly.

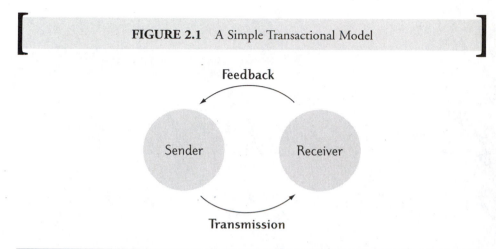

FIGURE 2.1   A Simple Transactional Model

As an example, think of a face-to-face conversation with a friend. As sender, you mention what you think is a funny comment made by another student named Maria. (Note that the basic transmission vehicle here is the sound waves that carry your voice.) As you refer to her, you see your friend's (the receiver's) face begin to cloud over, and you remember that your friend and Maria strongly dislike each other. This feedback makes you decide to start talking about something else. The model thus demonstrates an ongoing transaction between sender and receiver conditioned by both the type and effectiveness of the transmission and the impact of the feedback.

The more complex transactional model that appears in **Figure 2.2** on the next page has the following characteristics:

- The sender has an idea, which he or she must encode—that is, put into appropriate language.
- The sender uses a transmission vehicle (as in the previous model).
- When the receiver decodes, the transmission is susceptible to misunderstanding of structure and differing interpretation of words.
- Both sender and receiver may respond to feedback.
- Real-world communication is always subject to **interference,** which can be *external* and/or *internal.*

Traffic noise, people coughing nearby, a garbled e-mail file, and smudges on paper are some examples of external interference. Examples of internal interference include the receiver's having a migraine or having a strong bias against either the sender or the topic. Interference can impede the encoding, the transmission, the decoding, and/or the feedback, thereby greatly reducing the effectiveness of communication.

Here is a simple example. In an exam, you have to answer a complex question. While you have a clear idea of what you mean, you have to find the right way to express it. You have to **encode** your idea in language that is logical, clear, and

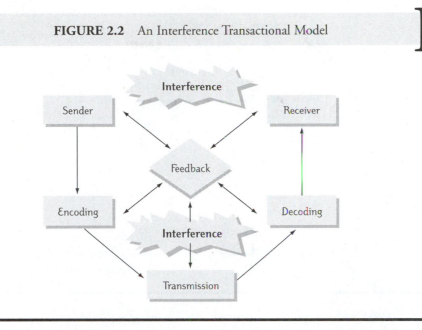

FIGURE 2.2   An Interference Transactional Model

concise. External interference while you are encoding might include the coughing of other students and the hum of the fluorescent lighting. Internal interference could come from your nervousness during the exam or from your fatigue after having been up all night studying.

The transmission vehicle is the exam paper—the composition you are writing. An example of external interference at this stage would be your pen leaving an ink blot or a smudge.

Your instructor—the receiver—will have to **decode** what you have written—that is, interpret your words and assess your knowledge. During this process, there might be external interference from other people's conversations or even from the difficulty of deciphering your rushed handwriting. Internal interference might stem from your instructor's irritation at the poor quality of the papers already marked.

In this example, feedback cannot be immediate: You will receive it only when you get your exam back. When that happens, your dissatisfaction with your mark might interfere with your understanding of your instructor's comments. Finally, the late arrival of several students might annoy your instructor and thus interfere with the delivery of his or her subsequent feedback.

The CMAPP Communication Model

The simple and interference transactional models appear to work for most types of communication. By contrast, the model shown in **Figure 2.3** on the next page is designed specifically for technical communication. The **CMAPP model,** which does not include the terms *sender, transmission,* or *receiver,* reflects the deceptively simple nature of real-world technical communication.

Tech Link

About.com's Technical Writing Guide features a wide variety of articles, links, and resources for writers. Visit *http://techwriting.about.com/ careers/techwriting*

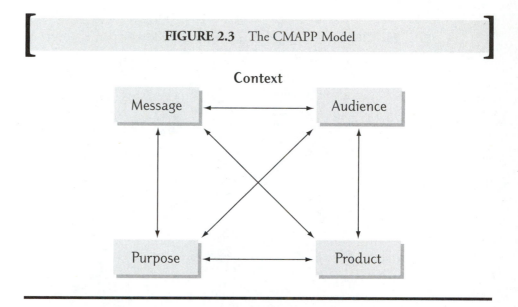

FIGURE 2.3   The CMAPP Model

The CMAPP approach incorporates the following ideas:

◆   Situations (the **context**) in which people find themselves affect their communication.
◆   What people say (the **message**) is affected by the person or group with whom they are communicating (the **audience**).
◆   What people communicate is affected by their reason for communicating and their expectations (the **purpose**).
◆   The physical form of the communication (the **product**) affects the way in which the communication is formulated and received.
◆   All these ideas affect each other all the time.
◆   The first step in creating effective technical communication is conducting a CMAPP analysis.

Definitions

Following are explanations of the CMAPP model's terminology.

◆   **Context** refers to the surrounding situation. It may include (but is not limited to):
  ◆   Personal relationships.
  ◆   Time and place.
  ◆   All circumstances that may influence the people and the communication involved.
  ◆   External and internal interference that might have an impact.
◆   **Message** refers to the content of the communication, and might include:
  ◆   An overview of the situation.
  ◆   The most significant facts, issues, and questions.

- Relevant details.
- A primary message (the main thing you wish to communicate) and, potentially, a secondary message (ideas that might appear in parentheses).

- **Audience** is similar to the receiver in the transactional models. Here, however, it can include:
  - A primary audience, which refers to the person or people you want to reach first.
  - A secondary (and perhaps even a tertiary) audience, which refers to other people you wish to reach as well (e.g., your boss's boss, the manager who receives a copy of all interoffice memos, your facilitator when you are delivering a presentation to your class).

- **Purpose** refers to why you are communicating. The concept includes:
  - Your motive or motives—potentially, both overt and covert—for communicating.
  - The possibility of a secondary (and perhaps even a tertiary) purpose.
  - The reaction that you expect from your audience.
  - The response you wish to elicit.

- **Product** is the "shape" of the communication, or the physical form it takes (e.g., a particular appearance on paper). The choice of product will affect and be affected by the context, message, audience, and purpose. Thus, the term would include (but not be limited to):
  - Memos.
  - Letters.
  - Reports.
  - Summaries.
  - Faxes.
  - E-mails.
  - Telephone conversations.
  - Face-to-face conversations.

Knowing Your Audience

Before beginning to write, you must know who your potential audience will be. Your potential audience affects everything you write—content (what should and should not be included), length (how long or short your work should be), and graphics (what diagrams, charts, pictures, and so on, are needed).

Here are five basic questions you should ask yourself before beginning to write. The answers will help determine what kind of writing you need to do.

1. *What is the reader's purpose and need in reading?* The reader may need to gather information, make a decision, or complete some action. The reader's purpose impacts the amount of information you share and the format in which you share it.

Tech Link

Austin Community College's Online Technical Writing Course features an excellent discussion of audience analysis, *www.io.com/~hcexres/ tcm1603/acchtml/ acctoc.html*

2. *What does the reader already know about the topic?* Your reader's level of experience tells you how to treat your topic. For example, if your audience is already knowledgeable about your subject, you can provide less background information and fewer illustrations.

3. *What is the reader's educational level?* Generally, a person who has completed higher levels of education will have a higher reading level. You must adjust the level of difficulty to the audience's ability to comprehend.

4. *What is the reader's attitude?* A reader's feelings toward a subject may be positive, negative, or neutral. How the reader feels will influence his or her reception of your material. This assessment may affect the order and timing of your message.

5. *What is the best format for the reader?* How best can you communicate your message? What form is expected and what will be most effective? The answer to this question will determine the form your writing takes. For example, you might choose an e-mail, a manual, a brochure, a memo, or a newsletter, depending on your reader's interests and needs.

Attitude

One common pitfall when adjusting to your audience is writing with an **I-attitude** rather than a **you-attitude.** A you-attitude focuses on the needs, interests, and concerns of the receiver. An I-attitude focuses on the sender. Consider the following examples:

I-Attitude	You-Attitude
I am pleased to inform you that your Tech Credit Card has been approved.	Welcome to the Tech family. Come in and use your Tech Credit Card soon.

Analysis Tips

To use a CMAPP analysis, ask yourself questions about the CMAPP components before you begin drafting your product. Make sure that you have adequately defined the particular context, the principal message, the primary audience, the overall purpose, and the appropriate product. Examine each of the elements closely. As you find one component affecting others, modify each accordingly until your product is ready for delivery.

There is no predefined set of questions you should ask yourself in your CMAPP analysis. The questions are determined by the interrelationship of context, message, audience, purpose, and product. Recall, however, that the specifics of your message should respond to what you think your audience will need and/or want to know.

The following Checklist features just some of the questions you might ask as you consider each CMAPP component.

✓ Checklist

CMAPP Analysis

Context

✓   What is the underlying or surrounding situation?

✓   What are the physical conditions (lighting, noise, and so on)?

✓   How will the context affect how my audience responds to me or my message?

✓   What is my relationship with my audience?

✓   What other relationships involved might have an impact?

Message

✓   What exactly am I trying to communicate?

✓   Is it a message worth communicating?

✓   Is my message self-contained, or is it the initial, middle, or final segment of a longer communication?

✓   Have I included all necessary and excluded all unnecessary information?

✓   Have I provided the specifics that my audience will need and/or want?

✓   Do I have more than one message (i.e., one or more secondary messages)?

✓   If I have more than one message, have I arranged them in an order that is appropriate for this context, audience, and purpose?

✓   Am I the best person to send this message, or should the message come from someone else?

Audience

✓   Who should receive my communication?

✓   Who will receive it?

✓   What does my audience know already?

✓   What does my audience need to know?

✓   What does my audience want to know?

✓   What assumptions have I made about my audience?

✓   How specialized (technical) is my audience?

✓   How will my audience benefit from my communication?

Purpose

✓   Why do I want to communicate?

✓   Why do I want to communicate at this particular time?

(Checklist continued on next page.)

Purpose (continued)

✓   Why would my audience need or want this communication?

✓   What do I want to achieve?

✓   Am I trying to inform, persuade, instruct, or describe?

✓   Was my communication explicitly requested?

✓   Are there deadlines involved?

✓   Have I identified and dealt with them?

Product

✓   Should I be writing, phoning, or visiting?

✓   Have I chosen a product (e.g., letter, memo, report, presentation) that is appropriate for this context, audience, message, and purpose?

✓   Do the wording and format of my product reflect the image I want to present?

CMAPP in Action

Consider the following scenario. You receive an envelope that is supposed to contain a check and an explanatory note. The note is there; the check is not. What do you do? According to the CMAPP approach, you would conduct a brief analysis before you actually do anything. Here's an example:

◆   *Context.*   Were you expecting the check, or was it a surprise? Was it on time or overdue? Was it a refund from the IRS, a birthday gift, a student loan installment, payment for overtime work? Do you have a personal relationship with the person who was to send it? If you do, is that relationship a good or a bad one? If the note was signed by more than one person, how do you determine to whom you should direct your response?

◆   *Message.*   What specifically should you say? Are you providing everything your audience will need in order to understand and respond? Should you mention your annoyance? (Think of the context.) How much detail should you include? What kind of language should you use—simple or sophisticated?

◆   *Audience.*   Are you communicating with a single individual? a company? a large bureaucracy? Will that audience know who you are—or care? Do you have reason to believe your audience is competent to deal with the situation? Are you trying to communicate with the person who forgot to enclose the check or with that person's boss?

◆   *Purpose.*   Are you communicating simply to get your check as quickly as possible? to voice your irritation? to obtain an apology? Do you expect an immediate response? Do you want to maintain a good relationship with your audience, or do you not care?

- *Product.*   Should you telephone? If so, would you be satisfied with voice mail? Would calling long-distance be acceptable to you? Should you—or can you—pay a visit instead? Would written communication be more effective? If so, should it be handwritten or word-processed? on personal or letterhead stationery? Which product is most likely to fulfill your purpose?

Interrelationships Among CMAPP Elements

Whereas most traditional models are linear in the sense that they progress from A to B to C (and then, for example, back to A), the CMAPP model is dynamic. In this dynamic, even the slightest change in one element has a ripple effect on all the others. In the missing check example, the CMAPP dynamic included the following interactions:

- Knowing more about your audience helped determine your context.
- That knowledge about context helped you identify the particular audience.
- Knowing your audience helped you identify and refine your purpose.
- As you refined your purpose, you got a better idea of the most appropriate product.
- Your conception of the product was also dependent on your audience, which in turn affected your message.

You may have noticed that CMAPP does not make explicit reference to a prime component of transactional models—feedback. The concept, however, is fundamental. Modifications to any one of context, message, audience, purpose, or product have an inevitable impact on the other elements, altering them over time. These shifts are, in effect, the manifestations of feedback. For example, your message affects your audience in a particular way, which alters the context, which has an impact on both your audience's reaction and your own response to that reaction. Technical communication, just like life, can get complicated.

Chapter Review. . . . .

CHAPTER SUMMARY

In a simple transactional communication model, the sender transmits the message to the receiver via a transmission vehicle. The receiver's feedback can affect the sender and the sender's future communication. In a more complex transactional model, external and internal interference can affect several areas and thus reduce the effectiveness of the communication.

The CMAPP model is designed specifically for technical communication and consists of five components—context, message, audience, purpose, product—that are the basis for analyzing your communications. Context refers to the surrounding situation. Message refers to the content of the communication. Audience refers to the receiver of the message. Purpose is why you are communicating. Product is the physical form of the communication.

To use a CMAPP analysis, ask questions to help you define the particular context, the principal message, the primary audience, the overall purpose, and the appropriate product before you begin drafting your product. The five components are interrelated, so a change to one component can affect the other four components. Always keep in mind that the specifics of your message should respond to what you think your audience will need and/or want to know. Modify each element until your product is ready for delivery.

KEY TERMS

Audience	Message
CMAPP model	Product
Context	Purpose
Decode	Receiver
Encode	Sender
Feedback	Transactional model
I-attitude	Transmission vehicle
Interference	You-attitude

CRITICAL THINKING ACTIVITIES

1. Two different scenarios follow. In Scenario A, you tell a student at another institution about your financial situation this term. In Scenario B, you communicate this information to a loan officer at your bank. For each scenario, provide answers to the CMAPP questions that follow. Invent any necessary details.

Scenario A: Fellow Student

Context
1. What is your relationship with the student?
2. Why would the student be interested in your message?
3. What is the student's own financial situation?

Message
1. What specific information will the student need or want in order to respond as you would like?
2. What details should you provide?
3. Should you exclude any details? If so, what details and why?

Audience
1. Is the student female or male? How might this make a difference?
2. What might the student know already?
3. What would the student want to know?
4. What do you know about the student's financial situation?

Purpose
1. Why are you telling the student about your financial situation?
2. What kind of reaction do you expect?
3. What do you want the student to do with the information?

Product
1. What product do you intend to use?
2. Why have you chosen to use that product?

Scenario B: Loan Officer at Your Bank

Context
1. What is your relationship with the loan officer?
2. Why might the loan officer even be interested in your message?
3. What kind of reputation do students have in the banking community?
4. How long have you been dealing with this branch and/or this person?
5. How might your history with the bank affect how your message is received?

Message
1. What specific information and explanations will the loan officer want?
2. What information should you provide?
3. What information might you want to withhold?
4. Should you withhold this information? Why or why not?

Audience
1. What is the sex and age of the loan officer? How might these make a difference?
2. Is the loan officer the only audience?

3. If there is a secondary audience, who is it?
4. What would the loan officer know already?
5. What would the loan officer want or need to know?
6. Is anyone else likely to see or use the information you provide?

Purpose

1. Why are you telling the loan officer about your situation?
2. What do you want him or her to do with the information?
3. Do you have a secondary purpose? If so, what is it?
4. What might the loan officer's purpose be?
5. Is the loan officer's purpose of any relevance to your situation?

Product

1. What product do you intend to use?
2. Why have you chosen to use that product?

2. The computer system you purchased from Acme High-Tech Products has given you considerable trouble. Angry, you dash off a letter (**Figure 2.4** on the next page) to Acme's sales manager, R. B. Kim. You do not mail this letter. Instead, you wait until you are calm, then decide to construct a letter that adheres to the principles of good technical communication. The first step is to conduct a CMAPP analysis. For the purposes of this exercise, do not write the new letter but simply answer the following CMAPP questions:

Context

1. What has prompted you to write a new letter?
2. How would you describe the relationship between you and your audience?
3. What are you prepared to do if your letter fails to meet its intended objective?

Message

1. What are your main points?
2. If you have any secondary points, what are they?

Audience

1. Who is your audience?
2. If you have a secondary audience, who is it?
3. What do you think your primary audience knows?
4. What do you think that audience needs to know?
5. What do you think that audience wants to know?

Purpose

1. What is your purpose?
2. If you have a secondary purpose, what is it? (Hint: Think long term.)

Product

1. What product might you have chosen instead of a letter?
2. Why have you chosen to use a letter? (Hint: You might have more than one reason.)
3. What kind of tone will you use?
4. How technical should your letter be?

FIGURE 2.4   Letter to R. B. Kim

Last month we purchased a computer from you, sold to us by your Mr. Webley when he came to our home after our phone conversation two days earlier. We spoke with him for a couple of hours, gave him coffee, and eventually decided to buy the PB-2 "User-Friendly Package" that he showed us in the many pages of advertising material he had brought.

When the merchandise arrived two days later, the delivery person, who said he replaced Mr. Webley on Fridays, really didn't seem to know what he was doing. He kept referring to the manuals that came with the package, and he wore a continual worried look while trying to make little jokes about the complex technology we have in our lives now. Eventually he seemed to get it all working and left. By then it was 8 p.m., some three hours since he'd arrived.

The next morning I had some spreadsheets to do. As I told Mr. Webley before he suggested the PB-2 package, I've had quite a bit of experience with the old Lotus 1-2-3. So I bought a copy of Office from Acme, as part of the package, along with Quicken, Quake, Encarta, and Front Page.

Unfortunately, I had one system error after another (I think that's what they were), never did get my work finished, and, to top it off, found the printer—the Printomatic 554, also part of the package—wouldn't accept the commands I keyed.

No one was at the service number Mr. Webley provided when I called that afternoon—a Saturday—nor the next day. On Monday, someone answered but got quite rude when I told my story and demanded that Acme either arrange for real support for its customers or pick up its lousy equipment and give me my money back! After that call, I gave up trying to contact anyone and wrote this--on my typewriter, not on your shoddy computer!

I better hear from you in the next couple of days, or you'll be hearing from my lawyer, who's getting a copy of this letter too.

---

3. Among RAI's products is the Minotaur, a popular luxury car manufactured by Global Vehicles. Having recently discovered a possible manufacturing defect in some Minotaur models, Global composed a notification (**Figure 2.5** on the next page) to deal with the problem. Based on your analysis of the notification, provide answers to the CMAPP questions that follow the figure.

FIGURE 2.5 Global Notification

A possible defect relating to the potential failure of a seal in the mounting of the left tie-rod-end assembly may exist in your vehicle. In the event of disconnection, this seal (configured as a supportive component to the front rack assembly) could result in at least partial loss of bilateral vehicle directional control, particularly during unusually significant intentional deceleration. In addition, your vehicle may require adjustment service to the front hub bearing where it comes into contact with the hub carrier beside the right caliper. Should this bearing be improperly aligned, unusually rapid acceleration during excessive directional change might result in a similar loss of bilateral vehicle directional control. In certain circumstances, either of these potential failures has the capability of causing unexpectedly severe vehicle handling. You are, therefore, advised to consider the benefits of contacting your reseller to arrange for relevant adjustment or replacement without personal expenditure on your part.

Context
1. What relationship(s) might exist between Global and the audience(s)?
2. How might the relationship(s) change as a result of the notification?
3. What kind of reaction to its notification might Global expect?
4. What impact might the situation have on RAI?

Message
1. Is the information clear and concise? Give examples to justify your response.
2. What do you think the primary audience needs and wants to know?
3. What can you say about the language used in the notification?

Audience
1. Who appears to be the audience for the notification?
2. At what other audience or audiences might the notification be aimed? (Hint: Look at the use of language.)

Purpose
1. What is the apparent purpose of the notification?
2. What secondary purpose might be involved?
3. How well do you think Global's current notification fulfills its purpose(s)?

Product
1. What product should Global use?
2. What would make the product effective?
3. Should Global use more than one product? If so, what should it use and why?

SKILLS APPLICATIONS

1. Think of a real-world situation, preferably one having to do with a business or an organization, that requires a written or verbal response from you. Based on your scenario, create a list of relevant CMAPP questions and answer them.

2. Use the CMAPP model to analyze a sales or promotional letter or another mailing you've received. How effective was the communication? Did it address your needs and interests as an audience? What changes might have made the letter or mailing more effective?

CONTEMPORARY ISSUES CASE

E-mail and Your Audience. As an employee of your company, you have an e-mail to send to a member of your staff; however, the would-be receiver of the e-mail is in a very bad mood. Does this factor impact your decision about sending an e-mail? If so, explain how. How might you approach your receiver in this situation?

CASE STUDIES

2A Ann Arbor University Student Association Function

Situation

During construction of the Student Association Building (the SAB), the Ann Arbor University Student Association (AAUSA) has continued to rent from the university the following premises:

- Office space in the Dominion Building (main administration building) for the ten members of the AAUSA Executive (AAUSAEx).
- A "student space" (a former classroom) on the main floor of Vanier Square (the engineering building), containing several video-game terminals, two football tables, a ping-pong table, an ATM, food and drink vending machines, and several tables and chairs.
- A small editorial office in the Confederation Building (used primarily for Department of Humanities faculty offices) for the editor and associate editor of the student newspaper, *The Muckraker*.

When it wishes to put on functions such as concerts, dances, or parties, AAUSAEx normally arranges to rent either Sassoon Hall, the university's main auditorium, or one of two conference rooms named after corporate benefactors Accelerated Enterprises Ltd. (AEL) and Radisson Automobiles Inc. (RAI).

After heated debate, AAUSAEx decides, on November 8, to celebrate the Thanksgiving holiday with a concert the Monday before the holiday. Jack Lee, the AAUSAEx functions coordinator, immediately sends an AAU room-booking form to the Room-Booking Office; he also confirms bookings with (and sends checks to) two popular local bands, Hodgepodge and Really Me. As usual, he contracts with a local company, Specialties, to produce and distribute posters and flyers advertising the event. He has to pay extra because the work is a rush job.

Checking the AAUSAEx mailbox on Wednesday of the following week, Jack is shocked to find his booking form returned and marked "rejected"; he is unable to decipher the signature on it. In a bit of a panic and angry at AAU administration, he tries to contact Dorothy Palliser, the AAUSAEx president, but discovers that she is in the middle of a two-day class field trip. Realizing that he has to take immediate action, Jack leaves a voice mail for Kulwinder Atwal, the administration room-booking clerk because he is unable to reach her personally. (A transcript of Jack's message is shown in **Figure 2.6** on the next page.) As well, because he once booked the RAI Conference Room by phone and was later told there was no record of the reservation, Jack decides to hand-deliver a handwritten memo to the Room-Booking Office (**Figure 2.7** on page 32). Finally, he pens a memo to Dorothy (**Figure 2.8** on page 33), and leaves it in her mailbox.

Issues to Think About

In analyzing this scenario using CMAPP, you have to consider the following interconnected communications involving AAU and AAUSAEx: the original booking form completed by Jack, Jack's voice mail to Kulwinder, Jack's memo to the Room-Booking Office, and Jack's memo to Dorothy.

Original Booking Form

Not having seen the original booking form, we don't know if it was completed incorrectly—a possible reason for its rejection. But we do know that it was submitted less than two weeks before the planned concert—another possible explanation for its rejection because Sassoon Hall might have already been reserved for another function. We also know very little about the relationship between AAU administration and AAUSAEx. Had there been problems before? Had the administration been unnecessarily rigid in its requirements? Had AAUSAEx been lax in submitting rental payments? Had there been incidences of damage to university property? Do you think that any of these details of context might have had an impact on the present rejection?

Voice Mail

Answer the following questions for analysis (see **Figure 2.6**). Then create a revised text for Jack's voice-mail message.

What can you say about the content of the message? Is it specific? Does it contain all the information that Kulwinder will need to look into the matter? For example, will she know that Jack is the AAUSAEx functions coordinator? Shouldn't he have given his last name too? Why hasn't he left a number and a time for her to reach him?

> [**FIGURE 2.6**   Transcript of Lee's Voice Mail to Atwal]

Hi! It's Jack from AAUSDAEx.

How come our booking was rejected? No one told us there was going to be a problem. We've already got Hodgepodge and Really Me coming, and Specialties has some stuff up already.

Can you call me and tell me what's wrong with it?

Is the message polite? Has Jack given sufficient thought to his audience? What might Kulwinder's reaction to the message be? Do you think that Jack's purpose is clear to Kulwinder? More importantly, do you think that Jack himself has a clear idea of his purpose? Does he simply want, as his message states, Kulwinder to call him back and tell him what was wrong with his booking form? Or does he really want Kulwinder to find a venue for the concert?

What about Jack's product? Is leaving a voice mail the best way for him to communicate? Should he have tried to reach someone else? Did he take likely delays into account when he decided to leave the voice mail? Do you think the voice mail is an effective product in this context? Why or why not?

Memo to Room-Booking Office

Answer the following questions for analysis (see **Figure 2.7**). Then create a revised memo for Jack. (This time, let's consider the product first.)

Is a handwritten memo acceptable, or should Jack have word-processed it? (Hint: Is it a personal or professional communication? How might the distinction be important in this context?) Did you notice the misspelling in the To line? Should Jack have included the year as part of the date? Why might these things matter?

Here are some other questions you might ask yourself about this memo:

- Does Jack's message contain all the necessary information? What significant information might be lacking?
- Will Jack's wording of the Subject line allow the Room-Booking Office to find the relevant information easily? How might this influence the context?
- How many requests does the memo contain? Are these clearly expressed?
- To whom is the memo addressed? Why did Jack leave a voice mail for a particular person (Kulwinder) but address his memo to "Room-Booking Office"? Do you think Jack knows whether AAU's administration has a section called "Room-Booking Office"? Why might this be important?
- Does the first sentence of the last paragraph imply that if the Room-Booking Office does not have questions, Jack does not want them to call?
- How might the likely audience respond to the last sentence? Who do you think that audience is? Do you think Jack knows who his audience is likely to be?

FIGURE 2.7   Lee's Memo to Room-Booking Office

AAUSAEx Memo

To: *Room-Boking Office, Administration*
From: *Jack Lee, Functions Coordinator*
Date: *November 16*
Subject: *Rock Concert*

I booked Sassoon Hall for our Thanksgiving concert and already hired the bands and got the publicity arranged. Now you've rejected our booking without saying why, and we don't have time to get our arrangements changed. I've already left voice mail for Kulwinder but can't get hold of her to do anything about it. The bands want to set up at 6 p.m., and we want to arrange with the caf to get food and refreshments. Would you please remake our booking?

If you have any questions, don't hesitate to call me. Otherwise, we'll just assume you made another mistake.

Memo to Dorothy

Answer the following questions for analysis (see **Figure 2.8**). Then create a revised memo for Jack.

How does the fact that Dorothy is another student (possibly a friend of Jack's) affect the context? Why didn't Jack simply copy Dorothy on his memo to the Room-Booking Office? Should he have attached a copy of that memo when he wrote to her? Why or why not?

Here are some other questions to ponder:

◆   What do you think Dorothy will do with Jack's memo?
◆   Might the Date line be a problem later?
◆   Words always carry two meanings: the denotation, which is the literal meaning, and the connotation, which is the emotional content or the impression created. Both meanings have an impact. What is the connotation of Jack's Subject line, and what do you think it says about him?
◆   Do you think Jack's wording says anything about his purpose? (Hint: Think about primary and secondary purposes.)
◆   Is the message clear? Is it specific? Will Dorothy find it useful? Do you think she will want other information? If so, what information?
◆   Is the language formal or informal? Is it appropriate for this audience, context, message, and purpose? Why or why not?
◆   Is the product effective? Why or why not?

FIGURE 2.8   Lee's Memo to Palliser

AAUSAEx Memo

To: Dorothy
From: Jack
Date: Wednesday
Subject: Another Admin Foul-Up

We got a problem with the booking for the concert on Thanksgiving, but I think I fixed it.

As usual, Admin goofed and rejected the booking I sent before. So I phoned the booking clerk and I sent a memo that I took over by hand so we don't take any more chances and left with Admin too.

I told them when Hodgepodge and Really Me need to set up and when the cafe is bringing over the stuff and that Specialties are already working too.

I guess you're just as ticked as I am. This isn't the first time they screwed up with us. Hope we can get it going fast, don't you?

I'll be in class Mon morning when you get back, but call me when you can.

2B Reorganization Notice at Radisson Automobiles Inc. (RAI)

Situation

At RAI's head office, Griffin Radisson, the president and CEO, has become concerned about what he sees as increasing decentralization of authority. He thinks that RAI's growing network of dealerships has diminished his own control over daily operations and overall company direction.

Recently Radisson persuaded the board of directors to impose in three months' time an organizational change that will have an impact on all seven RAI dealerships. As of January 1, 20--, each dealership vice president will report directly to Radisson rather than to the board. Furthermore, each dealership general manager will report not to the respective dealership vice president, but to the head office company manager, Celine Roberts.

The board members were reluctant to endorse this change. They foresaw considerable opposition on the part of dealership vice presidents and general managers over what might be perceived as a sudden lack of trust in their abilities. Over the last several years, all dealerships have been reporting increased profits and a decline in the number of customer complaints. Local dealership management has thus had good reason to believe that it has been instrumental in RAI's success.

The board also argued that three months did not leave sufficient time to work out all the inevitable administrative complications. But Radisson, who remains RAI's principal shareholder, prevailed. Now the dealerships must be notified of the coming reorganization. Radisson has decided to impose his will on the board once again and communicate the news personally. His memo to the dealerships appears in **Figure 2.9** on the next page. His attachments are shown in **Figure 2.10** on page 36 and **Figure 2.11** on page 37.

Issues to Think About

In deciding whether or not Griffin Radisson conducted an effective CMAPP analysis before communicating, consider the following issues. Complete your analysis of Radisson's message; then create a revised version.

- **Context.**   Radisson's position and forceful personality served him well in persuading reluctant board members to endorse his plan. Although we know little about his relationship with the dealership vice presidents, we can assume they will not be happy with a reorganization that will have a dramatic impact on two sets of relationships: those between Roberts and the general managers and those between the general managers and their local vice presidents. Another complication is geography. The physical distance between the players means that future communications are not likely to be face to face.

- **Product.**   What is your assessment of Radisson's choice of product? Because the communication is internal (within an organization), a memo is appropriate. On the other hand, what might have been the effect on the relationships if Radisson had first held a conference call and then followed up in writing?

- **Message.**   What do you think is the crux of Radisson's message? Can you identify any secondary message? What kind of impression is conveyed by the tone of the memo? (Hint: Think about connotation as well as denotation.) What might the message say to the audience about Radisson as a person? Do you think the two attachments help or hinder Radisson's message? Will his audience understand them easily, or will they need further explanation? If further explanation is required, what form should it take?

- **Audience.**   The memo is addressed to dealership vice presidents and general managers, with copies going to board members and the company manager. How many different audiences do you think are really involved? Which audience do you think is the primary one? Should they all receive the same message or messages? What differences in interpretation might there be on the part of these audiences?

- **Purpose.**   Does Radisson have more than one purpose? What do you think he is trying to do? What do you think he is actually doing? What do you think the various audiences will identify as his purpose or purposes? How do you think they will view the attached organizational charts in terms of perceived purpose?

FIGURE 2.9   Radisson's Reorganization Memo

Radisson Automobiles Radisson

Memorandum

To: Dealership Vice Presidents and Général Managers

From: Griffin Radisson, CEO

Date: December 1, 20--

Subject: Reorganization

cc: Board of Directors, Company Manager Celine Roberts

As you know, I believe in being concise and straightforward in all my dealings with both clients and company personnel. Therefore, I am announcing to you now the reorganization of Radisson Automobiles.

As of January 1, 20--, the Current Organizational Chart (copy attached) will be superseded by the Revised Organizational Chart (copy attached).

The board of directors and I recognize that administrative details must still be worked out. Nonetheless, we are confident that the new organization will be to the benefit of the company, a goal we are sure you all share.

Celine Roberts is looking forward to receiving annual operational plans from the dealership general managers. I am likewise looking forward to receiving annual business plans from the vice presidents.

I know I can count on your cooperation.

Attachments

FIGURE 2.10   RAI's Current Organizational Chart

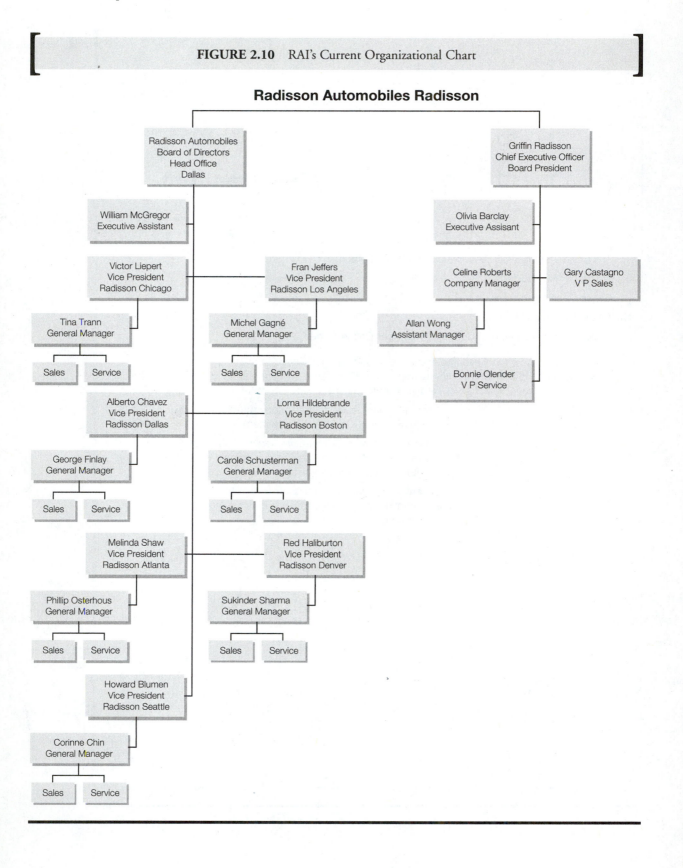

FIGURE 2.11   RAI's Revised Organizational Chart

Radisson Automobiles Radisson

CHAPTER 3

The Technical Writing Process

This chapter deals with the writing process—organizing and outlining your communications, drafting, revising, editing, and publishing them. You'll learn to use the CMAPP approach to convert data into useful information for your audience.

Good writers recognize that writing is a process or a cycle of tasks. In this chapter, we'll look at the following interrelated stages or tasks in the process:

- Prewriting
- Drafting
- Revising
- Editing and proofreading
- Publishing

Prewriting

Have you ever sent a message you wish you had not sent? Maybe you wished you had stated your ideas differently. Do you feel uneasy about your written communication? The problem may be that you don't take time to plan before you write.

The **prewriting** stage is the part of the writing process dedicated to planning. This stage begins with your CMAPP analysis and, based on your analysis, may include researching and collecting data, organizing your information, and outlining your communication. We'll discuss the process for researching and documenting information in Chapter 4. Here we'll focus on organizational patterns and outlining.

Organizing Your Message

Before starting any writing, you must decide on the sequence, or order, in which to present your information. Some common patterns of organization are as follows:

- Chronological
- Spatial
- Comparison-and-contrast
- Most-important-to-least-important
- Cause-and-effect

Chronological organization means that your information is organized according to time or according to when an event occurred. Usually, events are described from the earliest to the latest, or in **ascending order.** The reverse, moving from latest to earliest, is called **descending order.** The following example shows chronological organization for the history of photography. In this example, the events are in ascending order.

Example of Chronological Organization

1. Joseph Niepce, 1826, pinhole camera
2. Louis Daguerre, 1837, highly detailed picture
3. William Fox Talbot, 1839, light-sensitive paper negatives
4. George Eastman, 1888, celluloid roll film

Spatial organization means that ideas are arranged according to placement or geography. For example, a piece of equipment might be described as being composed of a number of parts; a description would explain how each part works in relation to the other, going from front to rear, top to bottom, or left to right. As another example, sales figures might be presented according to geographic region. Consider the following example featuring spatial organization.

Example of Spatial Organization

If the copy machine jams, first check the paper-feed tray on the left side of the machine to be sure all paper is aligned properly. Directly above the paper intake are the paper-feed rollers. Remove any paper stuck inside these rollers.

In spatial organization, **transitions,** or bridge words, are used to help the reader locate various parts. Examples of transitional words include *below, next to, overhead, behind, adjacent to,* and *above.* Visuals are particularly helpful when you're using a spatial organization; they can help your audience see the physical relationships between parts.

Comparison-and-contrast order arranges information according to similarities and differences. When you talk about the advantages and disadvantages of something, you are using comparison-and-contrast order. When you describe the ways objects, processes, or policies are similar, you are comparing. When you explain how items are different, you are contrasting. Investigative reports that discuss two or more items often use the comparison-and-contrast arrangement.

Example of Comparison-and-Contrast Order

Cars that run on steam are fast and easy to start. However, the water tank has to be refilled every 50 miles, and you have to wait 20 minutes after lighting the boiler before you can drive. Cars that run on electricity are quiet and clean. They require little servicing, and the motor starts easily. However, an electric car has a limited driving range and is slower than other types of cars.

A **most-important-to-least-important order** is simply a listing of points. This arrangement is used in reports that examine an issue and reach a conclusion or recommendation, such as determining the location of a new factory or selecting a vending machine service for the employee lounge. When more than one point is given, the most important idea is presented first and the consecutive points are listed in descending order of importance.

Example of Most-Important-to-Least-Important Order

After studying several presentation graphics software packages, I recommend that our company purchase Show-Off for the following reasons:

1. The clip art library is the most extensive of any currently available.
2. The help and tutorial programs provide excellent assistance to the novice.
3. The user can define the color palette.
4. The program automatically creates legends.
5. The program provides a spell checker.

When information is arranged according to factors and the results of those factors, a **cause-and-effect order** is used. Many scientific reports use this type of organization. The scientist begins by collecting data to support an unproven hypothesis. After the data is organized and studied, the scientist reaches a conclusion. Recommendations are made based on the conclusion. Common transition words used in a cause-and-effect order are *therefore, consequently, based on, because of, due to, as a result,* and *if . . . then.*

Example of Cause-and-Effect Order

Eggs, beef, lamb, and poultry were cooked at different temperatures to determine the lowest internal temperature that protects against food-borne illness. Cooking food to an internal temperature of 160 degrees was found sufficient to prevent most illnesses. Because some foods are most tasty when cooked to a higher degree of doneness, lamb, pork, and beef should be cooked to 170 degrees. Due to a new resistant strain of salmonella, which still lives at temperatures of 170 degrees, poultry should be cooked to an internal temperature of 180 degrees.

Outlining

Outlining is a key part of your prewriting process. In order for your audience to grasp your meaning, your thoughts must be organized and your understanding of what you want to convey must be absolutely clear. A well-organized outline can help you achieve this goal.

Numbering Systems.   A formal multilevel outline takes the form of a series of headings of different levels. These headings are called **level heads.** Two level-head numbering systems, the **alphanumeric system** and the **decimal system,** are shown in **Figure 3.1** below. In the alphanumeric system, the level 2, level 3, and level 4 heads may use parentheses, as shown in the figure, or they may use periods after the introductory letter or number.

 Tech Link

For more information on creating an outline, visit the Purdue University Online Writing Lab, *http://owl.english.purdue. edu/handouts/general/ gl_outlin.html*

FIGURE 3.1   Alphanumeric and Decimal Numbering Systems

Alphanumeric System

I.   **Level 1 Head**
  (A) Level 2 Head
  (B) Level 2 Head
      (1) Level 3 Head
      (2) Level 3 Head

II.   **Level 1 Head**
  (A) Level 2 Head
  (B) Level 2 Head
      (1) Level 3 Head
          (a) Level 4 Head
          (b) Level 4 Head
      (2) Level 3 Head
  (C) Level 2 Head

III.   **Level 1 Head**

Decimal System

1.   **Level 1 Head**
  1.1 Level 2 Head
  1.2 Level 2 Head
      1.2.1 Level 3 Head
      1.2.2 Level 3 Head

2.   **Level 1 Head**
  2.1 Level 2 Head
  2.2 Level 2 Head
      2.2.1 Level 3 Head
          2.2.1.1 Level 4 Head
          2.2.1.2 Level 4 Head
      2.2.2. Level 3 Head
  2.3 Level 2 Head

3.   **Level 1 Head**

Organizing Data for an Outline. Imagine that you need to report on your day's activities and that the list of activities in **Figure 3.2** below is the data you have compiled. How you translate the data into useful information for a report will depend on the answers to the CMAPP questions you devise.

FIGURE 3.2   Day's Activities

1. Woke: 7 a.m.
2. Fed my dog Prince
3. Did homework: 1.5 hours
4. Breakfast
5. Lunch in the cafeteria
6. Ate supper at home, as usual
7. New jacket looks great
8. Drove car to campus
9. Attended BusMgmt. 305
10. Comm. 302 class
11. Was a bit late for Acct. 313
12. Marketing 315: interesting today
13. TV: one hour only
14. Went to bed
15. Carlos told me about his new car
16. From Comm. instructor—info about next assignment
17. Spoke to BusMgmt. instructor about term paper
18. Continued Chapter 3 of Marketing project
19. Read part of latest issue of *Business Week* magazine
20. Internet search on micromarketing
21. Bought new Marketing textbook
22. Researched Acct. project in library
23. Taped TV program on Discovery Channel
24. Saw results of last Marketing midterm: awful!
25. What the 3 new library books are about
26. Composed part of Comm. assignment on computer
27. Spoke to Jan on phone
28. Asked Dad for loan: unsuccessful
29. Walked Prince: 1/2 hour
30. Finished Chapter 2 of Marketing project
31. Cover article in *Business Week* useful for Marketing project
32. Discovered that Accounting term paper relates to Marketing project
33. Outline for Marketing project needed adjusting
34. Got cash from ATM
35. Had coffee with Marge
36. Downloaded search results

Drafting an Outline. Assume that your CMAPP analysis reveals that your marketing instructor has asked you for an update on your project. You decide that your product will be a memo and that you will concentrate on three main topics:

- Marketing project itself
- Other courses that have a bearing on the project
- Related activities

You conclude that many of the items in **Figure 3.2** might be relevant. The others will not translate into useful information, so you ignore them. Your next step is to organize under appropriate headings the data elements you have kept, along with the introductory information your instructor will expect to see in the memo. This stage is often complicated by the fact that some data items may appear to fit under more than one topic, so you have to make content decisions as well. Completion of these tasks will result in a first draft of a formal multilevel outline similar to the one shown in **Figure 3.3** below.

FIGURE 3.3   Initial Multilevel Outline

I.   Why I'm Writing a Memo
      A.   Instructor asked for it

II.   Marketing Project Itself
      A.   Finished Chapter 2 of Mktg. project
            1.   Continued Chapter 3 of Mktg. project
            2.   Outline for Mktg. project needed adjusting
      B.   Bought new Marketing textbook
      C.   Mktg. 315: interesting today
            1.   Saw results of last Marketing midterm: awful!
      D.   Discovered that Acct. term paper relates to Marketing project

III. Other Courses That Have a Bearing on the Project
      A.   Comm. 302 class
      B.   From Comm. instructor—info about next assignment
      C.   Was a bit late for Acct. 313
      D.   Attended BusMgmt. 305
      E.   Composed part of Comm. assignment on computer

IV.   Related Activities
      A.   Spoke to BusMgmt. instructor about term paper
      B.   Researched Acct. project in library
      C.   What the 3 new library books are about
      D.   Did homework: 1.5 hours
            1.   Internet search on micromarketing
            2.   Read part of latest issue of *Business Week* magazine
                  a.   Cover article in *Business Week* useful for Mktg. project
      E.   Downloaded search results

V.   General Conclusion
      A.   Ask instructor to give me feedback

Finalizing an Outline.   After you organize the data elements under the appropriate headings, you should refine your outline. This stage in the process of translating data into useful information is a painstaking one, particularly if you are working with an outline for a longer, more complex document. Three principles—subordination, division, and parallelism—are central in revising and finalizing your outline.

1. *Subordination.*   The principle of **subordination** says that every item that appears under a particular level head must logically be a part of the subject matter of that level head. Conversely, the item must not deal with a different issue and must not be of equivalent or greater importance or scope.

    Your CMAPP analysis will allow you to determine what is appropriate in your circumstance. When you find an entry that violates the principle of subordination, you may decide to change the sequence of items, to create another separate level head, or to change the wording of a level head so that it reflects what you really mean.

2. *Division.*   The principle of **division** states that you cannot subdivide the content of any level head into fewer than two parts. For example, if you have a I.A head, you must have at least a I.B head.

    How you fix a division problem also depends on the results of your CMAPP analysis. You might decide to remove an item, to add an item (taking care not to contradict the principle of subordination), or to make the item a higher level head. What you do depends on what you decide you really mean.

3. *Parallelism.*   The principle of **parallelism** requires that all level 1 heads exhibit the same grammatical structure, that all level 2 heads exhibit the same grammatical structure, and so on. Note that the structure of level 1 heads may be different from the structure of level 2 heads, which may be different from the structure of level 3 heads, and so on.

    The solution to a parallelism problem is to reword items until each of the same-level heads exhibits the same grammatical structure. When applying the principle of parallelism, you may well find that the easiest grammatical structure to work with is a noun or noun phrase.

    The principle of parallelism applies not only to outlines, but also to bulleted and numbered lists in a document. Each item in a list must have the same grammatical structure.

Figure 3.4 on the next page offers a possible completed outline that is finalized from the initial multilevel outline shown in **Figure 3.3.** There is no single correct version because you may have several possible ways to fix any subordination, division, or parallelism problems. The final version of your outline should always be based on your CMAPP analysis.

Drafting

After you have finalized your outline, you can begin to develop your ideas. As you write your draft, remember to use words that promote goodwill and encourage your receiver to accept your message.

FIGURE 3.4 Completed Outline

I.   Rationale for Memo

II.   Marketing Project (Marketing 315)
      A.   Outline (completed)
      B.   Chapter 2 (completed)
      C.   Chapter 3 (partially completed)
      D.   Accounting course term paper (mentioned)

III. Related Coursework
      A.   Marketing 315
           1.   Issues related to project
           2.   New textbook
      B.   Accounting 313
      C.   Business Management 305
           1.   Course relevance
           2.   Conversation with instructor
      D.   Communication 302
           1.   General relevance to Marketing project
           2.   Instructor's comments re assignment

IV.   Complementary Activities
      A.   Library research re Accounting 313
      B.   Relevance to Marketing project
      C.   Usefulness of three library books
      D.   Homework
           1.   Internet search on micromarketing
           2.   *Business Week* magazine cover article
           3.   Complementary sources

V.   Conclusion
      A.   Summary
      B.   Request for feedback

It is best to try to write your draft all in one sitting. Keep your outline and prewriting notes nearby. If you find that you need more information, don't stop to do research. Instead, write yourself a note and move on to the next idea in your message. The whole point of drafting is to develop your ideas. You are not yet concerned with typographical errors, grammar, or spelling. You do, however, want to achieve the appropriate tone, or voice, for the message.

While you can always change things later, include as many specific details in your draft as possible. Choose your words carefully because the words you use help shape the tone and style of your message. However, try not to spend a lot of time on any particular word or phrase. Make a note to go back and check a thesaurus or dictionary later.

Revising

To revise is to make changes. Many writers spend as much or more time revising as they do creating their first draft. It is in the revision stage that a writer makes sure the message says exactly what it should.

Before you revise a draft, put it aside for at least a few hours, if possible. You'll come back to the document with a fresh perspective. To begin the revision process, read your draft all the way through, focusing on your original CMAPP analysis. Try to step back and put yourself in the place of the receiver. Is the message focused? Do you see gaps in logic? Do the paragraphs flow well? Have you included all of the vital information? Did you stray from your point? Reorganize sentences or paragraphs as needed and read the draft again.

The ABCs of CMAPP

As you revise your message, keep the ABCs of communication—**accuracy, brevity,** and **clarity**—in mind. These elements are always essential parts of your CMAPP analysis.

Accuracy. When composing and revising your message, ask yourself the following questions:

- Have I chosen the right facts for this situation? In other words, are all my facts pertinent to my context, my audience, and my purpose?
- Is all my data correct? (Have I checked?)

Remember that your audience "needs" your information. As you learned in Chapter 1, technical communication is audience-driven. But your audience does not need data that will muddy the issue. Recall as well that your message represents you to your audience, and thus your reputation hangs on it. Imagine the consequences if your audience were to find an error in your information: Your message would lose credibility, as would you, the "messenger." Once lost, your credibility with this audience may be hard to regain.

Brevity. A practical definition of brevity might be "Say what you need to say and then stop." If you include material in your document or presentation that is not relevant to your context, message, audience, and purpose, your audience may be confused, irritated, and/or bored—and all your efforts will have been wasted. Consider the following examples:

Poor: During the month of June, employees can preview the full and complete Annual Report for the year 20-- before it is distributed to stockholders.

Better: During June, employees can read the complete 20-- Annual Report before it is distributed.

Poor: When you present complex information, you need to ask yourself if a graphic illustration would make it easier to understand.

Better: Use a graphic illustration to make complex information easier to understand.

Tech Link

These web sites offer a wide variety of resources for improving your writing:

Guide to Grammar & Writing
http://ccc.commnet.edu/grammar/

Purdue University's Online Writing Lab (OWL)
http://owl.english.purdue.edu/

To cut down on wordiness, use the active voice rather than the passive voice. When you write in the **active voice,** the subject of the sentence performs the action of the verb. In the **passive voice,** the subject receives the action. Consider the following example:

Passive: The best idea was submitted by Vernon.
Active: Vernon submitted the best idea.

Clarity.   Clarity is a function of the words and grammatical structures you use, of the organization of your information, of the logic and cohesion of your arguments, and of the way you present your message to your audience. When examining your message for clarity, ask yourself the following questions:

- Is everything as clear as I can make it?
- Can I safely assume that my message will be as understandable to my audience as it is to me?

Consider the following example:

Poor: For the majority of people who comprise our society, money is perceived in but two states of tangible matter, either as currency or as coins.
Better: Most people think money is currency and coins.

Bias-Free Words

In today's diverse workplace, it is particularly important that you not offend your audience by showing biases. **Bias-free words** are free of prejudice, or unfair assumptions, and do not influence the audience in any particular or unfair direction. Courteous communications are sensitive to stereotypes and biases that involve gender, race, age, and disability.

Gender Bias.   In today's workforce, women work as pilots, air traffic controllers, police officers, and construction workers. Men work as nurses, administrative assistants, and kindergarten teachers. The words used for today's workers should be free of gender bias to reflect these realities. Note the difference between the gender-biased words and the neutral words in the following list.

Gender-Biased Words	Neutral Words
foreman	foreperson, supervisor
waiter/waitress	server
stewardess	flight attendant
salesman	salesperson
policeman	police officer
fireman	firefighter
manmade	manufactured
executives and their wives	executives and their spouses

Race and Age Bias.   A simple way to avoid biases of race and age is to avoid mentioning these factors at all unless they are essential to your meaning. The following sentences are examples of avoiding race and age bias.

Biased Words	Unbiased Words
We hired an Asian lawyer.	We hired a lawyer.
Have you met the little old man?	Have you met the man?

Disability Bias.   Avoid disability bias by avoiding reference to a disabling condition. If you must mention the condition, use unbiased words, as shown in the following examples.

Biased Words	Unbiased Words
afflicted with, suffering from	has
crippling defect, disease	condition

Editing and Proofreading

To **edit** is to alter or refine a written message to improve it. When you edit, you are fine-tuning your message with an eye on sentences, phrases, and words. Editing tools to keep on hand or to reference online include the following:

- A language handbook or style guide
- A dictionary
- A thesaurus

The Grammar and Style Handbook at the end of this text can help answer specific grammar and mechanics questions. An editing checklist is another useful tool. Consider the points in the Checklist shown on the next page whenever you edit your work.

Proofreading is the process of reviewing and correcting the final draft of your message. As you proofread your document, look for general content errors as well as mechanical errors, such as incorrect spacing, misspelled words, incorrect capitalization, or incorrect punctuation.

Nearly all word-processing software programs include a **spell checker** and a **grammar checker.** These programs are helpful, but do not assume that they will replace the editing and proofreading process. Spell checkers will not help you with most proper nouns or with word substitutions. Your spell checker won't know that you meant to key *being* instead of *begin*. Only careful proofreading can detect errors like this one.

Tech Link

Access the Merriam-Webster OnLine Language Center to find a complete dictionary and thesaurus, *www.m-w.com/*

Checklist

Effective Editing

✓ Read your document aloud and listen for awkward sentences. If you stumble over a phrase, chances are it needs editing.

✓ Check sentence types and lengths. Are all your sentences about the same length? If so, create some variety. Are any sentences long or complicated? Consider splitting them into two sentences.

✓ Look at sentence beginnings. If many sentences start with the same word, add some variety. Avoid starting sentences with *I, my, it is,* and *there is.*

✓ Use language appropriate for your audience. Avoid the slang, jargon, and informal language commonly used in everyday speech.

✓ Watch for overused words. Be original. Replace overused words and phrases with fresh, vivid language.

✓ Check for clarity, completeness, and tone. Look at your message from your receiver's viewpoint. Is the message clear? Will the receiver know exactly what to do or how to respond? Does the tone promote goodwill?

The following list describes six effective proofreading methods.

1. *Scroll the screen.*   Move the cursor down the screen of your computer as you proofread each line.
2. *Read aloud.*   Read aloud to slow down and examine words more carefully.
3. *Compare drafts.*   Check the final draft against the previous edited copy.
4. *Proofread the hard copy.*   Proofread the printed document even if you've already edited it on the screen.
5. *Proofread backwards.*   Read each line from right to left, or start at the end of the document and read the entire message backwards.
6. *Use two proofreaders.*   One proofreader reads aloud from the previous edited copy, while the other proofreader checks the final copy.

Publishing

When your proofreading process is complete, you're ready to prepare and publish the final document. To **publish** your message is to deliver it to the receiver or make it available to the public. Before publishing, evaluate your message from a visual viewpoint. Your finished product should not only sound good when your receiver reads it, it should look good too. Effective visual presentation of material in your technical communication is critical to your success. We'll look at this in Chapter 5.

Chapter Review

CHAPTER SUMMARY

The writing process consists of five stages: prewriting, drafting, revising, editing and proofreading, and publishing. In the *prewriting* stage, you organize your message and outline your information. Some common patterns of organization are chronological order, spatial order, comparison-and-contrast order, most-important-to-least-important order, and cause-and-effect order. A multilevel outline will help you organize your thoughts and define exactly what you want your message to convey. The first draft of an outline includes the data elements you want to include in your message organized under appropriate headings. To finalize your outline, correct any subordination, division, or parallelism problems.

The *drafting* stage is where you use your outline and any prewriting notes to develop your ideas. You are not concerned with grammar or spelling in this stage, but you do want to achieve the appropriate tone for your message.

In the *revising* stage, you make sure the message says exactly what it should. Keep the ABCs of communication—accuracy, brevity, and clarity—in mind as you revise. Focus on your original CMAPP analysis, and try to put yourself in the place of the receiver. Be sure that your communication does not contain any biases that involve gender, race, age, or disability.

Fine-tune your message in the *editing* and *proofreading* stage. Look at words, phrases, and sentences to be sure your message says exactly what you want it to say. After proofreading, you are ready to *publish,* or deliver, your message.

KEY TERMS

Accuracy

Active voice

Alphanumeric system

Ascending order

Bias-free words

Brevity

Cause-and-effect order

Chronological organization

Clarity

Comparison-and-contrast order

Decimal system

Descending order

Division

Edit

Grammar checker

Level heads

Most-important-to-least-important order

Outlining

Parallelism

Passive voice

Prewriting

Proofreading

Publish

Spatial organization

Spell checker

Subordination

Transitions

CRITICAL THINKING ACTIVITIES

1. List and briefly define the five ways that information can be organized. Give an example of how you might use each pattern of organization.

2. Discuss the best way to arrange information for each of the items listed below. Which organizational plan would you use?
    a. A description of furniture in a room decorated in Early American style
    b. A report giving reasons why a particular model of laser printer should be selected
    c. A report explaining which city streets should be resurfaced
    d. A scientific report explaining what happens to people who are deprived of sleep
    e. A report explaining the progress being made on a long-term project

3. List some of the benefits of using a multilevel outline in the creation of business and technical communication documents.

4. Define and briefly describe the principles of subordination, division, and parallelism.

5. In what parts of a business and technical communication document must you apply the principle of parallelism?

6. Rewrite these sentences to make them courteous and bias-free.
    a. Bring me the report.
    b. Ms. Jennifer Chang, Minister, will conduct the session.
    c. The old Indian attorney was an expert trial lawyer.
    d. The lady professor is afflicted with Lyme disease.
    e. An employee requesting family leave must file the required paperwork at least one month prior to her requested leave.

7. Rewrite the following memo to make improvements in clarity, tone, and style.

TO: All Employees
FROM: Human Resources Office
DATE: July 17, 20--

The new vacation request forms are available. You need to fill one out for each vacation request you want to make, and be sure to do it ahead of time. It gets tough processing so many vacation requests at the last minute right before the holidays.

---

8. Identify the wordy phrases in each sentence, and revise each sentence to make it more concise.
    a. Overall, in my opinion, Ralph Rodriguez is by far the best-qualified candidate for the job that is open.
    b. The many helpful new office supplies you will need for work are in the supply cabinet at the end of the hall.

c.   The house that was built during the Victorian era was renovated for office space.

9.   Use the Checklist for Effective Editing on page 50 to improve in the following paragraph:

Electronically prepared letters are becoming commonplace in today's society. Electronically prepared communications are an expected part of today's society. A major challenge for communicators will be to make these electronically prepared communications successful. They can make them effective by using the same skills as those needed for preparing communications in the traditional manner.

---

10. Describe the six methods of proofreading described in the chapter. Which proofreading method do you prefer? Describe the process you use, and explain why you prefer it.

11. Work in teams of two to proofread the following message for general content and mechanical errors. One person should read the message aloud, while the other person makes the needed corrections. Switch roles and repeat the process until you and your teammate agree the document is correct.

Welcome to Atten Motrgage compnay. For you're infromatoin and knowledge we have inclosed herewith a brochure to answer any questions I think you might have about you new mortgage laon? You loan number is located the uper left left cornor of the the payment coupon. payment coupons will be maled to You under separate cover and must acompany all payments.

SKILLS APPLICATIONS

1.   Examine a piece of technical or business writing, such as a report or a lengthy brochure. Based on your examination, create the multilevel outline that the author might have used while developing the communication.

2.   Select a card game or board game with which you are familiar. Compose a formal outline describing the following about the game: required materials, rules, strategy, minimum and maximum number of players, and minimum age requirements for players.

3.   Brevity, or conciseness, is one of the ABCs of effective writing. Visit the online Guide to Grammar & Writing (*http://ccc.commnet.edu/grammar/concise.htm*) to learn more about concise writing. Then take the quizzes at the end of the lesson to test your skills.

CONTEMPORARY ISSUES CASE

Dress for Success.   Atlee Corporation is a consulting company with offices in several major cities in the United States. An old firm, it is considered conservative and somewhat elite. The company directors have finally bowed to pressure and agreed to institute a casual dress day for employees. The directors issued the memo shown in **Figure 3.5** below.

FIGURE 3.5   Atlee Corporation Memo

MEMO

TO: All Employees of Atlee Corporation
FROM: Atlee Board of Directors
DATE: October 5, 20--
SUBJECT: Implementation of Casual Dress Day

After much consideration, we, the Board of Directors, agree that the implementation of a casual dress day will neither interrupt business nor damage our reputation. For that reason, employees may participate by wearing less than formal attire on the last first and third Friday or each month.

Should any employee violate any of the rules stated herein, disciplinary action may be taken. If this arrangement is to work in an acceptable manner, certain rules must be followed. First, employees who have contact with outside clients on the designated casual days may not participate in casual dress day under any circumstances. Women may not wear clothing that would be considered revealing. In additional short or mini skirts, shorts, halter tops, tight jeans, and anything resembling swimwear is not allowed. Male employees should wear comfortable slacks and shirts or sweaters, depending on the season.

If you have questions or comments regarding any information in this memo, direct them to Susan in the San Francisco office (415-555-1500, ext 237) or to Mr. Alzar in the Boston office (617-555-2300, ext. 526).

How do you think this memo will be received by employees? Consider the following questions, and then create a revised version of the memo.

1.   Does the message contain any bias? What evidence do you find?
2.   What is the tone of the message?
3.   What content and mechanical errors does the memo contain?

CASE STUDY

GTISU Facilities Leasing Report

Situation

For the last three years, the Grandstone Technical Institute Student Union (GTISU) has leased from GTI a large student common room and three small adjoining rooms for offices. The lease with GTI includes utilities (electricity and heat); GTISU contracts with the phone company for telephone, fax, and Internet connections.

On August 4, Heather Hong, executive secretary of GTISU, finds in her campus mailbox a formal notice from GTI informing GTISU that it must immediately vacate the facilities it has been renting. Vlad Radescu, the GTISU president, is on vacation in Hawaii, which means that Hong will have to deal with the crisis herself. Upset, she dashes off an e-mail (**Figure 3.6** below) to her friend Sally Johal, a member of the GTISU executive committee.

FIGURE 3.6   Hong's E-mail to Johal

Hi, Sal!

I guess I'm just venting here. Got a notice from Admin telling us to vacate right now. And Vlad is off on another of his Hawaii jaunts, of course! What are they doing? Term starts again in a few weeks! And now they've given us just a couple of weeks to get out. Can you believe it? And we've been here for years and years now too! The Institute keeps telling us that they need the space for more classes and that there was never any guarantee that we'd get to renew the lease and that they've been trying to do something else with the rooms for ages and that our reps just wouldn't get together with them — well, like why should they? Anyway, Admin's been totally unfair with the rent for ages. So what's to talk about? Anyhow, I think I'll try to get a petition together. We'll keep talking with them, I suppose, for all the good that'll do. But in the meantime, we can scout other places too, just in case we do have to find somewhere else. And all this just a month before term starts too! I'll keep you informed.

Well, hope your summer was better than mine. I guess I'll see you when you get back into town in a couple of weeks or so. By the way, how was Vegas? I loved it last year. See you! Oh, and by the way, it seems that in a pinch, we'd be able to rent a really big room from Apex Holdings just down the block. Pat Chen . . . you remember Pat . . . has an uncle who's a big shot there and can get it for us pretty cheap. I know . . . it is farther away. But it might work!

See ya!

After taking a break and calming down, Heather places a call to the law firm of Chung, Gomez, and McNamara and explains the situation to Franco Gomez, GTISU's legal counsel. Gomez is well aware that the relationship between GTI and the student union has for the last year been rocky at best. Thinking that things have finally come to a head, he asks Hong to prepare a report for him. Hong undertakes the task by gathering data and then working to convert it into information that will be useful to Gomez. The multilevel outline she creates appears in **Figure 3.7** on the next page. (The margin notes in the first column will assist you in analyzing her efforts.)

Issues to Think About

1. If you were Gomez, how might you explain the action taken by GTI?
2. To what extent would you expect to see GTI's reasons for the action reflected in the report you've requested from Hong?
3. How does the information in Hong's e-mail to Johal differ from the information in her multilevel outline? How do you explain and/or justify those differences?
4. What questions might Hong have been asking herself as she created her multilevel outline?
5. Refer to Hong's multilevel outline to answer the following questions:
   a. Who is Hong's primary audience?
   b. Might a secondary audience emerge at some point? If so, who?
   c. What does the primary audience already know?
   d. What does that audience likely need and/or want to know?
   e. What is Hong's primary purpose?
   f. What might her secondary purpose be?
6. Based on the information you have, are there any omissions in Hong's outline? Is it formatted correctly? Are there elements of Hong's outline that do not comply with the principles of subordination, division, and parallelism?

FIGURE 3.7   Hong's Multilevel Outline

Data > information: allows realistic interpretation.

Introductory information: takes CMAPP into account, allows audience to place situation in context.

Precise details are crux of most technical communication.

Graphic might be useful, but would it enhance? Would it be superfluous?

Balanced approach: Audience will likely need/want arguments of both sides.

Note: Use of "apparent" required for accuracy; information derives from second-hand data.

Options listed because CMAPP analysis reveals what reader will need to know.

Recommendations and deadline specify writer's purpose and specify action requested and time frame required.

Logical grouping of items throughout outline helps reader follow argument and see how items might be organized into bulleted or numbered lists in final document.

1. **Situation background**
   a) Agreement between Student Union (SU) and GTI
      i) Implementation date
      ii) Length of agreement
      iii) General terms of lease
      iv) Foreseen SU executive petition
   b) Premises
      i) Location
      ii) Size
      iii) Function

2. **Essentials of disagreement**
   a) SU perspective
      i) Value of SU location to GTI for attracting registrants
      ii) High rent
      iii) GTI's uncompromising approach
   b) Apparent GTI perspective
      i) Several tardy rent payments
      ii) Urgent space requirement for additional classrooms
      iii) Lack of responsible attitude on part of SU representatives
      iv) Lack of time: agreements with contractors

3. **SU's options**
   a) Continued negotiations with GTI
      i) Advantage: possibility of improved lease
      ii) Disadvantage: possibility of wasted time/effort
   b) Relocation to Apex Holdings' premises
      i) Advantage: resolution of problem with GTI and good lease terms
      ii) Disadvantage: distance from campus and lower student interest
   c) Abandonment of SU facilities—no real advantage

4. **SU's recommendations**
   a) Attempt at reconciliation/renegotiation with GTI
   b) If negotiations fail, relocation to Apex Holdings' premises

5. **Decision deadline: within 2 weeks**
   Must notify all parties by August 20

CHAPTER 4

Research and References

In today's information-rich workplace, the ability to find and use information is critical to success. With so many sources of information available via the Internet, libraries, databases, magazines, journals, newspapers, television, and more, determining the best source for your particular research project can be a challenge. Researching and finding information requires that you systematically sort through the data that is available in order to organize and analyze the information you need to produce a CMAPP product.

Reading for Information

Researching or reading for information requires a different approach than reading for pleasure. Your reading tasks may include reading narrative paragraphs, lists, or web pages, as well as reading charts, graphs, tables, and diagrams. Whatever the source, reading for information may require a variety of reading strategies or approaches.

To assess how to begin your reading task, survey the material in hand. This process might include:

- ◆ Reading the title and table of contents.
- ◆ Reading the introduction and/or summary.
- ◆ Looking for boldface headings and subheadings.
- ◆ Looking for graphics.
- ◆ Taking note of highlighted terms, which may be underlined, set in color, or set in italic or bold type.

Based on your survey, consider how the information source fits your research needs. Do the title or headings indicate you'll find information related to your topic? Did you see a graphic related to your research? This assessment will help you determine whether you need to scan, skim, or study the material to obtain the specific information you need.

When you read quickly to locate a specific piece of information, you are **scanning.** For example, you might scan the directory of a computer disk to locate a specific file. In contrast, when you are **skimming,** you are reading quickly to get the general or main idea. For example, a marketing manager might skim census and traffic-pattern reports to determine a desirable location for a franchise. When you read for detail and in-depth information, you are **studying.** An excellent tool for more detailed reading is the SQ3R technique, which includes surveying, questioning, reading, recalling, and reviewing.

When your reading includes visuals such as charts, graphs, and tables, keep the following points in mind:

- Look for a title to get an idea of the type of information being presented.
- Look for descriptions, headings, or labels for columns, lines, or circles.
- Determine what the numbers mean, where the information came from, and when it was collected.
- Determine how the information was measured and what is being compared.

Tech Link

MindTools offers extensive coverage of reading and information strategies. Visit
www.mindtools.com/ rdstratg.html

Finding Information

Determining the best source for your research project can be a challenge. Depending on your research question, your best source of information may be a library, an individual, or an organization. In most cases, you'll probably find that a combination of resources will yield the best results.

Your research will lead you to two basic types of information: primary information and secondary information.

Primary Information

Primary information involves the firsthand gathering of data. These unpublished sources of information can lead you to experts who can provide valuable insights, opinions, and access to information that may not yet be in published form. Primary sources of information include the following:

- Interviews
- Surveys
- Observations

Interviews.   Depending on your objective and the focus of your research, **interviews** can be an excellent source of information. By interviewing experts, or **SMEs** (subject-matter experts), in the field you are researching, you can acquire valuable firsthand information. Interviews offer the opportunity to ask questions and clarify answers as you go along. An expert can give you a unique perspective on a topic, something no reference book can match.

As you prepare for an interview with your SME, keep the following guidelines in mind:

♦ Become familiar with the subject matter so you know which questions to ask.
♦ Write out your objectives for the interview.
♦ Make a list of questions based on your objectives.

The best questions are broad and open-ended. A **closed question** can be answered by a respondent with a yes or a no. An **open-ended question** requires the person to respond with something more than a simple yes-or-no answer. When constructing open-ended questions, keep in mind the five Ws—who, what, when, where, and why.

With your questions in hand, the guidelines in the Checklist below can help you execute a successful interview.

 ## Checklist

Informational Interview

✓ Start and end on time. Arriving prepared with your questions shows that you respect the person's busy schedule.

✓ Be courteous in your speech and your manner. Express your appreciation for the interview and listen attentively.

✓ Begin with an overview. Restate the purpose of the interview, and explain how the information will be used.

✓ Summarize throughout the interview. Summarizing helps ensure that you understand what is being said.

✓ Probe for more information. Probing questions can help you get additional information.

✓ Ask for clarification. If you don't understand something that is said, ask for an explanation.

✓ Take careful notes. Write down all key information during the interview; then fill in any gaps as soon as possible after the interview.

Surveys. **Survey research** allows you to interview a group of people to gather information and draw conclusions. Surveys can be conducted in person, in writing, by telephone, or via the Internet. Knowledge gained from a well-produced survey can be invaluable; but the design, distribution, tabulation, and analysis of the information you gather can require considerable time.

As you construct your survey, you'll develop a set of questions called a **questionnaire.** The five types of objective questions commonly used in a questionnaire are either-or questions, multiple choice questions, graded-scale questions, short-answer questions, and rank-order questions.

Either-or questions give the reader a choice between two options, such as Yes or No, True or False.

Example: I would like the union to publish a monthly newsletter.

Multiple choice questions expand the number of possible answers by supplying three or more options.

Example: I would like the union to publish a newsletter that is issued (a) weekly, (b) monthly, (c) quarterly.

Graded-scale questions provide for degrees of response.

Example: I read the union newsletter (a) all the time, (b) occasionally, (c) not at all.

Short-answer questions are used only when the list of possible answers is too numerous to categorize.

Example: Some topics that I would like to see included in the union newsletter are

_____.

Rank-order questions are used when you have a series of items you want respondents to put in order according to a criterion, such as frequency of use or personal preference.

Example: Please rank the following topics on a scale of 1 to 5, using a 1 to indicate the most interesting topics and a 5 to indicate the least interesting topics.

Employee promotions   ____   Company officers   ____
New product development ____   Employee achievements ____

By using the Checklist for Effective Surveys on the next page, you will be able to create a well-designed questionnaire that can provide valuable information for your research.

Observations.   In contrast to survey research, **observation research** depends on watching what people do. Observations involve careful, systematic monitoring and recording of the activities of a person or persons without questioning or communicating with them directly.

Two common forms of people-watching-people research are mystery shoppers and one-way mirror observations. For example, at the Fisher-Price Play Laboratory, children are invited to spend 12 sessions playing with toys. Toy designers watch through one-way mirrors to see how the children react to the toys, and then modify their toy designs accordingly.

☑ Checklist

Effective Surveys

✓ Use simple, straightforward language that your audience will understand.

✓ Explain your purpose and give concise instructions for completing the questionnaire. Include a statement at the beginning of your questionnaire, or attach a cover letter or memo. Indicate the reason for the questionnaire and a deadline for completing the questionnaire.

✓ Define terms that your audience might not understand. Don't assume that people taking your survey will be familiar with technical terms or jargon.

✓ Make your questions easy to answer. Design questions so the answers can be easily categorized, and group related questions together. When a questionnaire asks questions in a logical order, it is easier for readers to respond.

✓ Whenever possible, develop closed questions that allow respondents to circle or check off their answers. These types of questions generally get a better response than open-ended questions that require written answers. You'll also find it much easier to tabulate your responses and draw conclusions.

✓ Use words that say exactly what you mean. For example, what does *several* mean in the statement "Benton Paper Towels have several advantages over their competitors"?

✓ Watch out for biased questions. For example, the question "Is the city's restrictive lawn-sprinkling ordinance affecting your business?" reflects your opinion and may bias your respondents. Instead, you might rephrase this question as "Is the city's lawn-sprinkling ordinance affecting your business?"

✓ Avoid linking two questions together. For example, if you say, "Was the instructor prompt and understanding of your needs?" you are really asking two things. Be careful to ask for just one piece of information in a question.

✓ When listing possible answers to questions, consider if all options have been included. You may want to add another option, called "Other," and allow respondents to write in an answer.

✓ Field-test your questions with a small number of people from the total group you'll survey. Have your field-testers complete the survey; then ask for their feedback. Was the questionnaire easy to complete? Were the questions clear? Did the group need additional direction? Revise your survey accordingly.

Another form of observation research, job shadowing, can provide valuable information about the job duties of the person shadowed. In addition, by observing people on the job, you may learn about larger issues of work flow, organizational structure, operating procedures, morale, and productivity.

Tech Link

These sites feature extensive listings of online reference sources, including almanacs, dictionaries, encyclopedias, and atlases. Visit *www.infoplease.com/* and *www.refdesk.com/ fastfact.html*

Secondary Information

Secondary information includes sources of information that are already in published form. Secondary sources of information include the following:

- Books
- Periodicals
- Encyclopedias
- Dictionaries
- Handbooks
- Almanacs
- Directories
- Government publications
- Electronic databases
- Web sites
- Internet discussion groups and newsgroups

The indexes and directories listed below are just a few of the sources available to help you locate secondary information.

Index/Directory	Description
Business Periodicals Index	Arranges by topic the titles of articles published in more than 250 business-related periodicals.
Directory of Directories	Indexes several thousand business, industrial, and professional directories.
Dun & Bradstreet, Inc.	Lists more than 100,000 U.S. companies by net worth. Includes information about company officers, products and services, sales, and number of employees.
Readers' Guide to Periodical Literature	Lists by topic and author the titles of articles in approximately 200 periodicals.
Standard & Poor's Register of Corporations	Lists U.S., Canadian, and major international corporations.
Consumer Information Catalog	Lists in each issue the titles of free and low-cost federal publications of consumer interest.

Knowing Where to Look

The first step in your research project is usually to examine secondary sources of information. These sources contain a wealth of data that provide valuable background information for your project. In fact, depending on the scope of your project, secondary sources may provide all the information you need. However, your secondary research may lead you to the conclusion that you need additional information from primary sources. Interviews, surveys, or observations can provide the additional information you seek.

As you locate sources of information, you should organize the information in a systematic way. When you are ready to write, you'll have all the information you need at your fingertips. List each source on an index card or a separate piece of paper, noting key points, title, author, page references, publisher, date, and other relevant information. For your interviews, note the date of the interview, the name and title of your interview subject, and any facts or quotes that you'll use in your report.

Using Information

As you research, evaluate and document your sources to ensure that your final CMAPP product is accurate, complete, and ethical. When using information you have gleaned from a secondary source, it is necessary to cite your source and give credit to the author. Using the words or ideas of an author without crediting the source of the information is called **plagiarism** (see **Figure 4.1** below). It leads the reader to believe the words are your own. This is unprofessional and unethical behavior and can often lead to expulsion from a school or a job.

FIGURE 4.1   How to Know When You Are Plagiarizing

You are plagiarizing when

- Any material, ideas, results, or comparisons are taken from another source and not referenced appropriately.

- Materials taken from one source are referenced as another source to confuse the reader and make the work appear original.

- Materials are taken as a direct quote from another source and not indicated in quotation marks within your work.

- The words of the original author are replaced by synonyms, but the structure and content remains largely unaltered.

You are not plagiarizing when

- The original text is digested, summarized, reworded, and referenced by you.

- The concepts or ideas are so general that they are considered common knowledge in a technical/professional area.

Tech Link

The University of Texas's statement on Academic Integrity offers an excellent discussion of plagiarism, including examples of the right way and the wrong way to paraphrase and cite sources. Visit *www.utexas.edu/depts/dos/sjs/academicintegrity.html #plagiarism*

Visit the web site for the U.S. Copyright Office at *www.loc.gov/copyright/* for more information on copyright laws.

Using the work of an author without authorization and without crediting the source is also a violation of **copyright law.** The authors of original works, both published and unpublished, are guaranteed copyright protection under the law of the United States as provided by the U.S. Copyright Office.

Crediting the author of information you have gathered from a web site can be tricky. The author or the source of the information may not be clearly spelled out at the site. Nevertheless, it is irresponsible to use the information without citing your source. If the author is unclear, at least note that the information was retrieved from a web site and list the URL of the site. Likewise, if the information is provided to you by way of an interview or e-mail, make those notations when crediting the information.

Evaluating Information

When gathering information from secondary sources, you should constantly evaluate the information you find. Ask yourself the following questions:

- Is the information valid?
- Is the information reliable? Is it provided by a reputable source?
- Is the information current or is it dated?
- Is the information biased?

Always check the validity and reliability of your sources. **Validity** means that the information presented is an accurate representation of facts. **Reliability** indicates that the information is free of error and that, if repeated, the research would result in the same findings. If most of the information you find offers the same or similar information, your source is probably reliable; but it's still a good idea to verify your facts. If there is one source that offers dramatically different data, you should question its reliability.

Bias in communication can be defined as "a preference or an inclination, especially one that inhibits impartial judgment." Even seemingly unbiased sources can introduce prejudice with a simple word or phrase. Consider the following excerpt from a news magazine: "The President angrily said . . . ." The use of the word *angrily* here is an interpretation. It is biased. Rewritten as "The President seemed angry when he said . . . ," the statement at least acknowledges the writer's interpretation. However, the statement "The President said . . ." is completely unbiased, leaving no room for interpretation.

Researchers must be especially careful when evaluating information from Internet sources. Today anyone can launch a web site and publish information in a professional-looking format. However, the information may be completely inaccurate. Responsible researchers constantly ask questions to determine if information is valid and reliable before using it.

Use the following Checklist to help you evaluate information you find on the Internet.

✓ Checklist

Evaluating Internet Sources

✓ Who publishes the web site? Is the source clearly an authority with verifiable credentials?

✓ Is the web site current? When was it last updated?

✓ Does the web site clearly indicate the author's name, title, affiliation, and contact information?

✓ Is the information balanced? Is the purpose of the web site to inform, to entertain, or to sell?

✓ Do the facts presented seem reliable to you? Do you see evidence of bias? Are facts clearly and completely referenced?

Documenting Information

Most organizations strive to achieve a consistent image in the documents they produce. Their document style is likely to include specific criteria for document formats and visuals (e.g., for letters and memos).

The compilation of "rules" for a consistent image is usually known as a house style. Although any organization can develop its own house style, well-established styles have been adopted by many institutions and companies. Widely used style guides include the following:

- *The Publication Manual of the American Psychological Association,* commonly referred to as the APA, has guidelines that are used in producing documents for the social science disciplines (psychology, sociology, and so on). You will probably need to follow the **APA style** for any documents that you prepare in these disciplines. See **Figure 4.2** on the next page, for examples of the APA style. APA's web site features a section on electronic reference formats: **www.apastyle.org/elecref.html**.

- *The Chicago Manual of Style,* published by the University of Chicago Press, is the reference guide used by most publishers and editors. Many North American organizations have modeled their house style on this style guide. See **Figure 4.3** on page 69 for examples of the **Chicago Manual of Style.**

- *The MLA Handbook,* published by the Modern Language Association of America, has guidelines that are commonly used in producing documents for humanities subject areas (literature, fine arts, philosophy, and so on). You will most likely have to follow the **MLA style** for any documents that you prepare in these subject areas. The handbook also offers guidance in handling documents in electronic form. See **Figure 4.4** on page 70 for examples of the MLA style.

⊠ Tech Link

Capital Community College's web site features guidelines for using MLA and APA documentation styles. Visit *http://webster.commnet.edu/mla.htm* and *http://webster.commnet.edu/apa/apa_index.htm*

FIGURE 4.2 References Using the APA Style

Reference Type	Reference Format
Annual Report	Willamette Company, Incorporated. (2000). *2000 Annual Report.* Seattle, WA: The Willamette Company, Incorporated.
Book, one author	Logan, P. (1998). *Small Winners.* New York: Stallings Publishing Co.
Book, two authors	Parker, Erica M., and T. M. Gauge. (1998). *Winning Is Not the Only Thing.* Phoenix, AZ: McDougle Press.
Book, edited	David, Gill A. (Ed.). (1999). *The Horse that Won the World.* Kansas City, MO: Lopes and Kinner Publishing.
Brochure	Collision Center. (2000). *Accidents Do Happen.* [Brochure]. Ruston, LA: Louisiana's Collision Center.
CD-ROM encyclopedia article, one author	Lee, Tyler (1996). Filing Systems. *Fileproof '99* [CD-ROM]. Silicon Valley, CA: FoolProof Systems, Inc.
Encyclopedia article, one author	Callens, Elizabeth. (1999). Database systems. *The Computer's Users Encyclopedia.* Dallas, TX: Automated Press.
Film, videotape, or audiotape	*Successful Computer System Projects.* (1999). [Film]. Atlanta, GA: Systems Development Resource Center.
Government publication	U.S. Department of Defense. (2000). *The Cost of the B-1 Bomber.* Washington, DC: National Press, Inc.
Internet, Web	Combining ethics and your travel. (1999). *Ethnic-o-Travel.* [Online]. Available: http://www.travelsites.com/dogood.htm. Cited 1999 May 13.
Interview	Susanboy, Martha, professor, Clever City State. (1996, January 12). Interview by author. Clever City, UT.
Journal article	Jiang, J. J. (1998). Systems success and communication. *The Journal of Computer Intelligence, 9,* 112–117.
Magazine article	Johnson, K. (1998, April 10). Losing and the loser psychology. *Successful Challenging 45,* 43–45.
Newspaper article, no author	"Is the weather really cyclical?" (1998, December 28). *Ruston Daily Journal,* B-7.
Newspaper article, one author	Marks, Amy. (1998, December 21). "Successful Weddings in Modesto." *Modesto Daily Times,* C-12.
Online newspaper	Adams, B. M. (1999, February 10). "The exciting international lawyer." [Online]. *Lawyers Journal 34,* 23–26. Available: http: www.alajournal.com/realworld.htm.

FIGURE 4.3 References Using the Chicago Manual of Style

Book, one author

Logan, P. *Small Winners*. New York: Stallings Publishing Co., 1998.

Book, two authors

Parker, Erica M., and T. M. Gauge. *Winning Is Not the Only Thing*. Phoenix, AZ: McDougle Press. 1998.

Journal article

Jiang, J. J. "Systems success and communication." *The Journal of Computer Intelligence* 9 (1998): 112–117.

Magazine article

Johnson, K. "Losing and the loser psychology." *Successful Challenging,* 10 April 1998, 43–45.

Newspaper

This type of citation is commonly incorporated into the text of the report; for example,

An article in the *Modesto Daily Times* of December 21, 1998, describes recent weddings in the Modesto area. Common elements in these weddings included . . . .

Unpublished interview

Susanboy, Martha. Interview by author. Clever City, UT, 12 January 1996.

FIGURE 4.4   References Using the MLA Style

Reference Type	Reference Format
Annual Report	Willamette Company, Incorporated. *2000 Annual Report.* Seattle, WA: The Willamette Company, Incorporated.
Book, one author	Logan, P. *Small Winners.* New York: Stallings Publishing Co., 1998.
Book, two authors	Parker, Erica M., and T. M. Gauge. *Winning Is Not the Only Thing.* Phoenix, AZ: McDougle Press, 1998.
Book, edited	David, Gill A., ed. *The Horse that Won the World.* Kansas City, MO: Lopes and Kinner Publishing, 1999.
Brochure	Collision Center. *Accidents Do Happen.* Ruston, LA: Louisiana's Collision Center, 2000.
Encyclopedia article, one author	Callens, Elizabeth. "Database systems." *The Computer's Users Encyclopedia.* 1999 ed.
Film, videotape, or audiotape	*Successful Computer System Projects.* Film. Atlanta, GA: Systems Development Resource Center, 1999.
Government publication	U.S. Department of Defense. *The Cost of the B-1 Bomber.* Washington, DC: National Press, Inc.
Internet, Web	"Combining Ethics and Your Travel." *Ethnic-o-Travel.* 1999. 4 Mar. 1999. <http://www.travelsites.com/dogood.htm>.
Interview	Susanboy, Martha. Personal Interview. 12 Jan. 1999.
Journal article	"Systems Success and Communication." *The Journal of Computer Intelligence* 9 (1998): 112–117.
Magazine article	Johnson, K. "Losing and the loser psychology." *Successful Challenging* 15 Aug. 1999: 43–45.
Newspaper article, no author	"Is the Weather Really Cyclical?" *Ruston Daily Journal* 28 Dec. 1998: B-7.
Newspaper article, one author	Marks, Amy. "Successful Weddings in Modesto." *Modesto Daily Times* 21 Dec. 1998: C-12.

Chapter Review

CHAPTER SUMMARY

Researching and finding appropriate information can be a challenge because of the many and varied sources available today. Reading for information uses different techniques depending on the information needed. Scanning is reading quickly to locate a specific piece of information. Skimming is reading quickly to get the general or main idea. Studying is reading for detail and in-depth information.

Research will lead to two basic types of information: primary information and secondary information. Primary information comes from the firsthand gathering of data. Primary sources of information include interviews, surveys, and observations. All of these primary sources can provide you with valuable information. The source you use depends on the type of information you need. An interview allows you to ask questions and clarify answers as you go along. By surveying a group of people, you can gather information based on your specific questions. Observation research is watching people and recording their activities and reactions.

Secondary information comes from sources that are already in published form, such as books, periodicals, directories, government publications, web sites, and so on. If you use secondary information, you must cite the source and give credit to the author. You should also evaluate secondary information in terms of the validity and reliability of the source.

The document you produce from your research may have to be formatted in a specific style so that your organization has a consistent image. Three common styles are the APA style, the Chicago Manual of Style, and the MLA style.

KEY TERMS

APA style
Bias
Chicago Manual of Style
Closed question
Copyright law
Either-or questions
Graded-scale questions
Interviews
MLA style
Multiple choice questions
Observation research
Open-ended question
Plagiarism

Primary information
Questionnaire
Rank-order questions
Reliability
Scanning
Secondary information
Short-answer questions
Skimming
SMEs
Studying
Survey research
Validity

CRITICAL THINKING ACTIVITIES

1. How does reading for information differ from reading for pleasure?
2. List and discuss three methods of reading for information.
3. Discuss three methods for obtaining primary information. When are you most likely to include primary information in your research process?
4. Define a subject-matter expert. Give an example.
5. What is the difference between open-ended and closed questions? Give an example of each.
6. Pick one of the instruction manual topics listed below, and develop a list of at least ten open-ended questions that you could ask an SME.

   ◆ How to Use the Computer Catalog in the Public Library
   ◆ How to Landscape a New House
   ◆ How to Administer First Aid
   ◆ How to Create Effective PowerPoint Presentations
   ◆ How to Train a Dog to Be Obedient

7. List ten sources of secondary information. When are you most likely to include secondary information in your research process?
8. Many research tools are available in print form at the library and on the Web. What criteria would you use to choose one resource over another?
9. If you were investigating a specific potential career, what method of gathering information would you use first? Why?
10. List five questions you can ask to evaluate the information on a web site.
11. Would you consider a web site with the suffix *edu* to have more reliable information than a site ending in *com*? Why or why not?
12. Why is it always important to credit the source of your information?
13. Name two or more commonly used styles. What are the critical differences between these two styles?

SKILLS APPLICATIONS

1. You've been asked to make an important presentation to a potential client. To prepare, you need to learn more about the company. You know only that this large software company is headquartered in Chicago. The company has been in business since 1979 and is publicly held. Based on the information you need, where should you begin your search? What types of resources might provide the information you need? List at least five possible sources.
2. Choose a contemporary topic of interest (for example, legal issues, technological change, or the economy). Locate a minimum of five articles about the topic, and create a bibliography page with each entry in the appropriate format. Consult a variety of sources for information, including the Internet, if possible.

3. Choose a career area in which you're interested, and identify an SME to interview. List at least ten open-ended questions, and arrange an interview with your SME. After the interview, use your notes to summarize the meeting.

4. Choose a current event or issue in the news. Find news articles, editorials, and commentaries on the topic from at least three different sources, including the Internet. What are the similarities and differences among the sources? How do the articles compare with the editorials and commentaries? Do some sources seem more biased than others? Do some sources seem more accurate than others? Prepare a summary of your findings.

CONTEMPORARY ISSUES CASE

Ethics on a Deadline.   David and Nico work for a foreign language interpreting and translating firm that has grown steadily since opening five years ago. The owners are planning to expand the business to at least two new cities within the next year and a half. David and Nico have been asked to work together to develop a list of ten potential sites for the new offices.

The timeline is tight, and David and Nico are pulling information together right up to the deadline. As David adds the final statistical information located on a web site, he realizes that he failed to note the source in his notes. Nico believes they should find the site again so they can include the proper reference. David says that it will take too much time and they'll miss the deadline. "After all," he says, "who will know?"

What do you think David and Nico should do? What are the possible effects of their decision?

CASE STUDY

Ann Arbor University Registration

Situation

A few years ago Ann Arbor University (AAU) instituted an automated telephone registration system referred to by the university as T-Reg, though often called T-rex by the students who have to use it.

After students obtain approved standing, they receive specific dates and times during which they must use the system to register for the next semester's courses. For security purposes, students are required to use their student number and their six-digit personal information number (PIN). As well, they must know the six-digit semester code (SC), the course identification number (CIN), and the section number (SN) for every course for which they wish to register. The system accepts credit card payments.

On May 17, Lester Mont, a 20-year-old AAU student, receives approval to register for his second year of Management Science, which is to commence in September. Telephone registration starts at 8 A.M. on Monday, June 5. Unfortunately, Lester's summer job as a help desk assistant obliges him to take a training course that day. He won't have the time or opportunity to make the lengthy and often frustrating calls that have characterized AAU's T-Reg.

At the beginning of June, Lester asks his father to register for him. Mr. Mont agrees but points out that he is unfamiliar with what Lester calls T-rex and, in fact, with the university. Lester assures his father that the procedure is simple and that he will fax him all the necessary information. In the late afternoon of Saturday, June 3, Lester faxes to his father a handwritten note that explains how to use the T-Reg system (**Figure 4.5** on the next page); a diagram of the T-Reg system taken from AAU's fall calendar (**Figure 4.6** on page 76); and an extract from the course timetable (**Figure 4.7** on page 77).

Issues to Think About

Lester's Note

Think about Lester's note in terms of CMAPP attributes, and answer the following questions: What do you think of Lester's organization of his message? Is the content of his message in keeping with his purpose? Is the form of the message appropriate given the audience? Is the format effective in terms of the message and the audience? Does the note reflect the aspects of accuracy, brevity, and clarity? (Justify your answer.) What improvements would you make to the note?

After you have analyzed the T-Reg diagram and the course schedule as directed in the following paragraphs, rewrite Lester's note to provide more specific and helpful direction for Mr. Mont.

T-Reg Diagram

Answer the following questions about the T-Reg diagram: To what extent do you think the diagram will help Lester's father? Will the form and format of the diagram make the message easier for Lester's father to read and use? How well does the diagram match the information Lester provided in his note?

Course Schedule

You often have to strike a balance between accuracy and brevity. To do so, you have to think about your context, your audience, and your purpose. As you answer the following questions, put yourself in Mr. Mont's position, keeping in mind that he has informed his son that he is unfamiliar with AAU. How is Mr. Mont likely to react to the format and content of the schedule information? What elements might present the greatest difficulty for Mr. Mont? For example, to what extent will he understand what each column represents? What do you think Mr. Mont, as Lester's audience, needs and wants to know?

FIGURE 4.5   Lester's Faxed Note

Saturday, June 3

Hey, Dad!

Sorry it took me so long to get this off to you. Things got hectic. Thanks very much for registering for me. It'll be a snap. Particularly since I'm only taking 4 regular courses this coming term. I made arrangements last term when I took an extra one so I'd have an easier time this Sept when I'm going to be really busy anyway, what with the part-time job and all. I'm also hoping to have the time to get back out to the big city to see you and Mom and Brenda, by the way. That'll be fun. Maybe we can get out to the island again, like we did when Brandon and I were kids.

Anyway, here's the info you need to do T-rex for me. You can see that it's pretty simple. You'll find the SC, CIN, and SN on the info I've sent too. All you do is dial the number and then follow the prompts, just like you do for your own voice mail at the office. So just think that you're like one of those automatons I'm supposed to be learning to program. By the way, the job is just great. I'm learning all kinds of really neat stuff. I can't wait till I see you guys later on to tell you about it. The kind of stuff they're building out here is really awesome! In case you get stuck, I've sent a diagram of how T-rex actually works. And I've sent you a clipping from the AAU calendar. By the way, you're going to need a bunch of numbers. My SSN is 226980878, and my PIN is 833848. Do you mind putting all this on your own MasterCard? I'll pay you back later in the summer. So you'd better have the card handy when you're phoning.

I'm going to need either one of the two accounting courses and either one of the marketing courses, plus the two computer sci courses. If you can, I'd prefer to get my classes over with earlier rather than later, but sometimes it's hard to get the sections you want. Oh, please try to get me Goldberg and Cornelian. They're both really good.

I'll give you a call when I get back. Had to go out of town over the weekend, but I'll be back at work dark and early on Monday for that training session that keeps me from registering myself. So I guess I'll phone you after supper on Mon. Don't forget that you have to phone in my reg at 9 on Mon. If you leave it until later, a lot of the sections will likely be filled up and I won't get what I want. The whole thing should take you about half an hour I figure.

Thanks again, Dad! Love you guys!

Les

FIGURE 4.6 Diagram of AAU T-Reg System

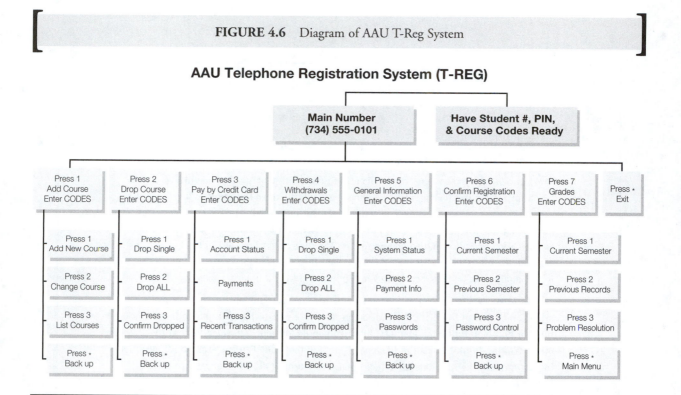

FIGURE 4.7   Extract from AAU Course Schedule

ACTG2100 Principles of Accounting 2

A339940	001	M W	08:30 10:00 F2100	Shen, A.
A339941	002	M W	11:30 13:00 F2239	Sayers, R.
A339942	003	T H	10:00 11:30 F2100	Parl, R.
A339950	004	W F	15:30 17:00 R2240	Singh, B.

ACTG2200 Statistical Analysis 2

A489901	001	T H	10:00 11:30 F2100	Goldberg, P.
A489903	002	M W	10:00 11:30 F2230	Parl, C.
A489905	003	W F	08:30 10:00 R2240	Singh, E.

CMPP2500 Comparative Languages

| C11100 | 001 | T H | 10:00 11:30 P1000 | Harby, I. |
| C11103 | 002 | W F | 15:30 17:00 P1005 | Weischart, F. |

MKTG2112 Marketing Trends

M22001	001	W F	11:30 13:00 A1100	Gatmar, E.
M22003	002	T H	08:30 10:00 A1115	Dijani, F.
M22005	003	T F	10:00 11:30 A1115	Hollings, A.
M22007	004	T F	14:00 15:30 A1100	Porseau, R.

MKTG2118 Research Methodology

M32222	001	M W	08:30 10:00 A2110	Dijani, F.
M32233	002	T F	08:30 10:00 A2100	Cornelian, W.
M32244	003	W F	14:00 15:30 A1100	Atwal, A.

CHAPTER 5

Communicating with Graphics and Visuals

For many people, the term *visuals* refers to pictures—photographs, clip art, sketches, and the like. In technical communication, however, the term has a much broader definition and includes the following:

- Typographical elements and other features that affect the appearance of a document.
- Visuals and graphics that illustrate specific ideas within a document or presentation.

Effective information design requires the integration of each of these elements. **Information design** is the use of specific, strategically chosen design features that help you communicate more effectively with your audience. By using white space, type fonts, and graphics in strategic ways, you can make your communication more appealing and meaningful to your readers. Basic elements of information design include the following:

- Sizes and styles of type fonts
- Headings, lists, and design attributes used for emphasis
- White space
- Justification and column widths
- Selection and presentation of visuals

Document Features

To make effective use of document features, you need to be familiar with relevant terminology and have a working knowledge of the various features of your computer software. Spreadsheet programs (such as Microsoft Excel, Lotus 1-2-3, and Corel QuattroPro), presentation programs (such as Microsoft PowerPoint and Lotus Freelance Graphics), graphics programs (such as Adobe PhotoShop), desktop publishing programs (such as Microsoft Publisher), and web-page authoring programs (such as Microsoft Front Page) make it easy for you to create visuals for your documents and presentations. However, even with all these options, you will likely create most of your documents with a word processor (such as Microsoft Word or Corel WordPerfect). While there are variations among the different software programs currently available, most programs allow you considerable control in manipulating a documents visual features.

Body Text and Level Heads

The term **body text** refers to the text that makes up your document's paragraphs and bulleted or numbered lists. Body text can be thought of as the main text of your document.

The term **level heads** refers to titles, subtitles, headings, and subheadings of all kinds. The term is useful in that it permits a ready numerical reference. In this chapter, for example, the heading "Document Features" is a level 1 head and the subheading "Body Text and Level Heads" is a level 2 head.

Headers and Footers

A **header,** also known as a running head, is text that appears at the top of every page. While the content of a header will depend on the nature of the document, the author's name, document title, and page number are standard elements of a header. In general, a header does not appear on the first page of a document. If the document is printed on both sides of the pages, left- and right-hand pages may feature different headers.

A **footer,** also known as a running foot, has the same elements as a header but appears at the bottom of every page.

White Space

White space refers to the portions of a printed page that are blank. Two examples of white space are margins and line and paragraph spacing.

Some word processors measure the margins of a document from the top, bottom, left, and right edges of the page. Others measure the bottom margin from the top of the footer and the top margin from the bottom of the header. No matter which software you use, you should normally set your margins at no less than 1" on all sides of the page.

Line spacing, or line space, refers to the space between each line of text. Your word processor will apply a preset line spacing automatically each time the text wraps to the following line as you key. To create particular effects, however, you can adjust the line spacing.

Paragraph spacing is the space between the last line of one paragraph and the first line of the next. On a typewriter, it was common to hit the return key twice between paragraphs. Most word processors allow you to set paragraph spacing so that it conforms with that of printed books: greater than a single line space but less than two line spaces. A common practice is to set paragraph spacing at 1.25 to 1.5 times the line spacing.

Justification

Justification refers to how lines of text relate to the left and right margins of the page. Examples (and descriptions) of left, center, right, and full justification appear below.

Example of Left Justification

When you write longhand on loose-leaf paper, you begin each line at the left margin and conclude it when you run out of room at the end of the line. This is **left justification,** also known as flush left or ragged right. (An exception would be an indented first line of a paragraph, of course.) This paragraph, like those of many documents, is left-justified.

Example of Center Justification

Sometimes lines of text, particularly titles and subtitles, appear equidistant from the left and right margins. This arrangement, not surprisingly, is known as **center justification,** or center-justified text. These lines are center-justified.

Example of Right Justification

To create certain visual effects, lines of text may be aligned with the right margin. This is **right justification,** also known as flush right. This paragraph is an example of right-justified text. Right justification is generally not suitable for body text.

Example of Full Justification

In most books, the text is aligned with both the left and right margins. This is known as **full justification,** or fully-justified text. The problem with this format is that, with certain fonts, different combinations of letters form words of different lengths that, in turn, require different line lengths. Ensuring that each line fits precisely between the margins, while ensuring as well that the apparent space between the words remains constant, can be painstaking work. The problem is particularly difficult to solve for short lines of text. For example, most newspapers use full justification and also have fairly narrow columns. This can produce undesirable effects.

Fonts

Font, in the context of technical communication, refers to a particular style of letter, including size and shape. Some common font attributes are as follows:

- **bold**
- *italic*
- ***bold italic***
- <u>underscored</u>
- UPPERCASE
- SMALL CAPS

There are literally thousands of different fonts, and typographers are creating new ones every day. Samples of a variety of fonts are featured in **Figure 5.1** below.

FIGURE 5.1   Font Samples

Courier	The quick brown fox jumps over the lazy dog.
Times New Roman	The quick brown fox jumps over the lazy dog.
Bookman	**The quick brown fox jumps over the lazy dog.**
Arial	The quick brown fox jumps over the lazy dog.
AvantGarde	The quick brown fox jumps over the lazy dog.
Impact	**The quick brown fox jumps over the lazy dog.**
Metropolis	**The quick brown fox jumps over the lazy dog.**
Serpentine Sans	**The quick brown fox jumps over the lazy dog.**

Tech Link

Daniel Will-Harris offers an excellent discussion on the effective use of fonts titled "Choosing & Using Type" at *www.will-harris.com/ use-type.htm*

Fonts fall into three general categories. Times New Roman and Bookman are both **serif fonts.** If you look closely at the samples in **Figure 5.1,** you will see that the letters have tiny "tails" (the meaning of the word from which *serif* is derived) at their extremities. Serifs were reputedly designed by typographers long ago to help the eye move more easily from one letter to the next. In almost all books (including this one), the body text is set in a serif font.

Fonts that do not have "tails" are called **sans-serif** ("without serif") **fonts.** Examples in **Figure 5.1** are the Arial and AvantGarde samples. Sans-serif fonts are commonly used for level heads. Although some technical writers do set their body text in a sans-serif font (maintaining that it "looks cleaner"), most typographers feel that sans-serif type is harder to read than serif type.

The Impact, Metropolis, and Serpentine Sans samples in **Figure 5.1** are examples of **decorative fonts.** These fonts, which may be serif or sans-serif, are designed to create a special visual impression. When used for body text, decorative fonts tend to be difficult to read.

Unless you have a compelling reason to do otherwise, you should use a serif font for the body text of your documents and, in most cases, a sans-serif font for level heads. However, for text projected onto a screen (an overhead transparency or a 35mm slide, for example), most authorities recommend the reverse. Audiences seem to find it easier to read sans-serif text when it is "far away" and "large," as is the case with text projected onto a screen.

Other Attributes

Document visuals may also include features such as the following:

- *Rules.*   Vertical and horizontal **rules** are simply straight lines that are intended to help the audience recognize divisions on a page.
- *Boxes.*   Text may be enclosed in a blank or shaded box. For example:

> This center-justified line appears in a blank box.

> This shaded box encloses this center-justified line.

- *Reverse Text.*   **Reverse text** involves placing white or light-colored letters on a black or color background. While reverse text can be effective in certain circumstances (e.g., in a heading), it should be used sparingly because it is harder to read than black text on a white background.

> This is a sample of reverse text.

Lists

Technical communication makes frequent use of both **bulleted** and **numbered lists.** The two types of lists tend to serve slightly different purposes. Items in a list are often numbered to suggest a particular sequence for a particular reason—order of importance, for example. While bulleted items don't imply sequencing, it would be more difficult to locate the ninth of fifteen items in a bulleted list than in a numbered one.

Which list should you use? As always, your choice should take into account your analysis of context, message, and audience.

Document and Presentation Visuals

The ABCs of CMAPP (accuracy, brevity, and clarity) apply to your visuals just as they apply to your written communication. Your CMAPP analysis for visuals should include the following two key steps:

1.   Decide whether your presentation requires a visual.
2.   Choose the best visual for your purpose, message, and audience.

We'll talk more specifically about the use of visuals in presentations in Chapter 10. In general, though, if you can answer yes to any of the questions in the Checklist below, then visual aids should be included in your communication.

 Checklist

Use of Visuals

✓   Will visuals help clarify your message?

✓   Will visuals add interest?

✓   Will visuals help the audience understand and remember what you say?

Tim Altom of Simply Written discusses the use of a variety of graphics in his article "Using Graphics Effectively." You can read it at www.simplywritten.com/ graphics.pdf

Information, Impression, and Ethics

As mentioned in Chapter 1, audiences respond not only to the objective or factual meaning of words (their denotation) but also to their emotional effect (their connotation). The same holds true for visuals. When your audience sees your visual, they receive not only "information" from it—the facts that you are representing—but also a "visual impression" that evokes a particular response. These two meanings may be quite different.

When you choose visuals for either documents or presentations, you have to remain aware of both the information the visual contains and the impression it creates. For example, imagine a photo of someone accused of embezzling funds from a company. The photo provides "information" that allows you to recognize the person's face. Now imagine that the photo was taken from an unflattering angle, that the lighting created stark shadows on the person's face, and that the subject was scowling at the photographer. This photo will likely create a "visual impression" of guilt.

Considerations

As you choose and construct your visuals, keep in mind the points discussed in the Checklist on the next page. The visuals shown in **Figure 5.2, Figure 5.3,** and **Figure 5.4** on pages 86 and 87 are referred to in the Checklist.

✔ Checklist

Choosing and Constructing Visuals

✓   **Relevance.** A visual should reflect or advance each of the CMAPP elements: context, message, audience, purpose, and product. Your personal delight with a particular visual is of no consequence if your audience looks at the same visual and thinks, "Why on earth is that here?" In addition to being relevant, your visual should create interest.

✓   **Simplification and Emphasis.** Remember the adage "A picture is worth a thousand words"? Visuals help increase your audience's understanding of your message by simplifying concepts or data. A visual is particularly helpful for displaying and analyzing complex numerical data. However, you must be careful to choose or construct a visual that actually does simplify the data because, otherwise, the visual may confuse the audience. Similarly, a properly chosen visual can be effective in emphasizing a particular point in your message, but a visual that lacks focus tends to distract an audience.

✓   **Enhancement.** A visual should enhance your message, not overwhelm it. Your visuals will not be a success if your audience walks away from your presentation thinking, "I have no idea who the speaker was or what the topic was, but those sure were great visuals!"

✓   **Size.** Your visual must be large enough for its details to be visible to your entire audience. For example, a car engine diagram that has been reduced to 1" x 1" in your document will be of little use. Similarly, no one in an audience of 30 developers will benefit if you hold up a 4" x 6" photograph of a construction site. At the same time, your visual should not overwhelm your communication by being larger than is necessary

✓   **Legibility.** If its text is not readily legible to your audience, your visual will not contribute to your communication. Instead, it will detract from your message and generate impatience and frustration in your audience. While often a function of size, legibility also depends on clarity of reproduction. A poor-quality photocopy in a document or an unreadable projected image in a presentation can severely compromise an otherwise effective visual—so, of course, can a font that is difficult to decipher.

✓   **Color.** Decide whether or not color is necessary. For example, an illustration of the wiring of an alarm system probably requires the use of color. However, a graph comparing yearly sales figures may not need color. You also have to take into account how you are planning to reproduce your document. For the alarm system illustration, black-and-white photocopying would defeat the purpose of using color.

(Checklist continued on next page.)

✓ **Level of Detail.** Consider the cluttered appearance of the diagram shown in **Figure 5.2** below. If your purpose is to provide dimension measurements for an audience who wants to know how to lay out a public tennis court, you could likely have omitted terms such as *Singles Sideline* and *Service Line*. Conversely, an audience wanting to learn the rules of the game does not need to see the various measurements. When deciding how much detail to include in your visual, give careful consideration to your audience and your purpose.

✓ **Scale.** If you want to discuss transportation problems between Chicago and Vancouver, the map shown in **Figure 5.3** on the next page is an appropriate scale. If, however, you want to discuss transportation links around the Great Lakes, you will need a large-scale map like the one shown in **Figure 5.4** on the next page. Applying a CMAPP analysis to the selection and construction of your visual will help you determine an appropriate scale.

FIGURE 5.2   A Tennis Court

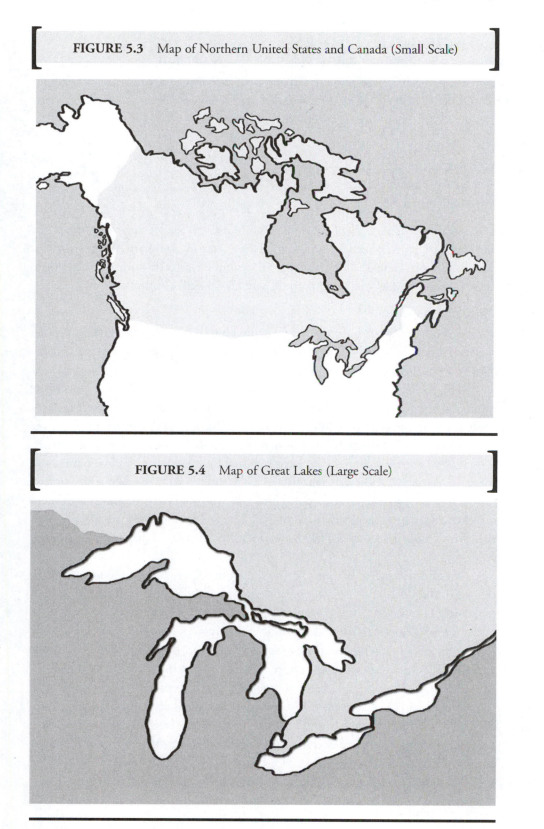

FIGURE 5.3   Map of Northern United States and Canada (Small Scale)

FIGURE 5.4   Map of Great Lakes (Large Scale)

Charts and Tables

Charts (often called graphs) are commonly created from the data generated by a spreadsheet or database program. In both documents and presentations, graphs allow a concise, visual communication of data. The most common types of charts used in technical communication are as follows:

- Pie charts
- Vertical bar charts
- Horizontal bar charts
- Line charts

A table consists of data arranged in columns and rows—an arrangement just like that of a spreadsheet. Like data in charts, data in a table may derive from a spreadsheet or database but may also be compiled directly into its final form. Tables are more likely than charts to display text as well as numbers.

Pie Charts

Whatever the information provided by a **pie chart,** the visual impression created is that of parts of a whole. Each segment stands for a different category, and the data in all of the segments combined totals 100 percent.

The pie chart in **Figure 5.5** on the next page is an attempt to represent the numbers of registrants in GTI's Business Program over an eight-year period. A pie chart is not an appropriate choice in this case. First, it is unlikely that we want the audience to think of the eight years as parts of a whole. Second, the eight segments, several of which are a similar size, create a visual impression of "some big ones and some small ones." Although percentage labels accompany the segments, precise differences are not visually apparent. Finally, the purpose of "exploding" a segment is to focus your audience's attention on it. There is no reason to focus attention on the two exploded segments (1994 and 1996), and so this distinction is merely confusing.

An effective use of the pie chart is shown in **Figure 5.6** on the next page. In this case, the data—the registration percentages for the four program areas that make up GTI's 2001 Co-op Program—lend themselves to representation in a pie chart. The 3-D perspective adds interest and enhances visibility. The use of only four segments avoids the confusing visual impression of **Figure 5.5.** The single exploded segment leaves no doubt as to which segment the audience should focus on. And finally, the use of a legend decreases the amount of clutter around the pie.

Note that the effectiveness of a pie chart also depends in part on the choice of fills or patterns, which should allow an audience to easily distinguish one segment from another. The chart in **Figure 5.6** uses four distinct fills, so it is easy to identify the various segments. The chart in **Figure 5.5** repeats the fills for various segments, giving the appearance that some segments are related to others.

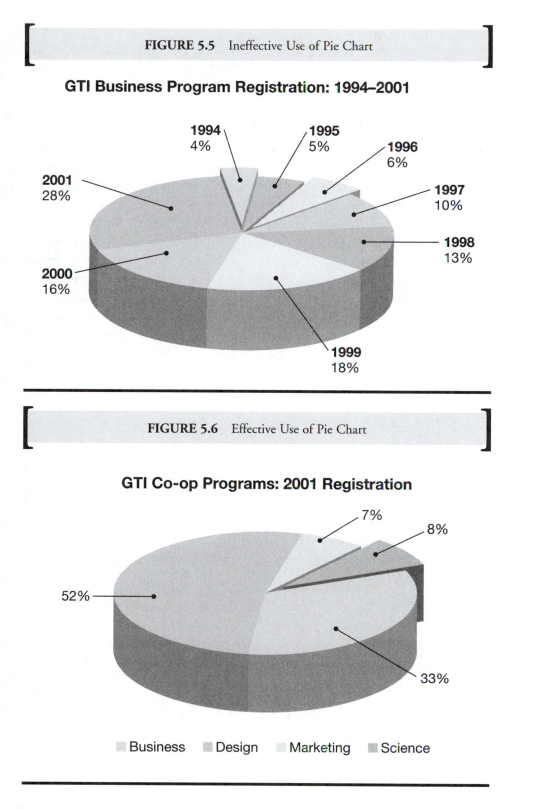

FIGURE 5.5 Ineffective Use of Pie Chart

GTI Business Program Registration: 1994–2001

1994 4%
1995 5%
1996 6%
1997 10%
1998 13%
2001 28%
2000 16%
1999 18%

FIGURE 5.6 Effective Use of Pie Chart

GTI Co-op Programs: 2001 Registration

7%
8%
52%
33%

Business   Design   Marketing   Science

Vertical Bar Charts

The visual impression created by a **vertical bar chart** (also known as a column chart) is that of discrete quantities. The audience expects to see sets of data (often called data categories and data series) ranging along the *x*-axis (the horizontal axis), and quantities increasing up the *y*-axis (the vertical axis). Negative amounts are often shown descending below the *x*-axis.

Vertical bar charts are highly effective in representing comparisons and contrasts. The visual impression they create makes them better vehicles than pie charts for representing precise differences. As well, vertical bar charts can be effective in displaying multiple comparisons and contrasts.

A common misuse of the vertical bar chart is to include too many sets of data. **Figure 5.7** below exemplifies the clutter and confusion that typically results. The figure, which attempts to compare and contrast eight years of registration figures for seven GTI programs, generates the visual impression of a city skyline. A far more effective use of the vertical bar chart is shown in **Figure 5.8** on the next page. Here the restriction of data to three sets (1994, 1995, and 1996) of two items (Arts and Business) enhances, condenses, and simplifies the message. The legend is far more legible than the one in **Figure 5.7**. Finally, the horizontal gridlines allow for a more accurate visual impression of the differences in quantities. Be cautious, however. Gridlines can lead to clutter.

FIGURE 5.7   Ineffective Use of Vertical Bar Chart

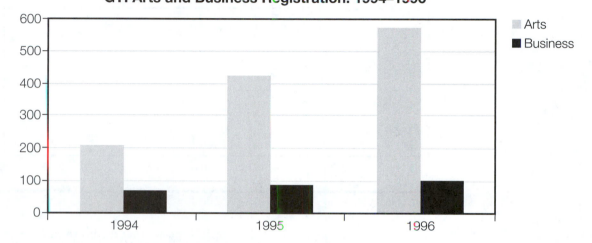

FIGURE 5.8   Effective Use of Vertical Bar Chart

GTI Arts and Business Registration: 1994–1996

Horizontal Bar Charts

The **horizontal bar chart** looks like a vertical bar chart turned 90 degrees clockwise. It, too, is effective for presenting one or more comparisons or contrasts (although, as mentioned, your audience's unconscious expectation is to see quantities increasing up the *y*-axis, rather than along the *x*-axis).

A horizontal bar chart's visual impression is conditioned by the overall shape of the chart. For an example, compare **Figure 5.9** below and **Figure 5.10** on the next page, which are derived from identical data. The *y*-axis in **Figure 5.9** shows

FIGURE 5.9   Horizontal Bar Chart with *y*-axis Showing Earliest Date at Top

GTI Registration Totals, 2000–1990

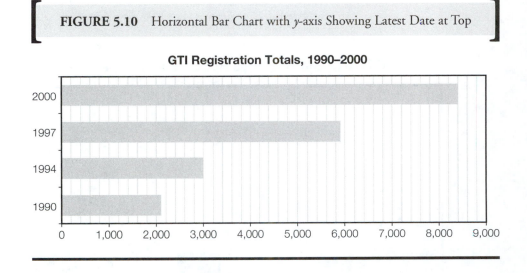

FIGURE 5.10   Horizontal Bar Chart with *y*-axis Showing Latest Date at Top

the earliest date at the top; whereas **Figure 5.10** places it at the bottom. Note how **Figure 5.9** creates a visual impression of stability, while **Figure 5.10** suggests a situation that is top-heavy (i.e., inherently unbalanced or unstable).

Line Charts

Like vertical and horizontal bar charts, **line charts** plot data along *x*- and *y*-axes. We are accustomed to reading from left to right in English, and we expect a line to progress in the same direction. The visual impression of a line chart is normally that of progression over time along the *x*-axis. Thus, a line chart is particularly effective in showing chronological change.

As **Figure 5.11** on the next page shows, you can plot more than one data series in a line chart by including more than one line. You can also increase the precision of the visual impression by using markers on the data points. Again, be cautious as you balance precision against clutter.

Note another aspect of **Figure 5.11**'s visual impression. The shape of the lines as they progress from left to right creates an image of partial convergence. Registration numbers for the Internship and General programs are growing more and more similar because of the simultaneous increase of the former and decrease of the latter, while Continuing Education appears to be growing independently weaker. Note also that the use of similar solid lines for the Internship and General programs emphasizes the impression of convergence.

Certain aspects of line charts can make them deceptive. Note that the span of years between the *x*-axis points in **Figure 5.11** changes even though the physical distance separating them does not. Note also that there are registration numbers for each of the indicated years but not for the intervening ones. An audience might

FIGURE 5.11   Line Chart Showing Multiple Lines

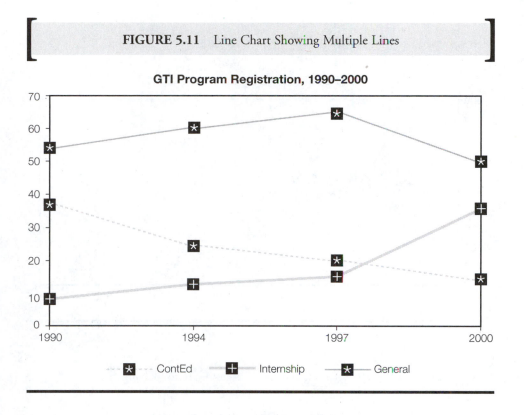

be tempted to extrapolate the registration numbers for the intervening years by using the visual impression of a continuous line showing progression as a guide. Such an extrapolation would be little more than an assumption (and likely an inaccurate one) because we have no data for the intervening years.

Another important aspect of line charts has to do with the scale of the axes and the size of the increments. Consider **Figure 5.12** and **Figure 5.13** on the next page. Both charts represent identical GTI Business Program data. The only difference between them is found in their *y*-axes. The *y*-axis in **Figure 5.12** begins at 0, ends at 1,000, and progresses in increments of 100; by contrast, the *y*-axis in **Figure 5.13** begins at 50, ends at 500, and progresses in increments of 50. Simply as a result of the different *y*-axis scales and increments, the former chart suggests steady growth while the latter chart conveys an impression of rapid change.

Does taking advantage of this phenomenon mean that you are deceiving your audience? Recall our discussion of ethics in Chapter 1. If you deliberately mislead your audience, you are probably being unethical. If, on the other hand, you are merely making effective use of visuals to present your message in conformity with your purpose—and if that purpose is not deception—you are probably on solid ethical ground. In any event, when you construct line charts or interpret those of others, remember the distinction between meaning and visual impression.

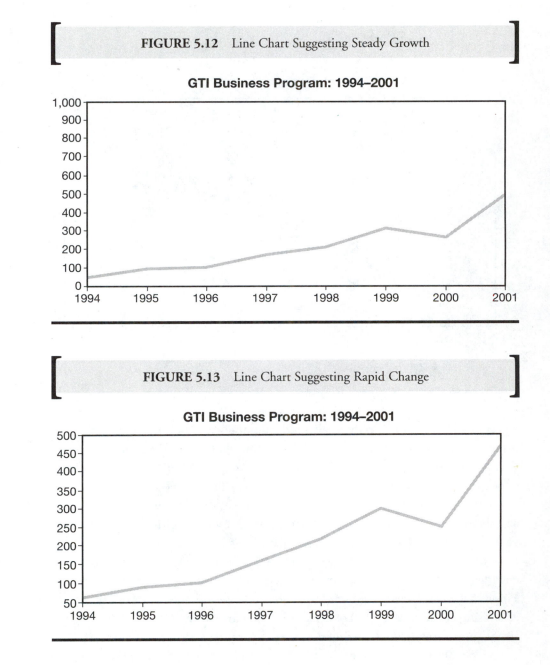

FIGURE 5.12   Line Chart Suggesting Steady Growth

GTI Business Program: 1994–2001

FIGURE 5.13   Line Chart Suggesting Rapid Change

GTI Business Program: 1994–2001

Tables

The rows and columns of data in a **table** can produce what we might call "visual information overload." The table shown in **Figure 5.14** on the next page is relatively uncomplicated, giving a visual impression of interrelated, if not readily understandable, numbers. Faced with a table in a document, a motivated audience can carefully examine every row and column in order to discern relationships,

> **FIGURE 5.14** Table Showing RAI Sales and Repair Data

Sales-to-Service-Event Ratio: 1990–2000

	Autos Sold / Leased	Repair / Service Events
1990	1,676	15,424
1991	1,745	15,377
1992	1,756	14,326
1993	1,748	14,114
1994	1,751	13,598
1995	1,763	13,112
1996	1,798	12,123
1997	1,895	11,112
1998	2,024	10,199
1999	2,135	10,168
2000	2,368	9,945

trends, and so on. But if you use a table as a projected visual, your audience will not have time to carefully examine every entry. The audience can only follow your lead as you discuss the data.

In discussing the numbers in the table in **Figure 5.14,** for example, you could leave two very different impressions. On the one hand, you could say:

> In 1990, almost 1,700 sold or leased vehicles accounted for the unacceptably high figure of more than 15,000 repair or service incidents. In 2000, a full decade later, the sales-to-service ratio showed moderate improvement, but the almost 10,000 repair or service events for the 2,000-plus vehicles sold or leased was still unacceptably high.

On the other hand, you could say:

> In 1990, we were forced to deal with approximately ten repair and service incidents for each vehicle we sold or leased. However, only ten short years later, we showed a dramatic improvement. In 2000, there were only about four repair and service incidents for every vehicle we leased or sold.

Thus, you could use the same table to leave a negative impression of ongoing difficulty or a positive impression of successful change. Use the results of your CMAPP analysis to guide your treatment of tables, but don't ignore ethical questions.

Tech Link

You can find an extensive set of free clip art (as well as links to other clip-art sites) at clipart.com. Visit **www.clipart.com**

Illustrations and Photos

You can import illustrations and photos into your communications using scanners, digital camera technology, software packages, and web sites. **Clip art** is electronic artwork—sketches, drawings, cartoons, line art, and pictures—that you can import and use as visuals for documents or presentation materials. Thousands of color and black-and-white images are available for your use.

A note of caution: A growing number of electronic formats exist; not all are compatible with every computer application, and not all illustrations can be effectively printed or projected. Also, you should consider the ethical—and legal—issue of copyright. While you may generally use public domain illustrations without seeking copyright permission, clip art and photos may be proprietary. Software licences are often ambiguous about what you may do with the clip art included with applications.

• • • • • • • • • • • • • • • • • • • **Chapter Review**

CHAPTER SUMMARY

In technical communication, visuals include typographical elements and features that affect the appearance of a document and visuals and graphics that illustrate specific ideas in a document. Document features to consider in preparing a message include body text and level heads, headers and footers, white space, justification, fonts, rules, boxes, reverse text, and bulleted and numbered lists.

When choosing and constructing visuals and graphics, you should consider the relevance of the visual, whether it simplifies or emphasizes a point, and whether it enhances your message. In addition, a visual must be an appropriate size and scale, be legible, use color effectively, and have a correct level of detail.

Several types of charts are commonly used in technical communication. In a pie chart, the visual impression is of parts of a whole, where the segments total 100 percent. The visual impression of a vertical or horizontal bar chart is of discrete quantities. A horizontal bar chart looks like a vertical bar chart turned 90 degrees clockwise. Both vertical and horizontal bar charts are effective in representing comparisons and contrasts. The visual impression of a line chart is of progression over time. A line chart is effective in showing chronological change.

Tables organize data into rows and columns in order to simplify groups of related numbers. For tables and all types of charts, you should be careful not to intentionally mislead your audience by how you present the visual information.

Various sources have visuals available for your use. If you import visuals, such as photos and clip art, be sure you have permission for their use.

KEY TERMS

Body text	Line chart
Bulleted list	Line spacing
Center justification	Numbered list
Clip art	Paragraph spacing
Decorative fonts	Pie chart
Font	Reverse text
Footer	Right justification
Full justification	Rules
Header	Sans-serif fonts
Horizontal bar chart	Serif fonts
Information design	Table
Left justification	Vertical bar chart
Level heads	White space

CRITICAL THINKING ACTIVITIES

1. Describe the main characteristics of serif, sans-serif, and decorative fonts.
2. Suggest the most common use in standard technical communication documents for each of the three font categories.
3. How might you qualify your answer to question 2 if "the most common use" was in reference to text projected onto a screen?
4. What are the different purposes served by bulleted lists and numbered lists?
5. Briefly explain the terms *information* and *impression* as they relate to the message carried by visuals.
6. Briefly explain why three or more of the following are important points to consider when choosing or constructing visuals.
    a. Relevance
    b. Simplification
    c. Enhancement
    d. Size
    e. Legibility
    f. Color
7. Find an example of a visual that includes too much or too little detail. Give reasons for your selection.
8. Find an example of a visual whose scale is too large or too small. Give reasons for your selection.
9. **Figure 5.15** below shows data obtained from Global Motors concerning the firm's national sales since 1980. Think of two different ways of presenting that data visually. For each of your suggestions, produce a brief CMAPP analysis. Then produce a draft of the visual you would use for each analysis.

FIGURE 5.15   Global Motor Sales

In 1980, 9% of Global Motors' vehicle sales came from its innovative *Traveler* line of sport utility vehicles. The *Trend* line of sport sedans accounted for 19% of sales, while the *Security* line of passenger vehicles accounted for the remaining 72%. In 1985, the *Traveler* line accounted for 14%, the *Trend* line for 23%, and the *Security* line for 63%. In 1990, the figures were 20% for *Traveler,* 21% for *Trend,* and 59% for *Security.* In 1995, the figures were 27% *(Traveler),* 25% *(Trend),* and 48% *(Security).* In 2000, 42% of sales were *Travelers,* 39% were *Trends,* and only 19% were *Securitys.* Global predicts that by 2005, fully 55% of its sales will be attributable to *Traveler* models, 30% to *Trend* vehicles, and 15% to the *Security* line.

Global sold 7,000 vehicles in 1980, 11,400 in 1985, and 22,900 in 1990. In 1995, sales totaled 35,400, rising to 48,400 in 2000. A total of 57,000 vehicle sales is predicted for 2005.

SKILLS APPLICATIONS

1. Find and analyze a user's manual for a home appliance or computer software. How effectively does the manual make use of information design techniques and principles? Discuss examples of effective and ineffective information design in the manual. Be sure to address all aspects of information design, including font selection, use of white space, graphics, and so on.

2. Look through a recent business magazine or newspaper, and identify three different examples of the charts or graphs discussed in this chapter. For each chart or graph, identify its type and write a critique of its effectiveness.

3. Use a software program of your choice (such as Microsoft PowerPoint) to create a pie chart that shows the following budget allocations. Title the chart "Budget Allocations," and represent the allocations as percentages.

   ◆   Rent, $950
   ◆   Utilities, $150
   ◆   Savings, $200
   ◆   Food, $250
   ◆   Clothing, $125
   ◆   Entertainment, $75
   ◆   Car payment, $225
   ◆   Miscellaneous, $90

   E-mail the chart to your instructor as an attachment.

CONTEMPORARY ISSUES CASE

Presenting the Facts. You are part of the team selected to prepare and present your company's annual report to the board of directors. At last year's presentation, the board indicated to your company president that they would like to see a 10 percent increase in sales in the coming year. They also indicated that, after several years of flat sales, this increase was necessary to avoid layoffs and cutbacks.

Unfortunately, your accounting department informs you that the company only had a 6 percent increase in sales this year. While you work on the text portion of the report, another member of the team works on preparing the visuals. You notice that the visuals do not create the impression that the sales increase is less than desired. They actually make sales look better than they are. Your job as well as others' may rely on this presentation of data. What would you do?

CASE STUDY

AEL Engineering Report

Situation

In January 20--, AAU's Department of Physical Plant, responsible for all university buildings, was notified by the university's principal real estate insurance company, Guardian Life and Property, of a problem in Vanier Place, a 35-year-old building used primarily as a warehouse. The insurance inspector, who had observed fissures in the concrete panels around the truck loading bays, indicated that a policy renewal would not be forthcoming until the necessary repairs were completed.

AAU contracted with Accelerated Enterprises Ltd. to investigate the damage and submit an engineering report. The assignment went to Deborah Greathall, an AEL senior associate specializing in civil engineering. During examination of Vanier Place, she discovered that the truck loading bays, installed in 1989, had been carved from what had been an exterior wall. Unfortunately, the construction had not taken into account the long-term impact of large trucks backing up into the loading bays. The ongoing shocks, Greathall concluded, had eventually led to cracking in the concrete panels that made up the west wall of the building.

Greathall considered various options for repairing the wall. (The situation was complicated by the fact that segments of the panels were below exterior grade. As well, the university had no alternative loading bays that it could use during reconstruction.) She eventually decided on a course of action. She submitted her preliminary engineering report, introduced by a cover letter, to Dr. Joan Welstromm, chair of AAU's Civil Engineering Department, who had been appointed by Dr. Helena Paderewski, AAU's president, to be the university's liaison. Greathall sent a copy of the report to Frank Nabata, the AEL senior partner who had arranged for her to take the AAU contract.

Greathall's cover letter and preliminary report appear in **Figure 5.16** on page 102, and **Figure 5.17** on pages 103–105.

Issues to Think About

Let's assume that Greathall is a competent engineer, that she is conscientious about her work, and that she wants to make a good impression on both Welstromm and Nabata. After you have analyzed Greathall's cover letter and preliminary report as directed in the following paragraphs, create improved versions of the letter and report based on your analysis.

Cover Letter

1. What kind of font is used for the letterhead?
2. Is the letterhead effective in conveying an impression of the firm's solidity and professionalism?
3. Is the body text font an effective choice? Why or why not?

4. What kind of document visual is used to present Avigdor's name? Would you have used that visual? Give reasons for your answer.

5. What can you say about Greathall's use of other document visuals?

Preliminary Report

1. How does the letterhead differ from that in the cover letter **(Figure 5.16)**? Should the two letterheads be the same or different? Explain your answer in terms of the CMAPP dynamic.

2. What kind of font has Greathall used for the report's body text? Explain why you think the choice is a good or bad one.

3. What type of justification is used for the body text? What are the advantages and disadvantages of the choice, given the context and the message?

4. Do you approve of the use of the two-column format in the "Note"? Give reasons for your answer.

5. Do the rules and the box serve a useful purpose? Why or why not?

6. What do you think of Greathall's use of bold and underline? Cite examples from the report in your answer.

7. The sketches referred to in the report are not, in fact, attached. How might this oversight affect Greathall's audience?

8. Evaluate the two visuals embedded in the report in terms of the following:
    a. Relevance of message
    b. Relevance to audience
    c. Size
    d. Level of detail
    e. Scale
    f. Overall usefulness

9. Evaluate Greathall's use of level heads in the report.

FIGURE 5.16   Greathall's Cover Letter

AEL Accelerated Enterprises Ltd.

Accelerated Enterprises Ltd.
342 Center Street West
Lansing, Michigan 48980-1720
Tel: (517) 555-0123 Fax: (517) 555-0124

Deborah Greathall, Senior Associate

March 30, 20--
Dr. Joan Welstromm
Chair, Civil Engineering
Ann Arbor University
5827 Dixie Road
Ann Arbor, MI 48106-0061

Dear Dr. Welstromm:
Having completed my examination of the west side of *Vanier Place,* I am pleased to present my preliminary report regarding proposed repairs.

Once you have had the opportunity to examine my findings, please contact AEL to advise us of how and when you would like to proceed.

Once you have had the opportunity to examine my findings, please advise AEL of your wishes. Since I must shortly return to our New York office, Dr. Noam Avigdor will be happy to assist you. Should you so wish, he could also recommend competent construction contractors. You may reach him at the numbers shown above or at his direct line:

Dr. Noam Avigdor
Senior Associate
555-0123

Yours sincerely,

Deborah Greathall

Deborah Greathall (Ms.)
Senior Associate, Civil Engineering

AEL will submit its invoice under separate cover.

c Frank Nabata

FIGURE 5.17   Preliminary Engineering Report

Accelerated Enterprises Ltd.

342 Center Street West
Lansing, Michigan 48980-1720
Tel: (517) 555-0123 Fax: (517) 555-0124

Preliminary Engineering Report

March 30, 20--

Specifications and procedures to rehabilitate lift-up panels at the industrial building called Vanier Place on the campus of Ann Arbor University at 5827 Dixie Road, Ann Arbor, MI.

The building was constructed on a preloaded site of approx. 4 acres in 2 phases

1. the first in 1972 and
2. the second in 1977.

At issue are the twelve 5½"-thick reinforced concrete lift-up panels that make up the west wall. <u>Each is 32' high and approx. 16' wide</u>.

The lower half of 9 of the lift-up panels, all dating from the 1977 construction phase, show signs of cracking and deterioration. The damage likely derives from trucks backing into the panels when

1. maneuvering to load or unload, and/or
2. from stresses during construction while the panels were being lifted by a crane into position onto their footing (probably before the reinforced concrete had fully matured).

These panels are marked on the attached sketches; note that in the original construction drawings that I consulted, they likewise appear within building lines 2–5.

Strengthening

It was decided to strengthen damaged panels by attaching them to newly formed 6" reinforced concrete retainer walls of approx. 8'6" height as measured from the top of the panel footing. As panel footings are competent and wide enough, they will also serve as a footing for the retainer walls. However, the above holds good only for the five panels marked A through E and one panel marked F. The panel marked G is very similar, but the height of the retainer wall is governed by an exhaust duct opening.

Retainer Wall

8'6"

FIGURE 5.17   (continued)

Note

Please note that panel F is, in effect, combined with panel B: A hollow steel rectangular column, 4" wide by 6⅜" thick, is attached to the footing by means of a ½"-thick steel plate bolted to the footing and welded to the column (¼" weld); this column is also attached to the south side of the existing reinforced concrete loading platform of panel B. It is intended to carry the weight of a horizontal retainer concrete beam attached to panel B above the door opening.

As panel C also contains an opening door with a cantilevered loading platform, its strengthening is in part achieved by another reinforced concrete beam, 6" thick, attached to the panel and resting on concrete retainer walls at both ends.

No retainer wall is attached to panel B or panel C below the loading platforms. Instead, two 8" reinforced concrete walls at right angles to the panels are being provided for both and connected to the panels.

Retainer Walls

The retainer walls are to be reinforced with 20-mm bars vertically at **2'** o/c and horizontally with 10-mm bars at **1'** o/c. The retainer beams above the doors are reinforced along their entire length with a 20-mm bar placed at the top and at the bottom. The reinforcement in the retainer walls is confined to its center by 10-mm L-shaped anchors. These anchors are placed at 2" each way into the panel. The anchors' legs are 6" long, one ensconced in a **12**-mm-diameter hole drilled 3" deep into the panel, with the other free leg parallel to the panel wall. The retainer beams are attached to the panels by the same type of anchors

Procedures Requested

1) Footing of panels of all 9 panels (approx. total length: 144") to be revealed.
2) Footing areas of panels "B" and "C" to be extended to the outline shown on the sketch.
3) All panels to be sandblasted to required height with "Black Pearl" coal slag to expose a visible profile and the aggregate of the concrete.
4) Holes of **12**-mm diameter, 3" deep, to be drilled at required spacing (**12**" e/w into panels) as required by retainer walls or beams.
5) All sandblasted areas to be power-washed.
6) Anchors to be placed into the drill holes after filling them with epoxy.
7) Panels to be soaked with water for a minimum of 24 hours and then let dry back to a "saturated surface dry" state, immediately prior to placement of concrete.
8) Dry-to-wet epoxy paint to be used for bonding top 15" of space for retaining beams and walls/panel location just before concreting.
9) Vibrator to be used to place concrete against panels within form work.

- 2 -

FIGURE 5.17   (continued)

10) Visible cracks in the panels (up to top of retainer beam height and outside of retainer walls or beams) to be cleaned out, washed, and then filled with epoxy paint.

11) All parts to be painted to the full height of the retainer beams with elastomeric paint to match existing light color.

12) Grade to be reinstated and asphalt to be renewed in the operation area.

Concrete Performance Requirement

1. Conform to CSA A231 type 10 normal Portland cement
2. Supplementary: class F Fly ash
3. Exposure class F2
4. Minimum compressive strength: 28 M Pa
5. Maximum concrete aggregate: 14 mm
6. Slump at point of discharge: 160 plus/minus 20
7. Air content 6 plus/minus 1
8. Minimum water ratio to cement: 0.55
9. Admixtures: normal dosage

Conclusion

This concludes my preliminary report.

Deborah Greathall

Deborah Greathall, Prof. Eng.

Sketches not quite ready; will be sent by courier within a day or two.

CHAPTER 6

Describing, Instructing, Persuading, and Summarizing

B ased on their CMAPP analysis, technical communicators use certain strategies to create messages. A strategy is, in effect, a template that provides a consistent approach to a variety of situations. A particular strategy can be appropriate for limitless variations of context, message, audience, purpose, and product. But because it is a kind of map for reaching a goal, your strategy will be based in large part on your purpose. In this chapter, you will learn strategies for creating messages that describe, instruct, persuade, or summarize.

Technical Descriptions

Technical communicators often describe an object or a process. The object might be as simple as a paper clip, described for a patent application or a new manufacturer, or as complex as the avionics system of a military jet.

You will apply the strategy for technical description to a variety of CMAPP products. In letters and memos, for example, you will often have to describe an issue. In reports, you may have to describe an object or a process. As always, your CMAPP analysis will help you determine how to approach your communication task.

Describing a Process

A **process description** explains how things work or are done or made. All processes consist of a series of steps that occur in a particular order. Processes can be carried out by machines, by people, or by nature.

Examples of Processes

Carried Out by Machines	Carried Out by People	Carried Out by Nature
how polygraph machines work	how law enforcement officials administer polygraph tests	how emotions alter breathing and blood pressure
how Doppler radar works	how the National Hurricane Center predicts the paths of hurricanes	how hurricanes form
how a bread machine works	how a baker makes croissants	how yeast makes bread rise

Process descriptions enable readers or listeners to make informed choices and sound decisions, to work safely, and to grow professionally. Even though the audience will rarely carry out the described process, other actions may depend on a clear understanding of the process.

A good process description is organized like a story—with a beginning, a middle, and an end. **Figure 6.1** on the next page shows a process description. The following Checklist outlines the process description strategy.

 Checklist

Process Description Strategy

✓ Organize chronologically. Present steps in the order in which they occur.

✓ Begin with an informative title and introduction. The introduction should define the process and provide an overview. It also might explain why or how the process is used, who or what performs it, and where or when it takes place.

✓ Include each step in the body of the description. If you use paragraph form, include headings and subheadings to distinguish important details. A long description may require a heading for each main step. If you use list form, follow an outline of main points and subpoints and use parallel structure.

✓ Use active voice for most sentences. Passive voice is acceptable.

✓ Define unfamiliar or technical terms.

✓ End with a closing. A long process description may require a paragraph summarizing the process and perhaps discussing its uses or advantages.

✓ Use visuals to make your description easier to understand. Drawings, diagrams, and flowcharts are especially useful in process descriptions.

FIGURE 6.1 Process Description

Clear and limiting title

How Data Is Transferred between a Computer and a Floppy Disk

A computer records information on a floppy disk in much the same way that a — Introduction
tape recorder records sound on tape. The computer has a read-write head with
a needle that can write new information on the floppy disk and later read information from the disk.

The Process

Step-by-step description

When you slip a floppy disk into its slot in the CPU, or central processing unit,
the disk rests on a turntable, or spindle, inside the CPU. When you decide to
save your work and key SAVE, the computer's read-write head lowers its needle to touch the disk. An electrical charge passes through the needle, magnetiz-
ing the iron particles on the surface of the disk. Each particle has a north pole
and a south pole, like a tiny magnet. The magnetic charge positions the particles into a specific, invisible pattern on the disk. This pattern represents the
data you are saving.

The read-write head remains stationary as the spindle spins the disk. On a new
disk, the head starts "writing" at a position close to the outer rim of the disk.
This is called track 0. When that track is filled with data, the head lifts and
moves to the next track, track 1, which is slightly closer to the center of the
disk. The head continues in this way until the disk is filled with data. On a
used disk, the head will search for available tracks and record on them.

Most computers now have two read-write heads. One writes on track 0 of the
disk's top surface; then the other writes on track 0 of the bottom surface. They
continue alternating until both sides of the disk are filled. A double-sided drive
requires a double-sided disk, marked DS.

When you open a file that you have saved on a floppy disk, the read-write
head moves to the correct track and waits for the disk to spin into the correct
position. Then it lowers its needle and "reads" the magnetic pattern on that
track, transferring it back into the letters and numbers that appear on your
computer screen.

A floppy disk provides a place to store a copy of the files on the computer's — Conclusion
hard drive so the files will not be lost if the hard drive "crashes." However,
floppy disks must be kept away from stereos, televisions, and telephones because their speakers contain magnets that can scramble the magnetic pattern
on the disk.

Describing a Mechanism

A **mechanism description** explains and describes an object or a system. A mechanism may be simple or complex and can have any number of parts. Each part has a specific function. The parts work together toward a definite purpose. Any system whose parts function separately to achieve an overall effect is a mechanism.

A mechanism has only this simple requirement: It has at least two parts that work separately, but together perform a single function. Mechanisms can vary from basic to elaborate, from miniscule to large, and from inanimate to living. The primary categories of mechanisms are the following:

- *Tools and machinery.*   For example, a claw hammer consists of a handle, claw, cheek, neck, and face.
- *Organisms.*   For example, a tree consists of roots, leaves, and bark.
- *Substances.*   For example, automotive paint contains chemicals such as toners, reducers, and hardeners.
- *Locations.*   For example, a construction site includes terrain and buildings.
- *Systems.*   For example, a plant includes its reproductive system.

Figure 6.2 on the next page is an example of a simple mechanism description. The strategy for writing mechanism descriptions is outlined in the following Checklist.

✓ Checklist

Mechanism Description Strategy

✓   Include a clear and limiting title.

✓   Introduce the item. Begin with the definition and purpose. Include basic information, such as what it looks like, how it works, and its principal parts.

✓   Specify all relevant details. Describe each part separately, and explain each part's appearance and function. List the parts in logical sequence. Include all relevant details, such as length, width, height, depth, weight, density, color, texture, and shape. State specific uses of the mechanism and any special features. Include a list or diagram of the main parts.

✓   Compare the familiar to the unfamiliar. For example, you might compare recording information on a computer disk to recording music on an audiotape.

✓   Include visuals if appropriate. Pay particular attention to document format and visual design. If your audience cannot readily follow and understand your description, your communication will not have achieved its purpose.

✓   Conclude. A brief concluding statement may be used to sum up the main parts and how they work together.

FIGURE 6.2   Mechanism Description

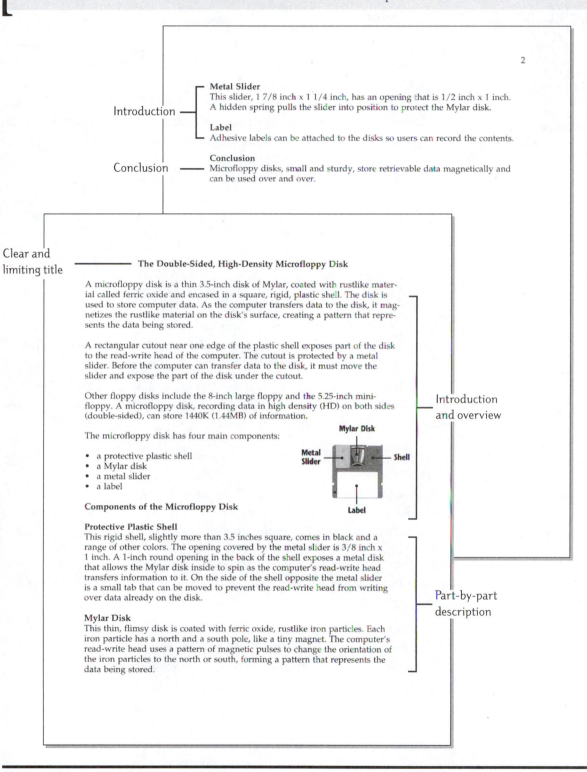

Introduction —

Metal Slider
This slider, 1 7/8 inch x 1 1/4 inch, has an opening that is 1/2 inch x 1 inch. A hidden spring pulls the slider into position to protect the Mylar disk.

Label
Adhesive labels can be attached to the disks so users can record the contents.

Conclusion —

Conclusion
Microfloppy disks, small and sturdy, store retrievable data magnetically and can be used over and over.

Clear and limiting title —

The Double-Sided, High-Density Microfloppy Disk

A microfloppy disk is a thin 3.5-inch disk of Mylar, coated with rustlike material called ferric oxide and encased in a square, rigid, plastic shell. The disk is used to store computer data. As the computer transfers data to the disk, it magnetizes the rustlike material on the disk's surface, creating a pattern that represents the data being stored.

A rectangular cutout near one edge of the plastic shell exposes part of the disk to the read-write head of the computer. The cutout is protected by a metal slider. Before the computer can transfer data to the disk, it must move the slider and expose the part of the disk under the cutout.

Other floppy disks include the 8-inch large floppy and the 5.25-inch minifloppy. A microfloppy disk, recording data in high density (HD) on both sides (double-sided), can store 1440K (1.44MB) of information.

The microfloppy disk has four main components:

- a protective plastic shell
- a Mylar disk
- a metal slider
- a label

Introduction and overview —

Mylar Disk

Metal Slider — **Shell**

Label

Components of the Microfloppy Disk

Protective Plastic Shell
This rigid shell, slightly more than 3.5 inches square, comes in black and a range of other colors. The opening covered by the metal slider is 3/8 inch x 1 inch. A 1-inch round opening in the back of the shell exposes a metal disk that allows the Mylar disk inside to spin as the computer's read-write head transfers information to it. On the side of the shell opposite the metal slider is a small tab that can be moved to prevent the read-write head from writing over data already on the disk.

Part-by-part description —

Mylar Disk
This thin, flimsy disk is coated with ferric oxide, rustlike iron particles. Each iron particle has a north and a south pole, like a tiny magnet. The computer's read-write head uses a pattern of magnetic pulses to change the orientation of the iron particles to the north or south, forming a pattern that represents the data being stored.

Austin Community
College's Online
Technical Writing course
features an excellent
"chapter" on writing
instructions. Visit
**www.illuminati.com/
~hcexres/tcm1603/acchtml/
acctoc.html**

Simple Instructions

In your professional and your private lives, you will undoubtedly have to write simple **instructions** from time to time. Examples would include instructions a fellow employee is to follow while you are on vacation, guidelines for the tenants of a building you own, or directions to your home for an out-of-town guest. You might think instructions should be process descriptions because, by definition, they refer to processes. Their purpose, however, is different. In standard process descriptions, you want your audience to see or understand how something works. In instructions, you want your audience to be able to perform a task. This distinctive purpose, of course, affects the message.

Note the differences between the following two examples.

Example 1:   At this stage, it is crucial that the power light be green. Gear A now activates gear B. Immediately thereafter, cam C, turning on shaft D, lifts rod E 3.5 cm, causing it to make contact with plate F.

Example 2:   **CAUTION:** Ensure that the power light shows green before undertaking the following steps. If it is not green, do not proceed; call the supervisor at once.
1. Allow gear A to activate gear B.
2. Turn shaft D clockwise until cam C lifts rod E 3.5 cm so that rod E makes contact with plate F.

The first example is appropriate for process descriptions; the second, for instructions. Notice the following differences, as shown in the two examples, between process descriptions and instructions.

- We recognize an instruction (which is similar to a command or an order) by the use of the imperative mood.
- Instructional steps are numbered and easy to follow.
- A warning is readily visible, appears before the step to which it applies, and is clearly distinguished from the instructions themselves.

In writing instructions, the wording and format used in the steps is especially important. In particular, the steps must be clear and specific. The following guidelines will help you write effective, easy-to-follow steps.

1.   Number each step and start it with a verb.

Instead of: 1. Alt and F1 are pressed simultaneously.

Write: 1. Press Alt and F1 simultaneously.

2.   Put the steps in sequential order.

Instead of: 1. Insert the disk into drive A: after turning on the computer.

Write: 1. Turn on the computer.

2. Insert the disk into drive A:.

3. Describe each step separately so readers will not overlook a step.

    Instead of: 1. Click Start, point to Programs, and click Uninstall.
    Write: 1. Click Start.
                    2. Point to Programs.
                    3. Click Uninstall.

4. Indent any explanations under the appropriate step.

    Instead of: 1. After you press F3, the screen will show the first menu.
    Write: 1. Press F3.
                    The screen will show the first menu.

5. If a step should be carried out only under certain conditions, describe the conditions first.

    Instead of: 1. Enter the order number in Field 6 if the order will be filled by our warehouse.
    Write: 1. If the order will be filled by our warehouse, enter the order number in Field 6.

6. Group multiple steps or procedures under subheadings.
7. Single-space the information within a step; double-space between steps.
8. Highlight warnings or cautions so readers do not overlook them.
9. Create a clear, inviting format by using numbers, letters, indentation, bold-face, and lots of white space.

The following Checklist outlines the strategy for instructions. **Figure 6.3** on the next page is an example of effective instructions.

✔ Checklist

Instructions Strategy

✓ Use a clear and limiting title. The title should explain what the reader will do.

✓ Introduce the instructions. Readers need a brief orientation. Explain what the instructions should accomplish, who should follow them, and when and why to follow them. Also list any needed tools, materials, special skills, or knowledge. Include a time frame, cautions, and definitions, as appropriate.

✓ Number steps in sequential order. Steps should provide everything readers need but not overwhelm them with details or unneeded information. Write in the active voice, and describe each step separately.

✓ Include diagrams or other graphics if they will clarify the instructions.

✓ Conclude by describing the expected results. This allows readers to determine whether they've successfully completed the procedure. If your instructions are lengthy, you might summarize the major steps.

FIGURE 6.3　Effective Instructions

Clear and limiting title

How to Install the DEBUG Anti-virus Detector on Your Computer

The DEBUG Anti-virus Detector was designed for use on personal computers. You can install the detector whether or not your computer already has a virus. This software will identify any files with a known virus and repair those files, keeping your computer virus-free.

Introduction and list of materials

Materials needed: DEBUG CD
　　　　　　　　 DEBUG Disks 1 and 2

CAUTION: Make backup copies of your AUTOEXEC.BAT files before installing this virus detector.

Numbered steps in sequential order

First, install the DEBUG Anti-virus Detector:
1. Choose and carry out one of the following:
   a. To install from a CD, insert the DEBUG CD into the CD-ROM drive.
      The detector setup program will start automatically.
   b. To install from a floppy disk,
      1. Insert the DEBUG Disk 1 into Drive A.
      2. Click Start on the Windows taskbar.
      3. Click Run.
      4. Key A:SETUP in the text box.
      5. Click OK.
2. Follow the instructions on the screen.

If the program detects an active virus during installation, follow these steps to remove it:
1. Turn off your computer.
2. Insert DEBUG Disk 2 into Drive A.
3. Turn on your computer.
   The screen will show this message: Emergency Virus Removal.
4. Press Enter to load the program.
   The program will scan for any active viruses and remove them.

Conclusion

After your detector is installed, it will automatically scan your files on a regular basis and detect and remove any viruses it finds.

CAUTION: Be sure to update your detector periodically. New viruses are constantly being created and spread.

Persuasive Messages

Persuasive strategies are vital in a variety of contexts, including creating brochures, presenting proposals, and writing sales and collection letters. All persuasive strategies are based on establishing a connection with an audience and providing something that the audience will relate to and respond to. Some persuasive strategies target the intellect and depend on logic and argumentation. Others target feelings and depend on emotional appeals.

Targeting the Intellect: Logical Argumentation

The essence of an appeal to the intellect is the logical progression from the assertion of a claim to its proof. This process follows one of two paths: deductive strategy or inductive strategy.

You should probably use the **deductive strategy** if your CMAPP analysis determines that your audience already knows the issue under consideration and/or is likely to react favorably to your message. This strategy consists of the three steps outlined in the following Checklist.

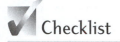 Checklist

Deductive Strategy

✓ Make your assertion. Provide statements that are accurate, brief, and clear.

✓ Justify your assertion. Your justification must consist of a series of cohesive points organized chronologically, topically, or spatially. Each point should be the logical consequence of the points that have come before it. (Try thinking of your argument in terms of the construction of a building, with a solid foundation required for each successive story. Just as a building will collapse if you do not build each story properly, your argument will collapse if you do not provide the proper basis for each point.)

✓ Conclude. Briefly summarize your argument. Then refer your audience to the necessary conclusion—your initial assertion. (You have thus come full circle.)

Note that the length and complexity of the second step of a deductive strategy will depend on your context and your message. Your level of technicality will derive from your audience analysis.

You should probably use the **inductive strategy** if your audience lacks the background necessary to follow your reasoning easily and/or is likely to be averse to receiving your message. The inductive strategy includes the steps outlined in the Checklist on the next page.

Tech Link

The Utah Valley State College Online Writing Lab features a detailed section on persuasive and logical writing. Visit *www.uvsc.edu/owl/ handouts/logic.html*

✓ Checklist

Inductive Strategy

✓ Introduce the issue. Describe it in a way that is relevant to your audience.

✓ Provide your arguments. Make your points just as you would if using the deductive strategy: Each point must stem logically from what has come before.

✓ Draw your conclusion. Briefly summarize your arguments, and then state your assertion as their logical conclusion.

As examples of inductive and deductive strategies, recall Case Study 2B, in which Griffin Radisson, Radisson Automobile's Chief Executive Officer, announces the reorganization of the firm. Assume that Melinda Shaw, one of RAI's vice presidents, would like to persuade Radisson to postpone the reorganization until discussions can be held with the vice presidents. Two versions of a persuasive memo that Shaw might send to Radisson are shown in **Figure 6.4** and **Figure 6.5.** The memo in **Figure 6.4** on the next page uses the deductive strategy. It reflects Shaw's recognition of Radisson's understanding of the issue and presumes that he will be amenable to feedback from his senior executives. The memo in **Figure 6.5** on page 118 uses the inductive strategy. Its premise is that Radisson may be unaware of all the implications of his decision or may view Shaw's remarks as inappropriate criticism from a subordinate. Although the different strategies presume different contexts and generate apparently different products, the basic message is the same.

Targeting the Emotions: AIDA

Particularly apt for targeting emotions is a strategy called **AIDA,** an acronym that stands for *attention, interest, desire,* and *action.* The elements tend to function as a continuum, with each element leading to the next.

Attention.   Your audience is constantly being bombarded with persuasive material, whether on television, radio, billboards, or the Web. Thus, if you want your message to be noticed, it must catch your audience's attention. In print documents, you can make use of the following techniques:

◆ *Color.* Possibilities include colored paper, colored type or graphics, and sharply contrasting colors.

◆ *Font.* Possibilities are decorative or otherwise unusual typeface or font size.

◆ *Shape.* Possible applications include a nonstandard envelope and/or stationery or contrasting shapes on the page.

◆ *Visual.* Possibilities are an eye-catching graphic or unusual visual.

◆ *Wording.* Words such as *free, new,* and *improved* are standards (look at the products on any supermarket shelf).

As well, cultural preferences and cultural referents (discussed in Chapter 1) are likely to play a role in what catches your audience's attention.

Tech Link

Dr. Joel Bowman of the Western Michigan University business faculty offers an excellent discussion of persuasion and persuasive messages. Visit *www.hcob.wmich.edu/bis/ faculty/bowman/ c4dframe.html*

FIGURE 6.4   Persuasive Memo—Deductive Strategy

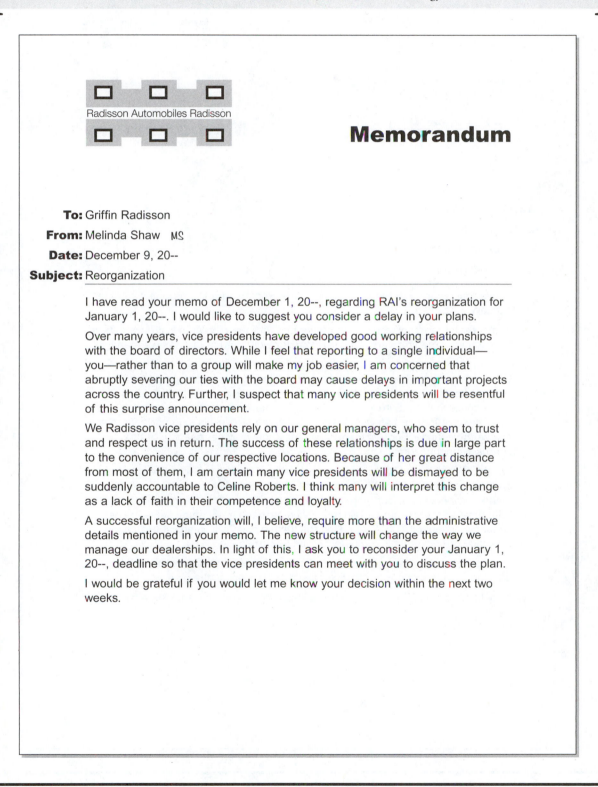

Radisson Automobiles Radisson

Memorandum

To: Griffin Radisson

From: Melinda Shaw   MS

Date: December 9, 20--

Subject: Reorganization

I have read your memo of December 1, 20--, regarding RAI's reorganization for January 1, 20--. I would like to suggest you consider a delay in your plans.

Over many years, vice presidents have developed good working relationships with the board of directors. While I feel that reporting to a single individual—you—rather than to a group will make my job easier, I am concerned that abruptly severing our ties with the board may cause delays in important projects across the country. Further, I suspect that many vice presidents will be resentful of this surprise announcement.

We Radisson vice presidents rely on our general managers, who seem to trust and respect us in return. The success of these relationships is due in large part to the convenience of our respective locations. Because of her great distance from most of them, I am certain many vice presidents will be dismayed to be suddenly accountable to Celine Roberts. I think many will interpret this change as a lack of faith in their competence and loyalty.

A successful reorganization will, I believe, require more than the administrative details mentioned in your memo. The new structure will change the way we manage our dealerships. In light of this, I ask you to reconsider your January 1, 20--, deadline so that the vice presidents can meet with you to discuss the plan.

I would be grateful if you would let me know your decision within the next two weeks.

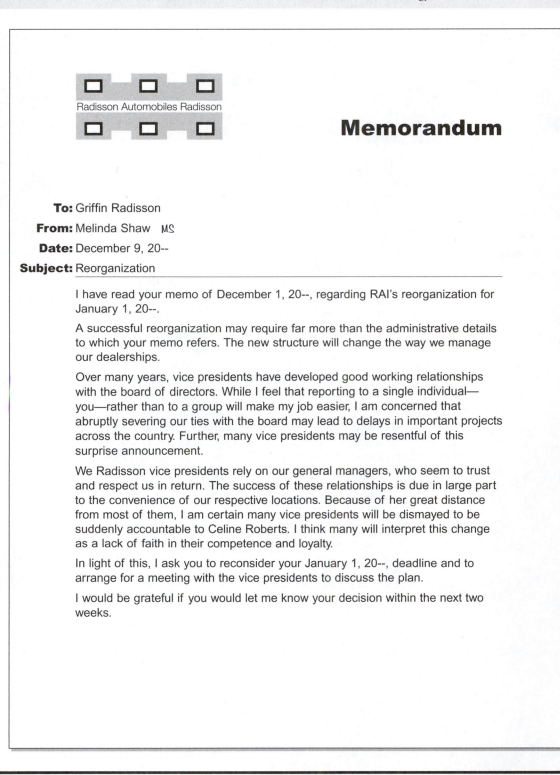

Radisson Automobiles Radisson

Memorandum

To: Griffin Radisson

From: Melinda Shaw   MS

Date: December 9, 20--

Subject: Reorganization

I have read your memo of December 1, 20--, regarding RAI's reorganization for January 1, 20--.

A successful reorganization may require far more than the administrative details to which your memo refers. The new structure will change the way we manage our dealerships.

Over many years, vice presidents have developed good working relationships with the board of directors. While I feel that reporting to a single individual— you—rather than to a group will make my job easier, I am concerned that abruptly severing our ties with the board may lead to delays in important projects across the country. Further, many vice presidents may be resentful of this surprise announcement.

We Radisson vice presidents rely on our general managers, who seem to trust and respect us in return. The success of these relationships is due in large part to the convenience of our respective locations. Because of her great distance from most of them, I am certain many vice presidents will be dismayed to be suddenly accountable to Celine Roberts. I think many will interpret this change as a lack of faith in their competence and loyalty.

In light of this, I ask you to reconsider your January 1, 20--, deadline and to arrange for a meeting with the vice presidents to discuss the plan.

I would be grateful if you would let me know your decision within the next two weeks.

Interest.   After obtaining your audience's attention, you must find a way of sustaining that attention by generating interest. You might ask, for example, "How would you like to see the world from your very own yacht?" You generate interest in this case by eliciting from your audience a feeling of curiosity about what your message is about. Once again, connotation is important; you are not trying to inform your audience, but to elicit an emotional response. As is the case with the attention element, your audience's cultural background will in part determine the effectiveness of this element. Remember always to ask yourself the appropriate CMAPP questions.

Desire.   Now that the people in your audience are willing to examine what you have to communicate, you need to convince them that they must have what you are offering. Advertisers traditionally create desire by suggesting that using their product or service will make us richer, stronger, healthier, happier, more beautiful or handsome, more sophisticated, and so on. We see this kind of message embodied in the television ads featuring young people whose happiness is dependent on a particular brand of soft drink. The aim of such ads is not to provide concrete information, but to target emotions.

Advertising slogans such as "Coke. It's the real thing!," "Mazda: It just feels right!," and "Just do it!" mean nothing in rational terms. In emotional terms, however, they are memorable and they work. In these and other slogans, connotation speaks more loudly than denotation, abstractions replace specific detail, and precision yields to vague promise. Experience has shown these tactics to be highly effective. As consumers, we are not all susceptible to the same emotional stimuli but we are susceptible.

Action.   Once you have created a desire for your product or service, you must tell your audience how to satisfy that desire. You need a clear call to action, which could range from the somewhat pushy "Operators are standing by. Call now!" to the more restrained "We hope to hear from you soon." Unless you specify an action, your persuasive message may be lost.

Writing Different Kinds of Persuasive Messages

Persuasive messages are common in the business environment. They might be sent from supervisor to employee, from employee to supervisor, from employee to employee, or from employee to customer or supplier. Sales letters and collection letters are two special kinds of persuasive messages. Proposals, a third type of persuasive communication, are discussed in Chapter 9.

Sales Letters.   A **sales letter** tries to persuade a potential customer to purchase a product or service. Like other persuasive messages, it involves:

- Gaining the reader's attention.
- Establishing a need.
- Showing how a product or service will meet that need or solve a problem.
- Presenting supporting information.
- Providing for an easy way for the reader to respond.

A sales letter might appeal to readers' senses by describing how something looks, sounds, feels, smells, or tastes. This appeal can range from the warm cinnamon smell of apple pie to the silky feel of a new blouse. As you construct a sales message, consider the following:

♦ *Audience.*   Put yourself in the customer's head. What will make your letter stand out? Approach each audience in a personal way suitable for that audience.

♦ *Product.*   The sales letter can create a solution, but first customers must believe they have a problem or conflict. Why would a customer buy your product? Find out and focus on that reason.

♦ *Competition.*   Know the competition. Emphasize the strengths of your product or company. Show customers why they need your product and not the competitor's.

Figure 6.6 on the next page shows how the steps of writing a persuasive message apply to a sales letter.

Collection Letters.   The purpose of a **collection letter** is to persuade a customer to pay a past-due bill. The collection letter should not offend the customer's goodwill but should appeal to his or her conscience instead.

Many companies use a three-stage series of communications for collections. These three stages are as follows:

♦ *Inquiry.*   A phone call or letter goes out to gently remind the customer the account payment is due. The writer asks directly or indirectly for the overdue payment and may mention a penalty for late payment.

♦ *Reasonable appeal.*   The company's message becomes stronger in this letter. The letter appeals to the customer's sense of fairness and explains the consequences if the customer leaves the account unpaid.

♦ *Firm appeal.*   This letter strongly urges the customer to pay the past-due account or to make payment arrangements with the company. Unpleasant circumstances, such as repossession, involvement of a collection agency, or instigation of a lawsuit, are mentioned as possibly following soon.

A collection communication made by phone or by letter should include the following three sections:

♦ *Goodwill greeting.*   Open with a general comment about the service or product to promote a feeling of goodwill.

♦ *Announcement of the problem.*   State the problem, the purpose of the letter, the payment due date, and the type of account or account number.

♦ *The next step.*   Close the communication by stating the next step if the payment or arrangements to pay are not made. This will vary from a mild warning to an ultimatum. Express the hope that the customer is willing to cooperate.

Figure 6.7 on page 122 is an example of an effective collection letter.

FIGURE 6.6   Effective Sales Letter

Comfy Feet, Inc.

October 1, 20—

Dear Friend,

On your feet for eight hours or more but not foot-weary? Isn't this how you'd — Gain attention and establish a need
like to feel at the end of your workday?

Through extensive research and testing, we have developed a new kind of shoe — Explain your solution to that need
with you in mind. These comfortable, attractive shoes have shock-absorbing
features that cushion and protect your feet all day. More than 80 percent of the
doctors and nurses who tried our shoes wanted to keep them! Many wanted to
order a pair for a friend or family member, too.

As an introductory offer, these Quality Label leather shoes are available for — Present the supporting information
only $29.95 a pair. As you can see from the enclosed photographs, they come
in styles and colors to please every need and taste.

To place your order, just call toll free at 1-800-555-0153. Or fill in the enclosed, — End by asking for specific action
addressed, postage-paid form. You will be slipping into your new shoes within
a week and enjoying new freedom from tired feet!

Melissa Konrad

Melissa Konrad
Sales Manager

Enclosure

FIGURE 6.7   Effective Collection Letter

SOUNDERS STEREOS
1211 Queens Court
Pittsburgh, PA 15228-8840

July 8, 20--

Mr. Joseph Miller
1806 Lane Street
Pittsburgh, PA 15228-8810

Dear Mr. Miller:

Paragraph 1
General comment to promote goodwill.

I hope that you are enjoying your new Sounders component stereo system. If you have any questions about the system, please contact either me or your local Sounders store.

Paragraph 2
Problem stated. Purpose of letter. Timeliness—2 weeks past due date.

Your long-term account requires a $40 monthly payment, due on the 20th. Sounders has not yet received your June payment.

Paragraph 3
Next step given. Tone—firm, not harrassing.

I trust that you will contact your local Sounders store immediately to make payment arrangements. Interest penalties add to the cost of your payment daily. If you have any questions, please do not hesitate to call me at 555-0110 or contact your local Sounders store.

Sincerely yours,

Marcos Hernandez

Marcos Hernandez
Account Supervisor

Summaries

If you were asked to tell what you've done during the last 24 hours, it's unlikely you would describe in detail every activity you could recall. (Such an account would be excruciating for your audience.) In all likelihood, you would select the activities you consider most significant and briefly recount them. You would, in effect, be creating a summary.

In the context of technical communication, a **summary** concisely conveys an original document's important ideas and, in some cases, its significant details. What are significant details? The answer lies in a CMAPP analysis. For example, imagine that you have to summarize a complex, technical report on weather conditions in the Los Angeles area during the past ten years. If the audience for the summary (not necessarily the same audience as the one for the report) is a group of graduate students in a meteorology program, they will likely think significant such things as the annual mean temperature and the average yearly rainfall. If the audience is a company that stages outdoor events, however, the significant details will likely include the amount of precipitation on holidays, such as the Fourth of July.

Categories

Summaries can be grouped into two broad categories: content summaries and evaluative summaries. **Figure 6.8** on the next page shows examples of the kind of material included in the two categories of summaries.

Content summaries, also known as informative summaries or informative abstracts, sum up the important elements of the original document. Objectivity is crucial in a content summary, which should not contain embellishment, opinion, or highly connotative vocabulary. Two special types of content summaries are minutes and executive summaries. **Minutes** are the record of what occurred at a meeting. They document decisions made; actions to be taken; and, on occasion, comments made. An **executive summary** is a summary found in the front matter of a formal report. Executive summaries typically do not exceed a single page.

Evaluative summaries, also known as analytic summaries or assessment summaries, provide not only the essential ideas of the original document but also the author's opinions, often in the form of recommendations. Two special types of evaluative summaries are abstracts and descriptive abstracts. An **abstract** is a standard front piece in reports. It presents a brief description of the report and offers the reader (typically the secondary audience) an evaluation of it (usually a very positive one). Abstracts tend to be shorter than executive summaries. **Figure 6.9** on page 125 shows examples of an executive summary and an abstract.

A **descriptive abstract** is most common in an academic context and is generally no longer than a few lines. It presents a synopsis of the original document, followed by a brief indication of the document's value or applicability to the project at hand. A descriptive abstract that follows an entry in a bibliography is

FIGURE 6.8   Content of Summaries

Content Summary

Often Includes	Typically Excludes
◆ Overall theme or goal	◆ Opinion
◆ Main points	◆ New information
◆ Significant details	◆ Insignificant details
◆ Reference to any conclusions in the original document	◆ Embellishments
	◆ Technical jargon (if possible)
◆ Reference to any recommendations in the original document	◆ Supportive examples or illustrations
	◆ Visuals
	◆ Quotations
	◆ Citation credits

Evaluative Summary

Often Includes	Typically Excludes
◆ Overall theme or goal	◆ Because the purpose here is evaluation or assessment, it is impossible to identify any exclusions without knowing the content or context.
◆ Main points	
◆ Assessment/evaluation of original's content	
◆ Assessment/evaluation of original's effectiveness	

often called an **annotation**—hence the term *annotated bibliography.* For example, if you wrote a report on the use of Windows NT versus UNIX in your company and your bibliography includes the book *UNIX for Dummies,* your annotation for that title might resemble the following:

> Part of the popular series of "Dummies" books, this is a 360-page primer on the operating system that still underlies a large part of the World Wide Web. Though the book is at times self-consciously populist and facetious, its 30 chapters provide a useful (and relatively nontechnical) introduction to UNIX.

Strategy for a Content Summary

The purpose of a content summary is to provide your audience with a report's important information. Most audience members who read the summary will not have time to read the entire report. You need to accurately reflect the report's content, order, and weight. Summarize its content without adding any new information. Cover the material in the same order as it is presented in the report.

> **FIGURE 6.9**   Executive Summary and Abstract

Personnel Strategies for RAI St. Louis Dealership

Executive Summary

In January 20--, RAI requested that AEL identify personnel strategies for a potential RAI expansion into the St. Louis market. That investigation has yielded the following two potential strategies:

1. Senior staff to be drawn from RAI's head office in Dallas. This strategy would involve the relocation to the St. Louis dealership of Vice President Alberto Chavez, General Manager George Finlay, and Sales Manager Mariela van Damm, with concomitant backfilling.

2. Senior staff to be drawn from:

   (a) RAI's Chicago dealership (involving the relocation of General Manager Tina Trann, who would become the St. Louis dealership's Vice President, and Sales Manager Ted Evans).

   (b) RAI's Atlanta dealership (General Manager Phillip Osterhous), again with concomitant backfilling.

Abstract

AEL recently identified two strategies for effectively staffing RAI's planned St. Louis dealership. Both meet RAI's budget provisions and take excellent advantage of local conditions. While either is likely to prove successful, one relies primarily on RAI in-house expertise in Dallas while the other draws on RAI's Chicago and Atlanta locations for the necessary expertise.

Give each piece of information the same weight it has in the report. Don't emphasize information that isn't given much attention in the report, and don't omit important information. Write a summary that allows your audience to feel they have read the report without actually investing the time.

As you can see, creating an effective content summary can be complex and painstaking. Here's some help for figuring out where to begin: Start by familiarizing yourself with the original text. Then identify the main points and significant details. Next, organize your data into useful information. Finally, write a first draft, and then revise it for your final draft. The Checklist on the next page outlines this process and offers details and suggestions.

Checklist

Content Summary Strategy

✓ **Familiarization.**   First, become thoroughly familiar with the original text. This will involve more than the one quick reading you might prefer. If you are the author of the original document, remember that writing something is not the same as reading it. Approach a document you have written as though you were not the author.

✓ **Identification and Marking.**   Identify the main points and significant details. While you will want to be as objective as possible, selection is by definition a subjective process. You are in a position similar to a television news director who has to choose which items to broadcast, how much time to devote to each, and how to present each one.

   You can make a concerted effort to try to be objective by making use of verbal cues in the original document. You can look, for example, for words or phrases that suggest importance in the mind of the document's author. These include:

- *Pointers:* 1st, 2nd, 3rd, next, last, and so on.
- *Causes:* thus, therefore, as a result, consequently, and so on.
- *Contrasts:* however, despite, nonetheless, and so on.
- *Essentials:* moreover, in general, most importantly, furthermore, and so on.

   As you identify the points you need to include, mark them. (You can make marginal notes, underline, or highlight on *your* copy of the document.) Try to identify single words or very short phrases. If you mark whole sentences, your task later in the process will be much more difficult.

✓ **Collection and (Re)organization.**   You must now organize your data into usable information. In effect, you will be creating a multilevel outline for what will essentially be a new document. This is an important point. A summary is an original document—not merely an abridgment. As such, it will not replicate phrasing used in the original document.

   As you develop your outline, you may find that in order to make your summary "flow" effectively, you have to reorganize some elements. Such reorganization is acceptable provided that your summary does not confuse an audience that is familiar with the original document and that it does not take on a slant or bias not apparent in that document.

✓ **Draft.**   Now that you have an outline, write your first draft, treating it like any other technical communication product you create.

✓ **Revision and Final Draft.**   Review, edit, revise, proofread, and check again. Remember that your summary, like every other CMAPP product, reflects on you and your credibility.

Content and Length

What you should include in and exclude from a summary depends on whether it is a content summary or an evaluative summary. In most cases, you can apply the criteria listed in **Figure 6.8.**

How long should a summary or abstract be? The answer is *as short as possible and as long as necessary.* As you saw in Chapter 3, technical documents often require you to balance the need to be precise against the need to be brief and concise. The more information you provide, the more you impose on your audience's time; the less information you provide, the more likely it is that your audience will not receive everything necessary.

Summaries typically run anywhere from 5 to 15 percent of the length of the original. However, keep in mind the **inverse proportion rule,** whereby the longer the original document, the smaller the percentage of its length that will be required for a summary. For example, a summary of a 3-page report might be just over half a page (close to 20 percent) while a summary of a 200-page report might run two full pages (only 1 percent). Remember, too, that most executive summaries still do not exceed a single page, regardless of the length of the original document.

Chapter Review ....

CHAPTER SUMMARY

Technical communicators use their CMAPP analysis to develop strategies for creating messages. These strategies are most often used to create technical descriptions, instructions, persuasive messages, and summaries.

Technical descriptions can be process or mechanism descriptions. Process descriptions explain how things work or are done or made. They are organized like a story—with a beginning, a middle, and an end. Mechanism descriptions explain objects or systems with at least two parts that work separately, but together perform a single function. Each part of the system is described in a logical order.

Instructions are similar to process descriptions. However, the goal of instructions is for your audience to be able to perform the task; the goal of process descriptions is for your audience to see how something works. Therefore, instructions are written in the imperative mood with numbered steps.

Persuasive messages are used to convince your audience to do something, believe something, buy something, and so on. The strategies used for these messages are based on connecting with the audience and providing them with something they will relate and respond to. Some strategies target the intellect, using deductive or inductive logic; others target feelings, focusing on attention, interest, desire, and action.

A summary is a message that conveys the important ideas and significant details of a document. There are two types of summaries: content, which objectively sum up a document's important elements, and evaluative, which include the author's opinions.

KEY TERMS

Abstract	Inductive strategy
AIDA	Instructions
Annotation	Inverse proportion rule
Collection letter	Mechanism description
Content summary	Minutes
Deductive strategy	Persuasive strategy
Descriptive abstract	Process description
Evaluative summary	Sales letter
Executive summary	Summary

CRITICAL THINKING ACTIVITIES

1. Specify the components of the strategies for process and mechanism descriptions.
2. Discuss the differences between a process description and instructions.
3. Locate a set of instructions, and rewrite them as a process description.
4. Discuss the differences between a deductive strategy and an inductive strategy. Give an example of when you might choose to use these strategies.
5. Identify and briefly explain the four components of the AIDA strategy.
6. Choose a magazine advertisement or a television commercial, and assess its use of each of the four AIDA components.
7. Identify and explain the three stages for collection letters.
8. Distinguish between a content summary and an evaluative summary.
9. Briefly describe each of the following types of summaries:
    a. Abstract (as front piece in a report)
    b. Annotation
    c. Executive summary
10. Write a set of instructions for making a peanut butter and jelly sandwich. The instructions should include a series of steps. Trade instructions with a partner, and try to make the sandwich following your partner's instructions.
11. Edit the following instructions for locating computer files to be printed. Format the instructions as they should appear.

---

1. The printer should be turned on.
2. The Search dialogue box will open after you choose File; then Find File.
3. You must make sure that the File Name box contains *.doc.
4. After you click the down arrow by the Location box, select the disk drive where your files are located.
5. The computer will search for the files as soon as you click the OK button.

---

12. You have been asked to write a summary for the school board based on the landscaping report that appears in **Figure 6.10** on the next two pages. Prepare a one- or two-paragraph summary.

FIGURE 6.10   Landscaping Report

Domingo Landscaping
P.O. Box 615
Dallas, TX 75214-9022
Phone: 555-TURF

July 15, 20--

Mr. Ramadan Dada
Business Manager
Morris School District No. 212
Martinsville, TX 75218-0344

Dear Mr. Dada

Turf for Proposed Football Stadium

Summary

The three best choices for the playing surface for the proposed football stadium are: Astroturf, Astroturf XL, and natural sod.

Introduction

Last spring you asked our company to examine the types of playing surfaces that would be suitable for a high school football stadium. You also requested that we discuss (1) the pros and cons of each, and (2) the type and frequency of injuries on each surface. We have now gathered the information you need to make an informed decision.

Details

Three surfaces are available. Recently, athletic fields have been designed to give maximum shock absorption for athletes, while minimizing the need for care of the field. The fields can be played on in all types of weather and provide sure footing when wet. Your choices are:

1. Astroturf: The surface has a 1/2 inch-high meshed nylon pile connected to a 3/4 inch-high foam pad. This tops a subbase of moldable asphalt.

FIGURE 6.10   Landscaping Report, *continued*

Mr. Ramadan Dada
Page 2
July 15, 20--

2.   Astroturf XL: The base is rubber and is covered by a 3/4 inch-high meshed nylon pile. The rubber eliminates the need for asphalt.

3.   Natural Sod: A top layer of grass combines with a root zone that is a blend of humus, sand, and peat. Cushioning is improved with shredded tires as a mulch brushed into the grass.

A number of pros and cons need to be considered when deciding between natural sod or astroturf. When the weather is hot and humid, the astroturf become hot and gives off heat. But, in cold weather, it won't freeze quickly like natural sod. Maintaining surfaces is always an issue, but natural sod can be torn up easily and must be repaired continually. Stadiums with heavy traffic need to consider this fact. Also, natural grass can't grow in domed stadiums because of the shading.

Another major concern when choosing a playing surface is the number of injuries reported. In a survey of several NFL franchises done in 1996, the total knee sprains were recorded by position and type of play. The results are:

Backs in rushing plays:	109 Astroturf injuries
	80 grass injuries
Linemen in passing plays:	104 Astroturf injuries
	72 grass injuries
Punting plays:	49 Astroturf injuries
	35 grass injuries
Kickoff	75 Astroturf injuries
	53 grass injuries

If you need further information, please call me. Domingo Landscaping Company will be glad to work with your school board to make your field the best in West Texas.

Sincerely

José Domingo

José Domingo
President

ro

SKILLS APPLICATIONS

1. Write a description of an object or a mechanism using a nonsense word such as *klane* in place of the object or mechanism. Then trade descriptions with a partner. See if your partner can identify the object or mechanism you described. Then work together to find ways to clarify, organize, and improve both of your descriptions.

2. Assume you work for a large company. Write an e-mail to your coworkers persuading them to join a new sports team that is forming at the company. (You can choose the sport.) Be sure to mention those benefits that will appeal to the wide range of people who work for your company.

3. Identify a process connected with your job or your educational institution. (Examples might include how orders are filled, how standardized tests are conducted, how the staffing process works, or how you register for a particular program.) Using visuals if appropriate, create a technical description detailing that process.

4. Austin Community College's Online Technical Writing course features an Instructions Planner (*www.io.com/~hcexres/tcm1603/ins_plan.html*). Use the interactive planner to define the key details for a set of instructions. When you are through, you can e-mail this planning information to yourself (and to your instructor, if requested).

5. Write a public service announcement to be aired on the radio. Choose a topic from the following: say "no" to drugs, read to your children, always wear your seatbelt, don't make biased jokes, and recycle your used bottles and cans. Determine whether your audience (the radio station's listeners) will react favorably to your message, and use the appropriate strategy (either inductive or deductive).

CONTEMPORARY ISSUES CASE

Ethics of Persuasion. As a copy editor and proofreader for an advertising agency, you review most of the radio and magazine advertisements prepared by your company. On several occasions, you have found persuasive ads that seem to mislead or deceive consumers. Your supervisor has told you to ignore these issues. "Whatever our clients claim about their products is their business," she stated firmly. "Your job is just to make sure the words are correct."

Do you agree with your boss? What responsibilities do you have to the clients of your agency? What responsibilities do you have to consumers? What would you do in this situation?

CASE STUDY

Persuasive Messages from AAUSAEx

Situation

At a series of meetings of the Ann Arbor University Student Association Executive (AAUSAEx), the executive president, Dorothy Palliser, has argued in favor of a special Student Association technology levy of $25 per term. This money would be used to purchase AAUSA-owned computers, peripherals, and software for student use on AAUSA premises. The hardware would be linked both to AAU's student-accessible network (currently available only through computers in the AAU library) and to the World Wide Web.

Despite strong opposition to her proposal, Palliser has managed to convince AAUSAEx to put the issue to a student vote. AAUSAEx has also set aside a small amount for campaign fees to be used by both sides in the debate. Part of Palliser's strategy is to send a form letter to every student. Seeking advice, she contacts Amy Booth, AAU's senior development officer, and asks for assistance. Booth agrees to help. A week later she provides two versions of text for a form letter, along with a note that says, in part, "You know your audience better than I do, Dorothy, so you'll have to decide between these." The two texts that Booth created are shown in **Figure 6.11** and **Figure 6.12** on the next two pages.

Issues to Think About

1. Why do you think Booth created two different versions? How would you explain her motivation in terms of context, audience, purpose, form (particularly the level of technicality), and format?
2. Examine each of the versions in terms of message. What differences can you identify?
3. How do the two versions differ with respect to level of technicality?
4. Does either version target intellect? If so, would you say the argumentation is deductive or inductive? Give reasons for your answer.
5. Does either version target emotions? If so, what specific features suggest this? (Think about the AIDA strategy and its emphasis on connotation, abstractions, and so on.)
6. Both versions include a mail-merge code, indicated by <Studentfirstname>.
   a. How do the two versions differ in their use of this item?
   b. In what ways do you think the uses are effective or ineffective?

FIGURE 6.11   Form Letter, Version A

Dear <Studentfirstname>,

As a mature university student, you will already have recognized the increasingly important role played by technology. From the efficient production of professional-quality class materials, such as essays and projects, to the research opportunities available through the World Wide Web, computer literacy and ready computer access have become a prerequisite for academic success.

If you have home access to today's generation of hardware and software, you are undoubtedly aware of your advantage—and concerned about those among your fellow students who lack such access. Although university computers are available—on a first-come, first-served basis—in a few campus locations, access to the university network and to the World Wide Web is available only through the computers found on the second floor of the library. Many of you have been frustrated by the strong competition for use of those computers or have had your grades lowered because of poor-quality printers.

As a member of both the university community and the community at large, you are keenly aware of the increasing costs of higher education. Your fees have risen more than 23 percent over the last two years. During the same period, the Student Association has managed to mitigate the impact of higher fees by imposing an 8 percent cap on increases to your Student Association allocation.

The fact that you have enrolled at Ann Arbor University demonstrates that you are committed to the long-term benefits of a postsecondary education, that you are willing to work hard to achieve those benefits, and that you appreciate their cost. Access to computers and the Web has become an indispensable feature of quality education. A modest $25 increase in the Student Association levy is a small price to pay for increased access for AAU students.

When called upon to exercise your franchise, let reason and compassion prevail over parsimony. Vote in favor of the AAUSA technology allocation.

FIGURE 6.12   Form Letter, Version B

WHO CARES?

I *think you do,* \<Studentfirstname\>, *because it's shameful*!

Costs have soared but you still need your education! Student fees keep skyrocketing, even though the Student Association tries to put some kind of lid on the cauldron by holding the line on AAUSA allocation. And what's the result? You still can't do the work you need to do when you need to do it.

You can't succeed unless your work looks good. But what if you don't have the latest hardware and software at home? You can use the campus computer rooms. But how often can you actually get in? How often can you get the computers to work? How often do the printers actually have ink or toner?

And what if you have to connect to AAU's network or if you absolutely have to do research on the Web? Well, the library lets you sit at one of its dozen stations—for less time than it takes to download just about any page or file you really need!

So what's the solution, \<Studentfirstname\>? AAUSAEx wants to have the com-puters that students really need. And we want them here in our own AAUSA rooms, hooked up to the AAU network, wired to the Web, and available 24 hours a day to any registered AAU student.

\<Studentfirstname\>, I know you care. Help us show AAU that we all do! Make sure that we **all** have the technology we need. When the ballot boxes come out, vote for the $25 ticket that will buy everyone access to a computer!

CHAPTER 7

Letters, Memos, and Electronic Correspondence

*I*n this chapter, we look at letters, memos, and electronic communication, including faxes and e-mail. These common CMAPP products share two principal characteristics: (1) they rarely exceed a few pages in length, and (2) they tend to follow an established format.

We might define the above-mentioned CMAPP products as follows.

- *Letter.* A **letter** is a hard-copy written communication from outside an organization to an audience within that organization. Although letters normally contain only text, they can include visuals as well.
- *Memo.* The word *memo* is an abbreviation of *memorandum,* a Latin word meaning "something to be remembered." A **memo** is a written communication within an organization. Hard-copy versions are common, although electronic transfer is gaining popularity. Memos tend to consist of only text but can include visuals.
- *Fax.* The word *fax* is an abbreviation of *facsimile,* meaning exact copy or replica. A **fax** is often created and received as a hard copy but transmitted electronically (most commonly across telephone lines). Faxes may contain text and/or visuals.
- *E-mail.* **E-mail** (short for *electronic mail*) is a written communication that is created, transmitted, and received electronically. While e-mail normally includes only text, a copy of almost any computer file can be attached to it. Also, some e-mail applications allow visuals to be included.

Strategies for Conveying News

The product you choose for conveying information will depend on your CMAPP analysis, particularly on your purpose for writing. Are you writing to share good news or to convey bad news? Or are you just writing to share information that will be neutral to the receiver? The following sections discuss the strategies you would use depending on your purpose (i.e., whether you are conveying good news, bad news, or neutral news).

Conveying Good News

The term *good news* applies to much more than the concept "Congratulations! You've just won the lottery!" Rather, it encompasses a broad variety of ideas, including the following:

- You have been appointed to the position.
- You have been accepted into the apprenticeship program.
- Your shipment will arrive on time.
- The repairs are covered by your warranty.
- Your materials have arrived in our warehouse.
- We are reinstating your membership.

In effect, good news is any information that your audience is likely to be pleased to receive. To convey it, regardless of the particular CMAPP product involved, you will normally construct your message to fit the **good news,** or direct, **strategy.** This strategy includes the three steps outlined in the following Checklist.

✓ Checklist

Good News Strategy

✓ State the good news in the first paragraph. Present the news directly, simply, and clearly. In doing so, you will communicate that part of your message that responds to what your audience wants to know.

✓ Explain the situation. Explain the main points and significant details of your message in the second segment.

✓ Conclude on a positive note. Although the second phase essentially completes your message, the conventions of the direct strategy dictate that you finish with a brief, positive comment of some kind. Your conclusion might be something as simple as "Thank you for choosing AEL." Or you might reiterate the good news itself, as in "Please accept my best wishes." Or your conclusion might be an expression of continued interest, as in "We look forward to serving you again in the future."

In the letter body shown in **Figure 7.1** below, Angelos Methoulios, the coordinator of GTI's Internship Program, uses the direct strategy to notify Karima Bhanji of her acceptance into the program. Notice that the first paragraph—one sentence only—conveys the good news; the second paragraph provides the explanation; the final paragraph offers the positive conclusion. As always, the specifics of your own message will be dictated by your context, your audience, and your purpose.

FIGURE 7.1   Direct Strategy for Conveying Good News

Congratulations. You have been accepted into the MIS Internship Program, which begins in September 20--.

Within the next week, I will send you the Internship Program Registration Kit. It details the registration procedures you should follow between July 5 and July 9 of this year. It also answers general questions about the program. If you have additional questions, please contact my office at 555-0105 during regular business hours.

In the meantime, please accept my best wishes as you join a program proven to provide personal and professional rewards. I look forward to working with you next term.

Conveying Bad News

You are likely to use the **bad news,** or indirect, **strategy** whenever you believe that your audience will not be pleased to receive your message. An extreme case of bad news is "You're fired." Less dramatic examples might include the following:

- We will not be contacting you for an interview.
- The new parts for your equipment still have not arrived.
- The photocopier I bought from you does not work properly.
- We are unable to ship the goods at this time.
- Your account is overdrawn.
- The text you requested is no longer in print.

Sometimes, as in the third example, your bad news will in fact be a claim letter—a statement of a problem with a product or service, coupled with a request for appropriate redress. The bad news conveyed in the fourth example might be followed up with the communicator's offer of some sort of compromise or recompense.

More complex than the good news strategy (and thus often resulting in a longer product), the bad news strategy is composed of the five parts outlined in the Checklist on the next page.

Tech Link

To learn more about writing strategies, review author Mary Ellen Guffey's PowerPoint presentations on writing routine and negative messages. Visit *www.westwords.com/ guffey/slds_bcp3.html*

Checklist

Bad News Strategy

✓ Describe the context. Explain the overall situation in the first paragraph.

✓ Provide details. Expand on the first paragraph by offering the main points and significant details that will prepare your audience for what follows.

✓ Deliver the bad news tactfully. Indicate the purpose of your communication, but try to do so diplomatically. Use language that is not as clear or direct as it could be. Communicators of bad news often use the passive voice because it permits more oblique expression. If your language is too circuitous, however, your audience may misinterpret it.

✓ Provide supplementary details. Depending on the circumstances, you may wish to include additional information that will further soften the blow.

✓ Offer conciliation and/or encouragement. You will normally have a secondary purpose—to maintain a working relationship with your audience. Thus, you should offer a "consolation prize" (e.g., a discount on repair charges or on goods shipped late, an offer of substitution, or an alternative course of action). At times, the consolation will be less tangible—for example, an expression of your commitment to service or a confirmation of your continued interest.

In the letter body shown in **Figure 7.2** on the next page, Methoulios is communicating rejection rather than acceptance. Many technical communicators dislike the indirect strategy, largely because its oblique presentation of information deviates from the CMAPP attributes of accuracy, brevity, and clarity. Nonetheless, use of this strategy is so widespread that a departure from its conventions may cause your audience to perceive your message as unfriendly or even rude.

Conveying Neutral News

A great many of the messages that form part of real-world communication convey neither good news nor bad news. They are simply information. The following are examples:

♦ Here is the catalog you requested.
♦ The meeting will take place on March 15.
♦ The report details the following points.
♦ Fourteen members attended the seminar.
♦ The price is $125.

These types of messages follow the **neutral news,** or modified direct, **strategy.** Like the direct strategy, the neutral news strategy has three parts, which are outlined in the Checklist on the next page.

> **FIGURE 7.2**   Indirect Strategy for Conveying Bad News

Thank you for your application, dated April 12, 20--, for the September 20-- Internship Program.

The Internship Program Criteria Bulletin specifies a minimum GPA of 3.2 for the year previous to joining the Internship Program and a grade of at least 80 percent in the relevant introductory course, in your case INFO 101. Our records show that although you received a grade of 84 percent in INFO 101 last term, the 66 percent you received in INFO 104 brought your overall GPA down to 2.87.

The Bulletin also specifies that a student's application must be accompanied by at least three letters of reference, two of which must be from GTI faculty. Only one of your referees, Ms. Pat Hayakawa, is on our faculty. Your two other referees, Dr. Janice Fleming and Mr. Edward Skoplar, appear to offer personal references only.

In light of the above, I am not currently able to further your application for the MIS component of the September 20-- GTI Internship Program.

I do note that most of your grades were entirely satisfactory and that Ms. Hayakawa's recommendation was highly favorable. Unfortunately, the number of applications we receive far exceeds the number of Internship Program places available; thus, we have found that we must apply the selection criteria quite rigorously.

Your record at GTI suggests that you are enthusiastic about a career in MIS and that you show some promise in the field. Consequently, I would urge you to make all efforts to raise your GPA this coming term and to seek appropriate references so that you may apply for next year's program. Grandstone's MIS Internship Program would welcome your reapplication.

 Checklist

Neutral News Strategy

✓ Introduce the content and intent. Briefly indicate what the communication is about, thereby situating your audience within the context.

✓ Explain the situation. Provide whatever main points and significant details are required. Keep in mind the complementary CMAPP attributes of accuracy, brevity, and clarity.

✓ Conclude with an action request or summation. Indicate clearly what you want your audience to do next. If you are looking for no real action on the part of your audience, provide a brief summation.

Angelos Methoulios's follow-up to his good news letter to Karima Bhanji appears in **Figure 7.3** below. Pay particular attention to the brevity of the content. Delivering neutral news does not require the elaboration that delivering good news, with the expected congratulations, or delivering bad news, with the necessary conciliation or encouragement, does. The delivery of neutral news in technical communication brings to mind the trademark line of Sergeant Joe Friday, hero of the 1950s television show *Dragnet,* "Just the facts, ma'am."

FIGURE 7.3   Modified Direct Strategy for Neutral News

The registration kit for the MIS Internship Program commencing in September 20-- is enclosed.

As you read through the entire kit, note in particular that (1) by June 16, you must arrange for your precommencement interview, which must take place on campus between July 5 and July 9, and (2) by July 16, you must have completed the automated course registration process (T-Reg).

In the kit, you will find detailed information regarding registration procedures, course and work-study requirements, and recommended extracurricular volunteer activities.

As soon as possible, please call my office at 555-0105 during regular business hours to set a date and time for your interview. I look forward to meeting with you.

Tech Link

For an excellent discussion of business correspondence, including letter formats and examples, visit Austin Community College's online technical writing course guide at *www.io.com/~hcexres/ tcm1603/acchtml/ genlett.html*

Letter Formats

Business letters are printed on **letterhead stationery,** which generally includes the company name and contact information. The letterhead and your letter's appearance and format are important because a receiver starts to form an opinion of you and your company by looking at your letter.

Block and Modified Block Formats

Two standard business letter formats are the **block format,** shown in **Figure 7.4** on the next page, and the **modified block format,** shown in **Figure 7.5** on page 144. (Note that in both letters, the body text is devoted to an explanation of the format.) The conventions for both formats are discussed in the following paragraphs.

Date.   The format of the date should be clear. It is standard practice in business letters to write the date in full. Position the date about 2" from the top of the page or at least two lines below the letterhead. The horizontal placement of the date depends on the letter format used.

FIGURE 7.4   Block Format with Mixed Punctuation

400 11th Street
Grandstone, Vermont 05824-4600
(802) 555-0141

April 3, 20--

Ms. Olivia Barclay
Executive Assistant
Radisson Automobiles Inc.
6134 Bank Street
Dallas, TX 75204-1010

Dear Ms. Barclay:

This letter illustrates the **block format** with **mixed punctuation.**
You will notice that all lines begin at the left margin. Paragraphs are not indented in this format.
You should also note the following common conventions.

Key the inside address four lines below the date. Use only one line space to separate the inside
address from the salutation and the salutation from the first paragraph of the text.

You should single-space the body of the letter and double-space between paragraphs. Place the letter
attractively on the page using side margins of 1", 1½", or 2", depending on the length of the
letter.

The complimentary close is keyed two lines below the body of the letter, and only the first letter
of the first word is capitalized. A company name may appear after the complimentary close if
company letterhead is not used. If used, the company name is keyed in all capital letters a double
space below the complimentary close. Key the writer's name four lines below the complimentary
close. Enclosure or copy notations should be separated by two lines.

Yours truly,

P.K. Hayakawa

(Ms.) Pat Hayakawa, Instructor, MIS

Enclosure

c Boris Milkovsky

FIGURE 7.5   Modified Block Format with Open Punctuation

AAU Ann Arbor University

5827 Dixie Road
Ann Arbor, MI 48103-0061
(734) 555-0198

April 3, 20--

Mr. Flavio Santini
Senior Consultant
Accelerated Enterprises Ltd.
342 Center Street West
Lansing, MI 48980-1720

Dear Mr. Santini

This letter uses the **modified block style** with **open punctuation.** Please note the following conventions.

In this form, all lines begin at the left margin except for the date, the complimentary close, and the signature block, which begin at the center of the page. This format is fairly efficient because only one tab setting at the center is required. Place the letter attractively on the page using side margins of 1", 1½", or 2", depending on the length of the letter.

Paragraphs may begin at the left margin, or the first line of each paragraph may be indented ½". The indentation is optional because paragraphs are separated by a double space. Key the inside address four lines below the date. Use only one line space to separate the inside address from the salutation and the salutation from the first paragraph of the text.

The complimentary close is keyed two lines below the body of the letter, and only the first letter of the first word is capitalized. Key the writer's name four lines below the complimentary close. Enclosure or copy notations should be separated by two lines.

Yours sincerely

Roger Concorde

Roger Concorde
Registrar

Enc.

c Nancy McDonald

Inside Address.   The **inside address** specifies the letter's primary audience. The standard formula for an inside address is shown below.

Standard Formula for an Inside Address

Personal or Professional Title + First Name or Initial + Last Name
Title
Company
Street Address
City + State + ZIP Code

Salutation.   The **salutation** acts as a greeting to the receiver. The salutation should agree with the first line of the letter address. If the letter is addressed to a job title, use the title in the salutation; for example, *Dear Service Manager.* The formality of the salutation depends on the relationship between the sender and receiver of the letter. As a guide, use the name that you would use if you were addressing the person face to face. A colon follows the salutation if **mixed punctuation** is used; no punctuation follows the salutation if **open punctuation** is used.

Complimentary Close.   The **complimentary close** is the formal closing. Only the first letter in the first word is capitalized. Use a comma after the complimentary close when using mixed punctuation; omit the comma when using open punctuation. Frequently used complimentary closes include the following:

◆   Sincerely
◆   Sincerely yours
◆   Cordially

Signature Block.   The **signature block** contains two elements: the signature itself and, immediately below it, the signature line, in which the sender's full name is keyed. The name is sometimes followed, either on the same line or the subsequent line, by the sender's professional title (see **Figure 7.4** and **Figure 7.5** on the previous pages for examples).

Simplified Block Format

The **simplified block format** omits the salutation and complimentary close. Designed for efficient processing, the simplified block format often is used when preparing letters by merging addresses from a database with a form letter. The letter shown in **Figure 7.6** on the next page is an illustration of the simplified block format. (Again, the letter's body text explains the format.)

The main disadvantage of the simplified block format is that some audiences respond negatively to it. Perhaps because of the format's origins in the advertising industry, many audiences equate its use with someone wanting to sell something. Again, consider the impact of CMAPP. What you know about your audience should determine your product.

FIGURE 7.6   Simplified Block Format

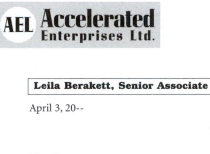

Accelerated Enterprises Ltd.
342 Center Street West
Lansing, Michigan 48980-1720
Tel: (517) 555-0123 Fax: (517) 555-0124

Leila Berakett, Senior Associate

April 3, 20--

Tina Trann
General Manager, Radisson Automobiles Inc.
4965 Madison Ave.
Chicago, IL 60602-0057

SIMPLIFIED FORMAT

The simplified block format omits the salutation and complimentary close. As in the block format, all lines begin at the left margin. The spacing between letter parts is the same as that in the block or modified block format.

Place the date 2" from the top of the page so that the letter address is positioned for use with a window envelope. Key the subject line in ALL CAPS or in uppercase and lowercase letters two lines below the letter address. Position the writer's name and title four lines below the body in ALL CAPS or in uppercase and lowercase, depending on your preference.

When writing a letter in this format, Ms. Trann, it is a good idea to personalize it by incorporating the receiver's name within the body of the letter.

Leila Berakett
LEILA BERAKETT
SENIOR ASSOCIATE

Memos

A memo is a quick, easy way to communicate with a colleague or a supervisor in your own department, in another department, or in another company office. Memos can be sent via hard copy (on paper) or via e-mail (electronically). More and more companies are using e-mail for sending and receiving memos.

Memos usually are more concise and less formal than letters. As you prepare your memos, keep the following points in mind:

The Writing Center at Rensselaer Polytechnic Institute features an excellent discussion of memos. Visit *www.rpi.edu/web/ writingcenter/memos.html*

- Remember that memos are used *within* an organization. If you are writing to an audience that is not part of your organization, use a letter.
- The word *Memo* or *Memorandum* should appear at or near the top of the form, often accompanied by the organization's name.
- Complete the To, From, Date, and Subject lines to indicate the recipient, sender, date, and topic of the memo, respectively.
- Many memo forms have a line headed "cc" or just "c" on which you can indicate any copies (in effect, you can identify secondary audiences).
- Most memos will address one topic only. Also, the information in the Subject line is usually not the same as that given in the introductory sentence of the memo. The former specifies the issue that the memo addresses. The latter introduces the situation, often by summarizing it.
- Memos are more likely than letters to have bulleted and numbered lists.
- The memo will be initialed or signed, often beside the keyed name of the originator. Memos do not contain an inside address, a salutation, a complimentary close, or a signature block.

Memos are designed to convey information quickly. In creating a memo, therefore, you should adhere to the principles of brevity and clarity. You should also regard a memo as you would a letter, as a product to which CMAPP strategies and analysis should be applied. The somewhat tongue-in-cheek memo shown in **Figure 7.7** on the next page provides further information about this CMAPP product.

Electronic Communication

When desktop computers started becoming a mainstay of offices and homes, pundits predicted the imminent death of the print medium. (Your use of this textbook refutes that prophecy.) Other so-called experts confidently foresaw the emergence of the paperless office. In fact, studies show that the volume of paper consumed by businesses worldwide has increased enormously since the entrenchment of computers in the workplace. At the same time, more technical communication is being carried out electronically. This apparent contradiction may be partially explained by the fact that many computer users prefer to edit and revise printed drafts and to print out copies of almost everything.

FIGURE 7.7   Traditional Memo Format

Formidable Forms, Inc.
Internal Memorandum

To: A. Lert
            Manager, Memo Division, Regional Office

From: Peter Carborundum   *PC*
            Supervisor, Effectiveness Branch, Headquarters

Date: April 3, 20--

Subject: Company Memoranda

For some time now, we have been considering the development and production of in-house memo forms. You will recall the following:

- The meetings were interminable.
- The points were irrelevant.
- The results were inconclusive.

Consequently, I have decided to take this bull by the horns and barge full steam ahead (please excuse the mixed metaphor). Following are some guidelines.

The word *Memo* or *Memorandum* will appear prominently.

A standard memo form contains provisions for indicating the date, the recipients, the sender, and the subject. To draw attention to the headings, you may want to use double spacing and capitalization in the heading components. The information following each component appears in uppercase and lowercase.

Memos need no salutation; simply double-space after the heading, and start the body of the memo. The body is usually single-spaced. There is no inside address, complimentary close, or signature block. If a document is attached to the memo, note this by adding the word *Attachment* two spaces below the body of the memo. The distribution list, if any, appears two spaces below any annotations.

Distribution: Virginia West
                Peter Donnelly
                Leon Garcia

The two main forms of person-to-person electronic communication are faxes and e-mail. Another form of electronic communication, the web page, is rarely used to communicate with a single individual. As you surf the Net, however, you might consider the CMAPP aspects of the pages you access. You may find that, all too often, web pages sport more sizzle than steak.

Faxes

Technically, a facsimile, or fax, machine is a method of telecommunication. The difference, of course, is that it transmits printed documents in digital form rather than as a voice message. The advantage of using a fax machine is that the transmission is immediate, unlike other means of sending print materials, which only offer delayed transmission.

Most organizations now require that their employees use standard fax cover pages, following conventions similar to the ones they follow when creating memorandums. Most current fax software is accompanied by a battery of modifiable cover-sheet templates, with designs ranging from the sedate to the outlandish. Fax cover pages frequently use bulleted or numbered lists and clearly indicate the following:

- Product (e.g., Fax transmission)
- Date of transmission
- Company name
- Primary audience, including phone and fax numbers
- Sender, including phone and fax numbers
- Number of pages being transmitted
- Topic of the fax

Elaborate fax cover pages, like the memos on which they appear to be modeled, are likely here to stay. Therefore, use the most professional-looking product that your organization offers.

Take special care when sending confidential documents by fax. Fax machines are usually shared by a number of people within an office. Anyone who walks past the fax machine has access to the contents of a document that has just been received. If a document contains confidential information, it is best to send it by courier or regular mail.

E-mail

In today's fast-paced business world, e-mail has become an essential technical communication product. More and more, it is supplanting letters (facetiously referred to as "snail mail") and memos as the preferred vehicle for rapid written communication. You can now expect all but instantaneous delivery of your message, regardless of where on the planet your audience may be, and you can also readily attach other electronic files to your message (documents, graphics, sound, video clips, and so on).

The following guidelines for planning and writing an e-mail are the same as those you use for a memo.

- Identify yourself and your company fully.
- State clearly the purpose of your message.
- State clearly who will take the next action, what that action should be, and when it should occur.
- Proofread. As always, business correspondence should be error-free.

The Privacy Issue.   Legislators are just beginning to recognize that existing communication law is not up to the task of dealing with the rapidly changing world of the information highway. They are still grappling, for example, with the legal and ethical issues surrounding the question of whether (and to what degree) employees' e-mail should be protected as private communication. Many people believe that e-mail should be subject to the scrutiny of the employers who provide the means to create and send it and who may reasonably expect that e-mail generated in the office will be work-related and therefore open to review by management.

Netiquette.   The use and abuse of e-mail has resulted in some common rules and conventions, often referred to as **netiquette.** The following Checklist highlights common netiquette conventions.

Tech Link

These Core Rules of Netiquette are excerpted from the book *Netiquette* by Virginia Shea at *www.albion.com/netiquette/corerules.html*

✔ Checklist

Netiquette

✓ Do not use all capital letters; they are the e-mail equivalent of **shouting.**

✓ To emphasize a word or phrase, enclose the word or phrase *in asterisks*.

✓ Proofread for grammatical, punctuation, and spelling errors. Because e-mails are written and sent so quickly, these mistakes are often ignored by senders.

✓ Remember that for your audience, what you see is what you get. Subtleties like irony and humor generally don't travel well.

✓ Do not overuse emoticons such as smiles :-) or frowns :-(. **Emoticons** are combinations of letters and symbols used to convey emotions in personal or informal e-mail.

✓ Keep your messages as brief as possible; many people receive scores of e-mails every day.

✓ Before sending a reply, delete the parts of the original message that are no longer critical. An exchange of several responses can produce a gigantic—and mostly useless—message.

(Checklist continues on the next page.)

✓ Before sending a file as an attachment, consider whether your audience has the software to open, view, or edit the file.

✓ If you want to attach a file, take into consideration your audience's download time. A lengthy download delays the receipt of other messages.

✓ Remember to check an attachment for viruses before you send it. Sending an infected file can have devastating consequences.

✓ If you are part of a network, do not overuse the option of sending messages (or replies) to every single member of that network. Remember the CMAPP injunction to consider your audience carefully.

✓ Do not **spam;** that is, do not send out unsolicited junk e-mail to a long list of recipients, regardless of the ease with which you can do so. Like junk mail and junk faxes, junk e-mail is usually resented.

✓ Don't send messages based on impulse or emotion (especially anger). Sending angry or insulting messages is called **flaming.** Take a moment to reflect (e.g., about possible consequences) before you click on Send. Also, make sure you think about CMAPP and your strategy.

Chapter Review . . . .

CHAPTER SUMMARY

News comes in three types: good, bad, and neutral. Good news is information your audience will be pleased to receive, bad news is information your audience will not be pleased to receive, and neutral news is simply information. The type of news you are conveying influences the communication strategy you should use.

To convey good news, use the direct strategy. First, clearly state the good news. Then explain the main points of the news. Finally, conclude with a brief, positive comment of some kind.

Use the indirect strategy when conveying bad news. First, explain and describe the situation. Use as much detail as is necessary for the reader to fully understand the context. Next, tactfully deliver the bad news. Use indirect language and provide details if they will help soften the blow. Finally, offer conciliation or encouragement. Offering a "consolation prize," either tangible or intangible, can help keep the relationship intact.

Convey neutral news with the modified direct strategy. First, briefly indicate the reason for the communication. Then explain the situation using the CMAPP strategies of accuracy, brevity, and clarity. Conclude by requesting action of your audience or, if you do not require any action, summing up the information presented.

Business letters are usually printed on letterhead stationery and can be in block format, modified block format, or simplified block format. Each format includes a date, an inside address, and a signature block. The block and modified block formats also include a salutation and a complimentary close. These two formats differ only in their spacing and indentation. Some audiences may respond negatively to the simplified block format because of its origins in the advertising industry.

Memos are designed to convey information quickly. They are used only within organizations. They can be sent via hard copy or via e-mail. Only one issue should be addressed in a memo, and the subject line should precisely indicate the topic. The most important thing to remember when writing memos is to be brief and concise.

Fax machines are useful because they can transmit printed documents immediately. All faxes should have a cover page, which often looks like a memo and indicates the date, the recipient's information, the sender's information, the subject, and the number of pages contained in the fax. Remember that most faxes are accessible to all employees, not just the recipient, so rely on more traditional methods (regular mail or courier) to send sensitive or confidential information.

E-mail is fast becoming the preferred method for rapid written communication. Delivery of messages is almost instantaneous, and you can easily attach other electronic files to them. E-mails are often used in place of memos and faxes. Remember, though, that an employee's e-mail is not usually considered private, so it should be used only for company business. Guidelines to follow when sending e-mail include the following:

- Always include a descriptive subject line.
- Do not use all capital letters.
- Proofread for grammatical, punctuation, and spelling errors.
- Keep your messages as brief as possible.

KEY TERMS

Bad news strategy	Memo
Block format	Mixed punctuation
Complimentary close	Modified block format
E-mail	Netiquette
Emoticons	Neutral news strategy
Fax	Open punctuation
Flaming	Salutation
Good news strategy	Shouting (in e-mail)
Inside address	Signature block
Letter	Simplified block format
Letterhead stationery	Spam

CRITICAL THINKING ACTIVITIES

1. Give brief definitions of good news, bad news, and neutral news. What are alternative names for each of these strategies?

2. Specify the components of the good news, bad news, and neutral news strategies. Give an example of when you might select each strategy.

3. Reexamine the acceptance letter from GTI to Karima Bhanji in **Figure 7.1** on page 139. Assume Methoulios wants to accept Karima's application, but there are problems with her transcript. What strategy might he apply? Construct an outline of the possible contents of this alternative letter.

4. Give brief definitions of the following components of business letters:
   a. Inside address
   b. Salutation
   c. Complimentary close
   d. Signature block

5. Name two or more common business letter formats, and provide a description of each.

6. Describe the principal differences between letters and memos.
7. Outline conventions for each of the following:
   a. Letter
   b. Memo
   c. Fax
   d. E-mail
8. Find out your organization's or institution's policy with regard to employee e-mail privacy. Express and defend your opinion of the ethics of its policy.
9. Do you think an educational institution that provides e-mail accounts for both faculty and students should apply the same e-mail privacy policy to both groups? (For example, should faculty be considered "employees" and students "clients"?) Give reasons for your answer.

SKILLS APPLICATIONS

1. Obtain a copy of the house style guide used by your company or educational institution, and refer to the guidelines for letter format and conventions, memo format and conventions, and fax cover pages. Assess the material in terms of the following:
   a. Consistency of image
   b. Audience's ease in obtaining information
   c. Potential audience reaction

   If your company or educational institution does not have a house style guide, refer to one of the style manuals cited in Chapter 4.
2. Review Welstromm's original memo in Case Study 7B (**Figure 7.9** on page 158). Put yourself in Roger Concorde's position.
   a. Construct a brief CMAPP analysis in planning a reply to Welstromm.
   b. Create a product that reflects your analysis.
3. Take the interactive netiquette quiz at albion.com's Netiquette site (***www.albion.com/netiquette/netiquiz.html***) to test your knowledge of the dos and don'ts for e-mail use. Write an e-mail to your instructor summarizing the results of your quiz.

CONTEMPORARY ISSUES CASE

Writing Across Cultures.   Maria Gonzalez is an administrative assistant for a financial services firm in Yuma, Arizona. Her responsibilities include editing and preparing letters for many of the workers in the office. Most of the recipients of these letters are in the United States; however, some recipients are in Mexico. Maria has noticed many inconsistencies in the letters, from format and length to tone and style.

Because of her Mexican heritage, Maria sometimes feels uncomfortable with the letters she prepares for recipients in Mexico. While she is comfortable with most of the longer letters, many of the letters sent to Mexico are short and seem a little blunt and tactless. She wonders if her concern with these letters is the result of her heritage.

Why do you think Maria considers some of the letters a little short and blunt for their audience? Should writers consider culture or nationality when writing their letters? Why or why not?

CASE STUDIES

7A Acceptance Letter from GTI

Situation

Karima Bhanji is a 20-year-old student registered at Grandstone Technical Institute. She chose Grandstone because of its highly regarded two-year Management Information Systems (MIS) Diploma Program with Internship option. Students who do well in their first year often gain a semester of real-world work experience with participating firms. After graduation, some of these students have obtained full-time employment with the companies in which they served as interns.

Midway through her first year of the MIS program, Karima applied for admission to GTI's Internship Program. On May 23, she received the letter shown in **Figure 7.8** on the next page. She is distressed to discover the following:

1. The letter was sent to her permanent address rather than to her temporary address at school.
2. Her parents redirected the letter, but postal delays have taken their toll.
3. She has missed the deadline for confirming her acceptance of admission to the Internship Program.

FIGURE 7.8   GTI Acceptance Letter

Internship Office
400 11th Street
Grandstone, Vermont 05824-4600
(802) 555-0141
Fax: (802) 555-0171

May 2, 20--

Ms. Karima Bhanji
1152 Ambrose Place
San Francisco, CA 94106-3712

Dear Ms. Bhanji:

Congratulations on your successful application to Grandstone's Internship Program.

I have examined your transcripts and studied the recommendation report submitted by your instructor, Pat Hayakawa. In the light of these documents, I have registered you in the MIS Group of the Internship Program.

Enclosed are profiles of the local firms among whom we hope to find a two- to three-month internship for you in the second semester of your second year. Please examine the company profiles and think about how one or more of them might benefit from the skills and personal qualities you believe you possess. Note that you will have to put your request for placement with particular companies in writing when you submit your Internship Placement Preference form in early June.

Note also that you must phone or fax me within the next two weeks to confirm your acceptance; otherwise, we may have to allocate your place to another student.
I look forward to working with you during your Internship Program and offer my best wishes for your success.

Yours sincerely,

Angelos Methoulious

Angelos Methoulios

Enclosure

c Mariana Lembo, Assistant Registrar

Issues to Think About

After you answer the following questions, write a response to Methoulios for Karima.

1. What communication strategy has Methoulios used in his letter to Karima? Give reasons for your answer.
2. Has Methoulios provided the right amount of information? Justify your answer.
3. How would you change the letter? Create an improved version.
4. What would you suggest Karima do now?
5. What specific CMAPP product(s) would you recommend she use? Why?

7B Ann Arbor University: Interdepartmental Memorandum

Situation

In July 20--, Kaz Lowchuk, a promising civil engineering student, received a letter from AAU's Admissions Office informing him that he would not be allowed to complete his registration for his third year because he had failed two of his compulsory second-year courses, Architectural Design 223 and Drafting Principles 200. Stunned, Kaz went to the Admissions Office and pointed out to the admissions officer that his grades before the final exams in those courses had been 78 percent and 82 percent, respectively. He stressed that he was certain he had done well on the exams and that his other course grades were all very good.

The admissions officer checked the computer record and informed Kaz that the two engineering professors had submitted his grades as required. According to the system, Kaz's marks for Architectural Design 223 and Drafting Principles 200 were 38 percent and 48 percent, respectively. The admissions officer told Kaz that both professors were on vacation but that he could launch a formal appeal of grades, although the process normally took six weeks.

Not wanting to lose admission to his third year because of what he was sure was an error, Kaz set up an appointment with Joan Welstromm, chair of the Civil Engineering Department. To prepare for the meeting, Welstromm examined Kaz's records and managed to contact the professors at their homes. At the meeting, she was able to reassure Kaz that he would be permitted to register.

After Kaz left, Welstromm composed the memo shown in **Figure 7.9** on the next page.

FIGURE 7.9   Welstromm's Memorandum

Interdepartmental Memorandum
Office of the Chair, Civil Engineering

AAU *Ann Arbor*
University

To: Roger Concorde, Registrar
From: Joan Welstromm, Chair   *JW*
Date: July 12, 20--
Subject: Kaz Lowchuk

It is <u>unfortunate</u> that another lapse on the part of your staff has once again created a situation that has caused a student worry and work and presented senior administrators with a problem they must resolve *despite their heavy workload.*

Your <u>*Admissions Office staff*</u> denied **Kaz Lowchuk** (Student Number **100888938**) admission to his third year of **Engineering** because of their own error in recording his grades. Their best advice to him was to "appeal"—a process that would have put him well beyond the <u>registration deadline</u> for this **September**.

I telephoned the two professors involved, **Vanetti** and **Scart**, interrupting their vacations, and received assurances from them that **Kaz** had, in fact, continued to do very well indeed in the courses in question. Their records—which, by astounding luck, they both had at home—confirm that **Vanetti** had entered a grade of **83 percent** and Scart a grade of **84 percent**. I am sure I need not further detail the sequence of careless events that led to **Kaz** being refused admission by your office.

I have assured Kaz that his registration will proceed without further delay. An immediate memo from you confirming this would be appreciated.

Distribution: John Vanetti
                Hans Scart

Issues to Think About

After answering the following questions, revise Welstromm's communication.

1. Why do you think that Welstromm used a memo for this communication?
2. What other product might she have used instead? Why?
3. To what extent does the memo reflect the conventions outlined in this chapter? In particular, what would you say about Welstromm's use of the following:
   a. Language (What does it say about her?)
   b. Document visuals (What improvements would you make?)
4. Conduct a CMAPP analysis of the memo. Then answer the following questions:
   a. What kind of relationship with her audience does Welstromm appear to presume?
   b. How well do you think she has gauged the context here?
   c. What effect do you think her content will have on the context?
   d. Will her purpose be clear to her audience? (Give reasons for your answer.)
   e. What secondary purpose does her memo suggest?

7C E-mail: Personal Communication at RAI

Situation

About a year ago, RAI's board of directors approved the creation of a Radisson intranet—a private electronic network connecting all Radisson dealerships and including an e-mail gateway to the Internet. Once up and running, the system allowed employees to send messages to each other and make use of Internet-based e-mail as well. Salespeople who gave clients and potential customers their e-mail addresses found that the additional communication option increased sales.

For the last 11 years, Walter Stephenson has been selling cars for Radisson Automobiles. Walter is popular with his colleagues and his customers. With repeat sales that are consistently among the highest in Radisson's seven dealerships, he has been named salesperson of the month more often than any of his colleagues.

When Victor Liepert, Stephenson's boss, received Griffin Radisson's curt memo announcing the impending reorganization (**Figure 2.9** on page 35), he decided to share it immediately with his staff. Among the most offended were the people who had been with the firm for a long time, including Walter Stephenson. The more he thought about it, the angrier he got. As far as Walter was concerned, the reorganization was a typically high-handed power grab by people in the head office who hadn't the faintest idea what things were like in local dealerships and had probably never sold a car in their lives. (In fact, Griffin Radisson has hands-on experience in every aspect of the firm's operations.)

One late December evening, Walter, still angry about the imminent changes, sent the e-mail message in **Figure 7.10** on the next page. On New Year's Day, 20--, Walter was at home. He decided to log on the Radisson intranet to see if any customers had sent him messages. What he found was the message in **Figure 7.11** on pages 162 and 163 from Celine Roberts, the head office company manager.

Walter is dumbfounded. The message makes him angrier than he has been in ages, confirming in his mind his suspicions about head office personnel. The tone of the message and its timing also leave him slightly apprehensive about going to work after the New Year's Day holiday.

Issues to Think About

1. Answer the following questions concerning Stephenson's use of e-mail as a product.
   a. Is his message clear?
   b. How many people might make up his intended audience?
   c. What do you think his primary purpose is?
   d. Do you think he has a secondary purpose? If so, what might it be?
   e. What kind of response might he have expected from his audience?
   f. Does his message comply with the general rules of netiquette?
2. Is Stephenson's use of company e-mail to criticize the company ethical? Why or why not?
3. What do you think Roberts' primary purpose is?
4. Do you think Roberts has a secondary purpose? If so, what might it be?
5. What changes in the context do you think these messages have generated? (Hint: Think of various relationships within the company.)
6. How do you think the messages will affect the context of Stephenson's meeting with Trann on January 4?
7. What do you think of the ethics of RAI's monitoring of e-mail?

FIGURE 7.10   Stephenson's E-mail

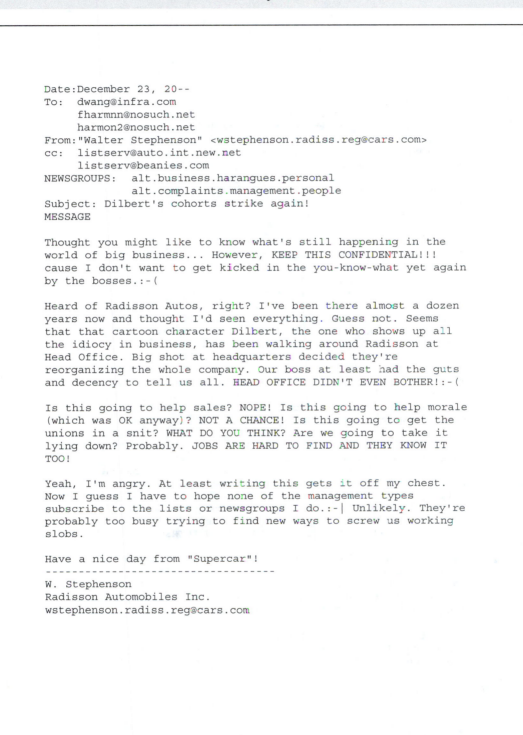

Date:December 23, 20--
To: dwang@infra.com
      fharmnn@nosuch.net
      harmon2@nosuch.net
From:"Walter Stephenson" <wstephenson.radiss.reg@cars.com>
cc: listserv@auto.int.new.net
      listserv@beanies.com
NEWSGROUPS: alt.business.harangues.personal
              alt.complaints.management.people
Subject: Dilbert's cohorts strike again!
MESSAGE

Thought you might like to know what's still happening in the
world of big business... However, KEEP THIS CONFIDENTIAL!!!
cause I don't want to get kicked in the you-know-what yet again
by the bosses.:-(

Heard of Radisson Autos, right? I've been there almost a dozen
years now and thought I'd seen everything. Guess not. Seems
that that cartoon character Dilbert, the one who shows up all
the idiocy in business, has been walking around Radisson at
Head Office. Big shot at headquarters decided they're
reorganizing the whole company. Our boss at least had the guts
and decency to tell us all. HEAD OFFICE DIDN'T EVEN BOTHER!:-(

Is this going to help sales? NOPE! Is this going to help morale
(which was OK anyway)? NOT A CHANCE! Is this going to get the
unions in a snit? WHAT DO YOU THINK? Are we going to take it
lying down? Probably. JOBS ARE HARD TO FIND AND THEY KNOW IT
TOO!

Yeah, I'm angry. At least writing this gets it off my chest.
Now I guess I have to hope none of the management types
subscribe to the lists or newsgroups I do.:-| Unlikely. They're
probably too busy trying to find new ways to screw us working
slobs.

Have a nice day from "Supercar"!

W. Stephenson
Radisson Automobiles Inc.
wstephenson.radiss.reg@cars.com

FIGURE 7.11   Robert's E-mail to Stephenson

```
Return-path: <radiss@cars.com>
Date: December 29, 20--
Sender:   owner- <radiss.cars.com>
From:"Celine Roberts" <croberts.radiss.ho@cars.com>
To:   "Walter Stephenson"
      <wstephenson.radiss.reg@cars.com>
cc:   "Victor Liepert" <vliepert.radiss.reg@cars.com>
      "Tina Trann" <ttrann.radiss.reg@cars.com>
      "Griffin Radisson" <gradisson.radiss.ho@cars.com>
SUBJECT:  Your misuse of company intranet e-mail and
consequences of your action

On December 23, 20--, wstephenson.radiss.reg@cars.com wrote:
>To: dwang@infra.com, fharmnn@nosuch.net,
>harmon2@nosuch.net
>From: "Walter Stephenson"
>wstephenson.radiss.reg@cars.com
>cc. listserv@auto.int.new.net, listserv@beanies.com
>NEWSGROUPS:   alt.business.harangues.personal
>              alt.complaints.management.people
>Subject: Dilbert's cohorts strike again!
>
>MESSAGE
>Thought you might like to know what's still happening in
>the world of big business... However, KEEP THIS
>CONFIDENTIAL!!! cause I don't want to get kicked in the
>you-know-what yet again by the bosses. :-(
>
>Heard of Radisson Autos, right? I've been there almost a
>dozen years now and thought I'd seen everything. Guess
>not. Seems that that cartoon character Dilbert, the one
>who shows up all the idiocy in business, has been
>walking around Radisson at Head Office. Big shot at
>headquarters decided they're reorganizing the whole
>company. Our boss at least had the guts and decency
>to tell us all. HEAD OFFICE DIDN'T EVEN BOTHER! :-(
>
>Is this going to help sales? NOPE! Is this going to help
>morale (which was OK anyway)? NOT A CHANCE! Is this
>going to get the unions in a snit? WHAT DO YOU THINK?
>Are we going to take it lying down? Probably. JOBS
>ARE HARD TO FIND AND THEY KNOW IT TOO!
>
>Yeah, I'm angry. At least writing this gets it off my
>chest. Now I guess I have to hope none of the management
>types subscribe to the lists or newsgroups I do. :-|
```

FIGURE 7.11   (continued)

```
>Unlikely. They're probably too busy trying to find new
>ways to screw us working slobs.
>
>Have a nice day from "Supercar"!

MESSAGE
You are no doubt aware that:

- The Radisson intranet is company property.
- All e-mail originating through that intranet must be work-
related.
- All such e-mail is and remains the property of Radisson
Automobiles Inc.

You may not, however, recall that Head Office conducts spot
checks on all intranet internal, incoming, and outgoing e-mail
to ensure its efficient and economical use and to verify that
the hardware and software are functioning as expected.

As it happens, your message of December 23 was one of those
chosen for scrutiny. In the opinion of the board of directors,
you have:

- Misused Radisson property for your own benefit.
- Brought shame on the Radisson good name.
- Without foundation accused the company of improper, unethi-
cal, and perhaps illegal activities.

I have been in communication with your vice president, Victor
Liepert, and with Tina Trann, your general manager. Please
report to Ms. Trann at 9 a.m. on Tuesday, January 4. She will
inform you of the action we have decided to take.

Note that I am sending copies of this message to Mr. Liepert,
Ms. Trann, and Mr. Griffin Radisson, President and Chief
Executive Officer of Radisson Automobiles Inc.

Celine Roberts
Company Manager
Radisson Automobiles Inc.
```

CHAPTER 8

Reports

A t some point in your career, you'll probably have to submit an income tax return, sign up for a medical or dental plan, keep track of sales statistics, record experiments you conducted, or list your company's activities over the last year. Each of these documents is a report. Every report, whether written or oral, can be defined as an organized set of information created in response to an expressed need. In other words, you create a report specifically because a particular audience has requested one.

Written reports can be grouped into two broad categories:

◆ Informal reports, also called short reports
◆ Formal reports, also called long reports

The terms *short* and *long* do not refer simply to length. (In fact, a long short report may be longer than a short long report.) Instead, the distinction between long reports and short reports relates to structural conventions.

Let's now look at some common characteristics of written reports, both formal and informal.

Characteristics of Reports

There are very few people who get up in the morning exclaiming, "I want to write a report today! Now what should I write about?" You do not produce a report because you feel like writing one; you produce a report because someone has asked for it. Thus, a report is an audience-driven document—a document whose content and style is determined almost entirely by its audience. As such, it requires you to focus particular attention on your audience and your context.

Rationale

The needs met by written reports are virtually limitless. For example, a report can:

- Keep others informed of developing situations (e.g., consecutive reports on traffic accidents at a particular corner or at a particular time of day).
- Maintain a permanent record of events (e.g., a scientist's detailed description of a series of experiments).
- Reduce errors stemming from faulty recollections or confused interpretations (e.g., witness statements concerning a laboratory accident).
- Facilitate planning and decision making (e.g., a comparison of the Linux and Windows computer operating systems).
- Fulfill legal requirements (e.g., a corporation's annual report for investors, an income tax return, or a workers' compensation report on an injury or accident on the job).
- Fulfill administrative requirements (e.g., a company's pay and benefits records or a medical expense claim form).

The transcript that appears in **Figure 8.1** on the next page is an example of a report that fulfills administrative requirements.

Hierarchy

If you are the originator of a report within an organization, one of your primary CMAPP considerations should be that organization's hierarchy. In general, you can consider your report to be either lateral or vertical.

- *Lateral.* Suppose you are the manager of the steel-detailing group in an engineering firm and have been asked to produce a report on your staff's progress on a particular job. If your primary audience is the manager of the structural drafting section, you are writing for an audience at approximately the same level in the organization; therefore, you should write a **lateral report.** Your audience, another manager, will have concerns similar to your own with regard to day-to-day activities, level of detail, and so on. These factors, part of the context, will influence not only your purpose but also your message (including the report's organization and the language you use).
- *Vertical.* If the principal audience for your report is the vice president of the design division, someone above you in the organizational hierarchy, your report will be **vertical.** The VP will likely be interested less in the minutiae of your staff's accomplishments than in the big picture (e.g., the effects on the bottom line). In fact, the VP may very well not have the technical expertise to appreciate the finer points of detailing. By tailoring your report to the results of your CMAPP analysis, you will create a product quite different from the lateral report.

FIGURE 8.1   Transcript, Example of Administrative Report

Ann Arbor University Transcript of Student Academic Record

Name: Rosalind Rebecca Greene   **Student Number:** 1123835988   **Page # 1**
Date of Birth: 03-15---   **Current Program:** General Studies   **Date of Issue:** 08-17---

CONFIDENTIAL COPY
Not valid if removed from sealed
envelope before delivery to
requesting institution.

Ann Arbor University

R.M. Concorde

Signature of Registrar

Course		Title	Crd	Grd	GPA	Course		Title	Crd	Grd	GPA
Fall Session 20--						**Fall Session 20--**					
CMNS	220	Bus&Tech Comm	3.00	B+	3.33	ANTH	320	Early Eastern Cultures	3.00	A–	3.67
LITR	210	19th Cent Amer Survey	3.00	B+	3.33	PHIL	150	Survey	3.00	A–	3.67
FRNC	220	Conversational French	3.00	B	3.00	SOCI	220	Histor.Ovrview	3.00	B	3.00
POLS	255	Party Politics	3.00	B	3.00	SPAN	100	Introduction	3.00	A–	3.67
SOCI	200	Intro Part 2	3.00	C+	2.33	TCWR	200	Report Writing	3.00	B	3.00
			Semester: 3.00						**Semester: 3.40**		
Spring Session 20--						**Spring Session 20--**					
MISY	214	System Design	3.00	C+	2.33	ENGL	352	Short Stcry	3.00	A	4.00
MISY	225	System Development	3.00	C+	2.33	ENGL	355	Drama Survey	3.00	A	4.00
MISY	229	System Evaluation	3.00	C	2.00	MISY	300	LAN Connectns	3.00	C+	2.33
PSYC	210	Intro to Statistics	3.00	C+	2.33	MISY	320	Advncd Design	3.00	C+	2.33
TCWR	110	Intro to Tech.Writing	3.00	C+	2.33	MISY	330	Advncd Develop	3.00	B–	2.67
			Semester: 2.26						**Semester: 3.07**		
Summer Session 20--						**Summer Session 20--**					
COMP	200	Basic Hrdware Design	3.00	A–	3.67	MISY	350	Intro OS Langs	3.00	B	3.00
COMP	210	Hardware Troubleshoot	3.00	A	4.00	MISY	355	Intro to SysTech	3.00	B	3.00
COMP	215	Intro to LAN/WAN	3.00	A	4.00	FRNC	200	Lang & Lit	3.00	A–	3.67
COMP	218	System Recognition	3.00	B+	3.33	PHIL	200	Ethics	3.00	A	4.00
PHYS	110	Intro to Physics 2	3.00	A	3.67	TCWR	300	Manuals	3.00	A	4.00
			Semester: 3.73						**Semester: 3.53**		
			YEAR:		3.00				**YEAR:**		3.33

Level of Technicality

Because the level of expertise of your primary audience will dictate the language of your report, the level of technicality is not necessarily dependent on whether the report is lateral or vertical. Suppose, for example, that your primary audience in the first example is the personnel manager, whose knowledge of steel detailing is negligible. Although your report in that case would be lateral, you would try to avoid technical jargon that the personnel manager might not understand. Conversely, if the primary audience for your vertical report is a vice president who is a practicing structural engineer, you would likely support some of your points by using the appropriate technical terminology.

But consider the following situation. Your supervisor, the drafting director, has requested your report and is thus your primary audience. Your supervisor can be considered a technical audience, but you've been told your report will also go to the vice president of public relations, a lay (nontechnical) audience. Common practice would be to write your report at a high level of technicality for your primary audience (your supervisor), who can understand the technical jargon, and to append to your report a brief, nontechnical document (often in the form of an abstract or executive summary, discussed later in this chapter) for your secondary audience, the vice president.

Purpose of Reports

Reports can be either informative (content) or analytical (persuasive). Your CMAPP context and purpose will help you choose which category is more appropriate.

Informative Reports

"Just the facts, ma'am." An **informative,** or content, **report** should comply with Sergeant Joe Friday's request: It should provide, as objectively and as precisely as possible, the facts.

Leaving your opinion out of a report is no easy task. Suppose that a recent fee increase at your school has left you and your fellow students angry. But suppose also that you are writing an informative report on the issue. If you refer in your report to "the unreasonable and unjustified hardship imposed on the unsuspecting student body by this untimely and disproportionate fee increase," you are not adhering to the rules for writing informative reports, which require you to provide unbiased information. Here the connotation of your words expresses your own opinion. Rather, you might have stated, "Approximately 35 percent of the students interviewed believe that the $275 per term fee increase will have an adverse effect." Such wording is objective and verifiable. It is informative without being biased or opinionated.

NASA's Glenn Research Center provides an excellent guide explaining the fundamentals of writing and reviewing technical reports. Visit *http://publishing.grc.nasa. gov/editing/ vidoli.htm#contents*

You should organize the body of your report clearly and logically with a pattern that is appropriate for the content and audience of the report. Common organization patterns include the following:

- Chronological
- Spatial or geographical
- Topical
- Importance—from highest to lowest or vice versa

When completing a prepared form, you are required to follow the organizational pattern of the form itself.

Analytical Reports

Also called evaluative or persuasive reports, **analytical reports** require you to narrate the "facts" and then comment on them. You voice your opinion through your analysis and/or recommendations. Suppose that you are asked to suggest ways for your student council to respond to an announcement of raised fees. You might create an analytical report that would examine the issue, analyze its ramifications, offer alternatives for the student council, and probably indicate which option you prefer.

Normally you organize an analytical report in one of two ways: using the deductive, or direct, pattern or using the inductive, or indirect, pattern. Very common in business settings, the deductive pattern attempts to provide as quickly and clearly as possible the recommendations that the audience has requested. The following sequence of elements is typical.

1. *Problem or Introduction.*   Very briefly sets out the reason for the report.
2. *Recommendations.*   Precisely and concisely states the recommendations resulting from the analysis.
3. *Background or Facts.*   Presents relevant details concerning the issues.
4. *Discussion or Solution(s).*   Discusses the issues, develops the arguments, analyzes the aspects of the problem, and demonstrates evidence for the report's assertions.

In the example described above, you would likely have organized your report so that the student council could quickly note the topic of your report and immediately examine your recommendations. Reading the rest of your report, and determining how you reached those recommendations, would be optional.

Note the CMAPP implications. Your audience is already aware of the subject and having requested your recommendations, will respond positively to receiving them, even if they are concerned about the content.

If your audience is unfamiliar with the issues or is likely to react negatively to receiving recommendations, you should choose the inductive, or indirect, pattern. It follows the steps you often use when you are thinking something through: You prepare the audience for your recommendations by first explaining the process you used. The inductive pattern incorporates the same elements as the deductive pattern, but the sequence is as follows:

1. Problem or Introduction
2. Background or Facts
3. Discussion or Solution(s)
4. Recommendations

The success of your analytical report will depend in large part on how well you organize items 2 and 3, the background and discussion segments. Suppose you have been asked to make recommendations on the issue of postsecondary fees. You could organize the background and discussion segments by option or issue, as illustrated in **Figure 8.2** below.

FIGURE 8.2 Organization by Option or Issue

Option	Issue
Raise Fees	**Impact on Students**
Impact on Students	Raise Fees
Impact on Taxpayers	Maintain Fees
Impact on Education	Lower Fees
Maintain Fees	**Impact on Taxpayers**
Impact on Students	Raise Fees
Impact on Taxpayers	Maintain Fees
Impact on Education	Lower Fees
Lower Fees	**Impact on Education**
Impact on Students	Raise Fees
Impact on Taxpayers	Maintain Fees
Impact on Education	Lower Fees

The first column shows **organization by option.** For the first option—raising fees—you would look at each issue:

- The effect on students because they will have to pay the fees
- The effect on taxpayers because they will also be affected
- The potential effect on the education provided at the institution

You would repeat the process for the second and third options, maintaining fees and lowering fees. By looking at the same issues for each of the options, you can compare apples with apples, not apples with oranges.

The second column shows **organization by issue.** The three issues are the impact of fees on students, taxpayers, and education. For each of the three issues, you would "compare apples with apples" by examining the same options: raising fees, maintaining fees, or lowering fees.

How do you decide which organizational pattern to use? Conduct a CMAPP analysis. In our scenario, your audience is state administrators. Because that audience would likely want to focus on financial implications, you would probably select organization by option, the organizational pattern that places emphasis on raising, maintaining, or lowering fees.

But suppose that your audience comprises members of your school's student council who want to stimulate public opposition to higher fees by focusing on the negative impact on students and (if they could make the argument) on taxpayers and education as well. This audience might well prefer a report organized by issue rather than by option.

Informal Reports

Informal reports share a number of common characteristics related to focus, format, length, and content.

Single Focus.   An informal report normally addresses a single issue. Note that *single* does not mean "simple." For example, Melinda Shaw, RAI's VP, might submit to Griffin Radisson a seven-page report with the Subject line "Decline in Sales of Global Minotaur, 1999–20--." Her report would certainly include sales statistics. But it might also examine related areas such as supply of new cars, service department concerns about deficient Minotaur components, parts availability, and customer complaints following a Minotaur recall notice. Because the report is a short report with a single focus, however, Shaw would not include an analysis of general advertising budgets for her dealership or her reaction to the RAI reorganization.

Varied Product Format.   Like proposals, informal reports can take the form of a variety of other CMAPP products, including the following:

- *Letter.*   Noah Avigdor, an AEL senior associate specializing in civil engineering, might use a letter as the format for the report on seismic upgrading to the Plumbing and Electrical Building at GTI he is preparing for Cal Sacho, GTI's senior facilities manager.
- *Memo.*   Before creating her report to Griffin Radisson, Melinda Shaw asked her manager of new car sales, Caroline Pritchard, to give her biweekly updates on both Minotaur sales and customer comments. As well, she asked Dean Wong, her service manager, to report every two weeks on Minotaur service incidents. Because both reports were written communications within an organization, Pritchard and Wong appropriately used the memo format.

- ◆ *Report.* Whether internal or external, an informal report may be a document titled "Report on . . . ." For example, Avigdor might have chosen as his product a document headed "Report on Seismic Upgrading Requirements for the Plumbing and Electrical Building at Grandstone Technical Institute." Similarly, Shaw might have produced a document entitled "Report on Decline in Sales of Global Minotaur, 1999–20--." Such a product is typically introduced by a transmittal memo or letter.
- ◆ *Prepared Form.* Many informal reports are communicated through prepared forms. Examples include the speeding ticket you received, the transcript in **Figure 8.1** on page 167, an income tax return, or a magazine subscription form. Such prepared forms proliferate in society. Whatever their intended use, they allow information to be recorded in a standard, well-organized format.

Length. Short reports normally do not exceed a few pages, although some may actually be longer than some long reports. Consider the following examples:

- ◆ When you receive a parking ticket, the official who fills out the form is completing, in effect, a short report: information with a single focus recorded on a prepared form. Such a report typically runs no more than half a page.
- ◆ The income tax return you prepare deals with a single issue: your income tax situation in a particular year. About four to eight pages in length, your tax return is also a short report.
- ◆ AEL submits an income tax return as well. The complexities of the firm's operations are such that the return is about 77 pages in length. Nonetheless, AEL's return has a single focus (just as yours did); despite its length, it qualifies as a short or informal report.

Content. The content of an informal report may consist of the following:

- ◆ *Text only.* For example, several paragraphs, perhaps with one or more bulleted lists, or a prepared form, such as a parking ticket.
- ◆ *Text and visuals.* For example, Shaw's report to Radisson, which consists of tables of sales figures integrated into several pages of text.
- ◆ *Visuals only.* For example, the sales report shown in **Figure 8.3** on the next page that was prepared for Melinda Shaw.

Classification

One way to look at informal reports is to classify them according to the main function they serve. The most common types include the following:

- ◆ *Incident Report.* An **incident report** documents what happened in a particular situation. It also assumes that the incident is not likely to be repeated. Examples of incident reports would include a safety officer's report on an accident in a large industrial operation or a report on the installation of a new telephone exchange.

- *Sales Report.*   A **sales report** presents sales figures for a particular business. Sales reports may consist entirely or almost entirely of visuals, often a table or a graph, as evidenced by the sales report shown in **Figure 8.3** below, which was prepared by Caroline Pritchard and submitted to Melinda Shaw.

- *Progress Report.*   A **progress report** indicates the extent to which something has been completed. Examples include the state of your investment portfolio, the condition of a patient, or your midterm grades.

- *Periodic Report.*   A **periodic report** appears at regular intervals and focuses on the same issue. An example is the annual *U.S. News and World Report* ranking of colleges and universities. If Caroline Pritchard were to produce regular reports on RAI sales, they too would constitute periodic reports.

- *Trip Report.*   A **trip report** might be an inspection of the condition of a building site, a hydro crew member's report on the repair of downed cables, or a manager's report on a recent conference.

- *Test Report.*   **Tests reports** are often completed on prepared forms or according to strict format and wording guidelines. Such reports include a biochemist's report on the testing of certain pharmaceuticals, a software engineer's report on debugging and recompilation of operating system subroutines, or an advertising executive's report on the results of a focus group session.

FIGURE 8.3   Sales Report

RAI: 1st Quarter Sales 20--

	Jan. 2 to Jan. 15	Jan. 16 to Jan. 31	Feb. 1 to Feb. 14	Feb. 15 to Feb. 28	Mar. 1 to Mar. 15	Mar. 16 to Mar. 31	Totals
Chevrolet Impala	12	10	15	13	14	9	73
Ford Windsor	15	18	22	15	19	20	109
Global Minotaur	49	55	56	58	21	15	254
Global Whirlwind	53	65	34	48	22	18	240
Jeep Cherokee	22	25	28	25	29	32	161
Pontiac Sunfire	18	22	15	35	22	32	144
Totals	169	195	170	194	127	126	981

There is considerable overlap among the six types of reports. For example, a biweekly report on car sales would be both a sales report and a periodic report, while a series of regularly scheduled reports on the various stages of developing a new drug would be test reports, progress reports, and periodic reports.

Formal Reports

Formal, or long, **reports** need not run hundreds of pages, although some—the annual report of a large business, for example—might well do so. Generally, length is dictated by content and structure. As **Figure 8.4** below shows, the body of a formal report mirrors the three-part structure of other technical communications.

FIGURE 8.4   Structure of Different Types of Communications

Formal Report	Other CMAPP Product	Business Presentation	Traditional Paragraph
Front pieces			
Body ♦ Introductory information ♦ Discussion ♦ Conclusion	♦ Introductory topic summary ♦ Body text ♦ Concluding summary	♦ Introduction ♦ Body ♦ Conclusion	♦ Topic sentence ♦ Supporting sentences ♦ Concluding sentence
End pieces			

Formal reports differ from informal reports in the following aspects:

♦ *Multiple Focus.*   The report deals with the interrelationships of a number of issues.

♦ *Complex Content.*   The message is complex and thus requires considerable analysis and synthesis. Not only will a secondary message almost inevitably complement the primary message, but a long report frequently harbors a secondary purpose as well. Often, the primary message will be informative, while the secondary message will be persuasive—for example, convincing shareholders how well management has run the company.

- *Detailed Organization.*   A multilevel outline (see Chapter 3) is used to develop the multiple focus and complex content.
- *Format.*   The long report never takes the form of a letter, a memo, or a prepared form; rather, it accompanies the transmittal memo (internal report) or letter (external report) that introduces it.
- *Content.*   The long report will always contain substantial text, often enhanced by visuals. It can never consist of visuals alone.

Structure

Most formal reports follow a three-part structure consisting of front pieces, body, and end pieces.

Front Pieces.   Also referred to as preliminary parts or front matter, **front pieces** help the audience deal with the complexities of the report. The pages are numbered separately from the body of the report, usually with lowercase Roman numerals.

Standard front pieces include the following:

- *Transmittal Letter or Transmittal Memo.*   The **transmittal letter** or **memo** introduces the report to the audience. It may also direct the audience's attention to particular passages or recommendations in the report. A transmittal letter or memo that runs longer than one page is numbered separately from the other front pieces. **Figure 8.5** on the next page is an example of a transmittal memo.
- *Title Page or Cover Page.*   The **title** or **cover page** typically presents the title of the report, the name of the author, the identity of the primary audience, and the submission date. The title page is not numbered. **Figure 8.6** on page 177 is an example of a title page.
- *Abstract.*   The **abstract** (discussed later in this chapter) is a brief description and assessment of the report. Most abstracts are printed on a separate unnumbered page.
- *Table of Contents.*   The **table of contents** lists the level heads of the report and the page number on which each head appears. It provides a clear picture of the organization of the document and helps the audience locate particular sections. **Figure 8.7** on page 178 is an example of a table of contents.
- *Executive Summary.*   The **executive summary** presents the main points of the report, often for the benefit of a nontechnical secondary audience. The executive summary always begins on a new page. **Figure 8.8** on page 179 is an example of an executive summary.
- *List of Figures.*   The **list of figures** (also titled list of illustrations, table of figures, or table of illustrations) indicates the page numbers on which the illustrations appear. It serves as a secondary table of contents and makes illustrations more accessible in a report whose message relies significantly on its visuals (e.g., a report that emphasizes comparisons and contrasts among tables of costs).

FIGURE 8.5   Transmittal Memo

Meade Legal Services

1100 Court Street
Cincinnati, OH 45201-1100

To :   Richard Bryce, Senior Vice President
From: Katie Goodman, Manager of Office Services
Date: May 15, 20--
Subject: The Effect of Information Processing

On March 23, 20--, you asked me to prepare a report on the impact of information
processing in selected legal offices in the United States. You also asked that my report
determine the impact of information processing on business education curricula offered
by NABTE institutions.

The completed report, which is attached, shows that information processing has had a
significant effect on legal offices and on business education curricula. The report also
includes recommendations for ways in which NABTE institutions can match their curricula to the needs of legal offices in their local areas.

Thank you for the chance to study this important issue. If you have any questions about
the report, please call me at extension 454.

tr

Attachment

FIGURE 8.6   Title Page

THE IMPACT OF INFORMATION PROCESSING IN SELECTED
LEGAL OFFICES AND NABTE INSTITUTIONS

Prepared for

Richard Bryce
Senior Vice President
Meade Legal Services

Prepared by

Katie Goodman
Manager of Office Services
Meade Legal Services

May 15, 20--

FIGURE 8.7   Table of Contents

TABLE OF CONTENTS

FIGURE 8.8   Executive Summary

EXECUTIVE SUMMARY

The purpose of the study was to determine the impact that information processing has made in selected legal offices in the United States. Further, the study sought to ascertain the impact that information processing has made on business education curricula offered by selected NABTE institutions.

Methods and Procedures

The participants for the study were information-processing specialists employed in legal offices throughout the United States and NABTE representatives from selected collegiate institutions. The legal participants were randomly selected from the Martindale-Hubbell Law Directory, 1998. The NABTE representatives were randomly selected from NABTE institutions located in or near the capital city in each state.

Each legal office participant completed a questionnaire, and each NABTE representative completed a business education questionnaire. The t-test, McNemar test, and Stuart-Maxwell test were used to analyze the data.

Results and Conclusions

The results of the study revealed that attorneys hired high school graduates or two-year secretarial graduates who knew how to answer the telephone, operate a workstation, file documents electronically, use various computer software packages, and key straight copy at speeds of 60 to 80 words a minute. The data also revealed that, in general, the firms had not established evaluation standards for information-processing specialists and had not increased the number of these specialists since purchasing electronic workstations. The firms also had not increased the salaries of information-processing specialists. Further, the findings revealed that the cost of processing information in legal offices had decreased since the implementation of electronic workstations.

The responses received from the NABTE representatives revealed that business educators trained office technology and comprehensive business education majors to operate information-processing equipment, use software packages, and key documents at production rates. No changes were noted for teaching basic business or basic English skills.

iii

Body.   The **body** constitutes the bulk of the formal report. When Roman numerals are used in the front matter, the body introduction begins with Arabic numeral 1. Mirroring the three-part structure of introduction, body, and conclusion, the body begins with an overview, proceeds to a description and analysis of the issues, and concludes with a short summation and, in some cases, a set of recommendations. **Figures 8.9, 8.10,** and **8.11** on the next pages are examples of the introduction, findings and analysis, and summary of the body of a report, respectively.

End Pieces.   Also called supplementary parts or back matter, **end pieces** furnish relevant information not included in the body. The end matter typically picks up the Arabic numbering where the body left off.

End pieces may include some or all of the following:

- *Appendix.*   A report may include one or more appendixes. (An alternative plural is appendices.) An **appendix** contains material not essential to an understanding of the report but of potential interest to the audience. Examples include a table that is too long or cumbersome to be included in the main body of the text, a transcript of an interview, or the full text of a document referred to in the report. **Figure 8.12** on page 185 is an example of an appendix.

- *Endnotes.*   Like a footnote, an **endnote** provides additional information about a particular part of the report. Unlike a footnote, though, an endnote is placed at the end of the report rather than at the bottom of the page. If you use endnotes in your report, you should follow the note form outlined in your chosen style guide.

- *Glossary.*   A **glossary** is an alphabetized list of words or phrases that the report's author believes may require definition or explanation. The choice of glossary items should depend on the results of a CMAPP analysis, particularly with respect to level of technicality.

- *Works Cited.*   If your report contains quoted material, you may use a **works cited** page to present the bibliographic credits for your citations. The format you use will, once again, depend on your style guide. See details in Chapter 4.

- *Bibliography.*   More comprehensive than a works cited page, the **bibliography** lists research sources such as books, periodicals, interviews, and web sites. The sources are typically arranged alphabetically by the last names of authors. Documentation is discussed more fully in Chapter 4. Again, be sure to consult your style guide.

- *Index.*   An **index** is a list of alphabetically arranged entries (consisting primarily of key words and concepts) that appears at the very end of the report. Whether you include an index will depend on the nature of your report. An index is particularly appropriate in the case of a report that is long, complex, and technically oriented.

FIGURE 8.9   Introduction to the Body of the Report

INTRODUCTION

Advanced technology caused many changes in the twentieth century. Equipment changed from manual to electric and, in the eighties, from electric to electronic. Information processing and communication methods progressed to an extremely high level of sophistication (Simcoe, 1999). Some legal offices became fully automated while others strove for a similar setting. According to Moody (1998), office automation is an extension of the technologies refined and developed to electronically process data and words.

Statement of the Problem

The problem of this study was to determine the impact that information processing has made in selected legal offices in the United States. Further, the study sought to ascertain the impact that information processing has made on business education curricula offered by selected National Association of Business Teacher Educators (NABTE) institutions.

Specifically, the study seeks to determine the training and entry-level skills needed for employment, the functions and operations performed, and the equipment and software used by information-processing specialists in legal offices before and after the implementation of the electronic workstation.

Scope

The report will study the impact that information processing has had on the legal office but will not include the impact of other automation technologies on the legal office. Participants identified in the study were from large cities; therefore, this study will not address the impact of information processing on legal firms in small cities.

The study also will determine any changes in tasks performed before and after information processing was implemented.

FIGURE 8.9   (continued)

2

<u>Limitations of the Study</u>

The limitations of the study are as follows:

<u>Legal Firms</u>. The legal office participants invited to participate in this study were randomly selected from the Martindale-Hubbell Law Directory, 1998. Also, the legal firms had to be located in the capital cities in the United States or the largest city in the state where an NABTE institution was located.

<u>NABTE Representatives</u>. The business educators invited to participate in the study were selected from the NABTE Directory. One NABTE institution located in the capital city or a city near the capital per state was identified for the study.

<u>Definitions</u>

These definitions were listed to assist the reader.

1. <u>After information processing</u> means after the implementation of information-processing operations (concepts, equipment, procedures).

2. <u>Before information processing</u> means before the implementation of information-processing operations.

FIGURE 8.10   Findings and Analysis Section of Report

3

FINDINGS AND ANALYSIS

The responses received from legal office participants relating to the cost of processing information since the implementation of information processing are shown in Table 1. The data presented are classified by National Business Education Association regions. Fifty percent of the legal office respondents indicated a decrease in the cost of processing information, while 28 percent reported no change had occurred in this area.

A summary of the data supplied by legal respondents reported an increase in the number of information-processing specialists employed in 21 percent of the legal offices since implementing information processing, while 23 percent revealed a decrease. Fifty-six percent of the office respondents reported no change in the number of specialists employed.

Table 1

PERCENTAGE OF LEGAL RESPONDENTS REPORTING
THE COST OF PROCESSING INFORMATION
SINCE ELECTRONIC OPERATIONS WERE
IMPLEMENTED IN LEGAL OFFICES

Legal Offices by Regions	Increase in Cost	Decrease in Cost	No Change	Total Percent
Eastern	29%	42%	29%	100%
Mountain Plains	19%	39%	42%	100%
North-Central	25%	63%	12%	100%
Southern	21%	49%	30%	100%
Western	19%	55%	26%	100%
Mean	23%	50%	28%	100%

FIGURE 8.11   Summary, Conclusions, and Recommendations

4

SUMMARY, CONCLUSIONS, AND RECOMMENDATIONS

This study was designed to determine the impact that information processing has made in selected legal offices in the United States. Further, the study sought to ascertain the impact that information processing has made on business education curricula offered by selected NABTE institutions.

The conclusions of this study provide the basis for the following recommendations:

1. The NABTE institution representatives participating in this research study and their business education department chairpersons need to study the skills, functions, and operations performed by information-processing specialists in legal offices. The study should determine if the needed skills, functions, and operations are being taught in business education programs.

2. The NABTE institution representatives participating in this study and their business education department chairpersons need to analyze the current business education curricula to determine a procedure to eliminate voids in the legal secretarial curricula.

FIGURE 8.12   Appendix of a Report

APPENDIX

Functions and Operations Performed by Information-Processing
Specialists in Legal Offices

Please place check marks in the appropriate columns to indicate functions and operations secretaries/word-processing specialists in your legal office perform BEFORE
INFORMATION-PROCESSING (IP) and AFTER IP.

R = Rarely
O = Occasionally
F = Frequently

BEFORE IP				AFTER IP		
R	O	F		R	O	F
____	____	____	1. Answering the telephone	____	____	____
____	____	____	2. Transcribing handwritten copy	____	____	____
____	____	____	3. Transcribing rough draft	____	____	____
			4. Transcribing from machine			
____	____	____	dictation	____	____	____
____	____	____	5. Transcribing from telephone	____	____	____
____	____	____	6. Receiving oral directions	____	____	____
____	____	____	7. Composing correspondence	____	____	____
			8. Transcribing material received			
____	____	____	from an attorney	____	____	____
			9. Transcribing material received			
____	____	____	from a paralegal	____	____	____
____	____	____	10. Proofreading others' work	____	____	____
____	____	____	11. Operating a computer	____	____	____
____	____	____	12. Using word-processing software	____	____	____
			13. Using software other than			
____	____	____	word processing	____	____	____
____	____	____	14. Filing manually	____	____	____
____	____	____	15. Filing electronically	____	____	____
			16. Performing other functions on			
____	____	____	a computer	____	____	____
____	____	____	17. Operating a photocopier	____	____	____
			18. Operating a microfiche			
____	____	____	reader/printer	____	____	____
			19. Operating an optical disk			
____	____	____	system	____	____	____
____	____	____	20. Other _____	____	____	____

Format

Formal reports generally follow specific formatting guidelines. A company may develop its own style manual, a set of guidelines for formatting documents, to help report writers plan the appropriate margins, spacing, headings, text formatting, and other details.

Margins.   Most format reports use 1" side and bottom margins. Reports that are stapled at the left side use a 1½" left margin. Preliminary and supplementary pages and the first page of the body usually have a 2" top margin. All other pages use a 1" top margin. MLA style specifies 1" side, top, and bottom margins. If the right margin is uneven, it should be no narrower than 1".

Spacing.   Formal reports may be double-spaced or single-spaced, depending on your organization's preference—a preference that should be stated in its style manual. If your report is double-spaced, indent paragraphs. If the report is single-spaced, double-space between paragraphs. However, in this situation, paragraph indentions are not required.

Headings.   Use headings to help organize and present data. Headings help the reader follow your line of thought as you move from point to point in the report. A first-level head is a heading that opens a major section; for example, a first-level heading is identified with a Roman numeral in your outline. A second-level heading introduces a subtopic below a first-level heading. **Figure 8.13** below shows one way to format report headings.

FIGURE 8.13   Format for Report Headings

FIRST-LEVEL HEADING

Key the words of a first-level heading in capital letters and center the heading. Making it **bold** is optional. Allow three spaces (two blank lines) before starting the first paragraph under a first-level heading.

Second-Level Heading

Place a second-level heading at the left margin of the report, capitalize all important words, and underline the heading or print it in bold. Making it **bold** is optional. Side headings are always preceded and followed by a double space (one blank line).

Third-Level Heading. A third-level heading is part of the paragraph. Making it **bold** is optional. Double space before it, underline it, capitalize the first letter of important words, and follow it with a period.

Fourth-level headings may be needed in your report. If so, capitalize only the first word, underline it, and run the heading into the text of the paragraph.

. . . . Chapter Review

CHAPTER SUMMARY

There are two broad categories of reports: informal (short) and formal (long). Despite the terms *long* and *short,* the distinction between the two types does not have to do with length, but with structural conventions.

Reports written within an organization are either lateral or vertical. Write lateral reports for audiences who are at approximately the same level in the organization as you are. Write vertical reports for audiences who are above you in the organizational hierarchy. Use your audience's knowledge of the subject and its associated jargon to determine the report's level of technicality.

Informative reports provide the facts without any bias or opinion attached to them. You can organize them chronologically, spatially, topically, or in order of importance. Analytical reports (also called persuasive or evaluative reports) provide an analysis of the facts and the author's opinion on the subject.

If the audience is familiar with the report's subject and will respond positively to suggestions, organize your report deductively (directly): problem or introduction, recommendations, background or facts, and discussion or solutions. If the audience is unfamiliar with the subject or will respond negatively to suggestions, organize the report inductively (indirectly): problem or introduction, background or facts, discussion or solutions, and recommendations.

Informal reports normally address a single issue. They can be letters, memos, reports, or prepared forms. They are usually no longer than a few pages, but some are much longer. Informal reports may consist of text only, text and visuals, or visuals only. Common classifications of informal reports are incident reports, sales reports, progress reports, periodic reports, trip reports, and test reports.

Rather than addressing a single issue, formal reports deal with the interrelationships of a number of issues. They require detailed organization to handle the complex content. Formal reports are always in report form. They always contain extensive text, and they never consist of visuals alone.

Most formal reports have three parts: front pieces, body, and end pieces. The front pieces help the audience deal with the complexities of the report. They may include a transmittal letter or memo, a title page or cover page, an abstract, a table of contents, an executive summary, and a list of figures. The body constitutes the bulk of a formal report. It consists of an overview, a description and analysis of the issues, and a short summation and recommendations. The end pieces of a formal report furnish relevant information not included in the body. They may include an appendix, endnotes, a glossary, a works cited page, a bibliography, and an index.

Formal reports generally follow specific formatting guidelines. Consult your company's style guide or a style manual for details on formatting your report.

KEY TERMS

Abstract	Lateral report
Analytical report	List of figures
Appendix	Organization by issue
Bibliography	Organization by option
Body	Periodic report
Endnote	Progress report
End pieces	Sales report
Executive summary	Table of contents
Formal report	Test report
Front pieces	Title/Cover page
Glossary	Transmittal letter/memo
Incident report	Trip report
Index	Vertical report
Informal report	Works cited
Informative report	

CRITICAL THINKING ACTIVITIES

1. Briefly describe four or more needs that are met by written reports.
2. Explain the difference between a lateral and a vertical report, and relate that difference to a report's level of technicality.
3. Identify and describe at least three of the six types of informal reports discussed in this chapter, and give an example of each.
4. Describe the differences between informal and formal reports with respect to focus, format, length, and content.
5. Distinguish between an informative report and an analytical report.
6. Identify at least two of the four common organizational patterns found in informative reports.
7. Describe the organizational difference between the deductive pattern and the inductive pattern used in analytical reports. Explain the CMAPP implications for each pattern.
8. Assume that you have been asked to write an informal analytical report on possible changes to the parking situation at your institution. Identify the two organizational approaches you might use. Explain which approach you would choose if your primary audience were:
   a. The senior administration of your institution.
   b. The student association executive.
9. Name the three main parts of a formal report. Identify and describe at least two elements in the first part and two elements in the third part.

SKILLS APPLICATIONS

1. Review Chin's report on Radisson participation (**Figure 8.14** on pages 191–193). Imagine that her investigation had led her to conclude that RAI's experience with GTI's Internship Program had been of no benefit to the company. Rewrite the report accordingly, paying particular attention to the information you provide about the students, the wording you use to do so, and your concluding segment and call to action.

2. Visit the Annual Report Gallery at ***www.reportgallery.com*** and view the International Gallery of annual reports housed there. Review and compare six to eight annual reports. Then select a single report to analyze. How effectively does the annual report speak to its audiences? Is the structure of the report effective? How are visuals used to enhance the report content? What changes would make the report more effective?

CONTEMPORARY ISSUES CASE

Reporting on Markets Abroad.   Your company does business abroad in a variety of countries. You have been asked to help prepare a training program for employees who deal with clients and coworkers from (select a country to research). Collect data on this country from a variety of sources, including the Internet as well as interviews with international workers and/or students. Your data should include information about formats for written communication, observance of holidays, customary greetings, business ethics, and other business topics. Prepare a memo report addressed to Meera Bhata, editor for the training program materials, summarizing your findings and recommendations for the program.

CASE STUDIES

RAI Report on Participation in GTI Internship Program

Situation

In 20--, Radisson Automobiles participated in Grandstone Technical Institute's Internship Program. Several students in GTI's Automotive Mechanics and Electronics programs secured work placements with Radisson's dealerships. Upon graduating in the early summer of that year, most of these students applied for positions with Radisson and a number were hired. The following year, as a result of union-related and financial issues, Radisson declined to participate in GTI's Internship Program. That summer Angelos Methoulios, the Internship Program coordinator, wrote to Howard Blumen, Radisson vice president, requesting (a) that Radisson report on its reaction to its participation in the program and (b) that the company consider participating again in the Internship Program in the coming year.

Blumen asked Corinne Chin, a general manager at Radisson, to take care of the matter. Chin consulted company records and sought additional input from Larry Cornetski, the service manager, and Emily Cardinal, the personnel manager. Having concluded that their previous participation in the program had been worthwhile and that it would be in Radisson's best interest to take part again, Chin created for Methoulios the report that appears in **Figure 8.14** on the next three pages.

Issues to Think About

1. How would you describe the context at the outset of this case study?
2. Why do you think that Blumen asked Chin to deal with the matter instead of dealing with it himself?
3. From your answer to question 2, what can you infer about the relationship between Blumen and Chin?
4. Is Chin's report formal or informal? What criteria led you to your answer?
5. How would you summarize Chin's primary message? Can you see a secondary message? If so, what do you think it is?
6. What do you think of Chin's choice of product? Would you have chosen a different one? If so, why?
7. How would you describe Chin's primary purpose? Can you discern a secondary purpose? If so, what might it be?
8. The primary audience is Methoulios. Do you see a secondary audience? If so, who is it?
9. Does the report reflect a deductive or inductive strategy? Did Chin make the right choice? (Give reasons for your answers.)
10. How would you describe the report's organizational pattern?
11. What "call to action" has Chin used to close her letter? How effective is it?
12. How do you think Methoulios will react to the report? What would you expect to happen next in this scenario?
13. Do you think Chin has made effective use of document visuals? (Support your answer with examples.)

FIGURE 8.14   Chin's Report on Internship Participation

Radisson Automobiles Radisson

Radisson Fine Automobiles
6134 Bank Street, Hartford CT 06176-3507
860.555.0180 Fax: 860.555.0181
Email: radisson@cars.com

September 13, 20--

Mr. Angelos Methoulios
Coordinator, Internship Program
Grandstone Technical Institute
400 11th Street
Grandstone, VT 05824-4600

Radisson Participation in Grandstone Internship Program

Dear Mr. Methoulios:

Thank you for your letter of August 16, 20--, to our Vice President, Mr. Howard Blumen. He has asked me to reply.

Your letter made two requests:
1. That we give you our views on our previous participation in your Internship Program
2. That we consider participating again later this year

First, here are our overall reactions.

Conclusions
1. As a whole, Radisson staff regard the internship experience as having been positive for the company.
2. Recorded feedback from the students who interned with us suggests that for the most part, they, too, found the experience productive and valuable.
3. Upon graduating, several students applied for full-time work with our company; three are now employees of Radisson.
4. Although we foresee little opportunity for full-time hiring in the coming year, we would be pleased to participate in the Internship Program in early 20--.

Let me now deal with each of your queries in detail.

Previous Participation
Fourteen students applied for internship positions with Radisson. As a result of the subsequent interview process and in the light of our own projected needs, we accepted eight for placement for the period of January 5, 20--, through March 6, 20--.

The students were assigned a variety of tasks, and their progress was monitored by assigned Radisson personnel, who then provided our management with written feedback. The following table summarizes the information collected.

FIGURE 8.14   (continued)

Methoulios, page 2

Student	GTI Area	RAI Work Sector	Comments From Staff
Peter Bennett	Automotive	Repair Shop Floor	Knowledgeable; conscientious; enthusiastic; learned quickly; good interpersonal skills; good communication skills; required little supervision. **Hired as apprentice mechanic.**
Penny Miller	Electronics	Administration	Excellent understanding of MIS electronics; broad operating system background; worked very quickly; thorough and meticulous; some difficulty accepting criticism; average interpersonal but excellent written communication skills.
Francine Orti	Automotive	Repair Shop Floor	Good independent worker; got along very well with mechanics and with customers; eager to learn; enthusiastic worker; intent on finding solutions to problems; excellent mechanical diagnostic sense; good interpersonal and communication skills. **Hired as apprentice mechanic.**
Jason Parak	Automotive	Parts Dept.	Competent worker but rather unenthusiastic; argued at times with supervisor and with mechanics; seemed very keen on coffee/lunch breaks; often unwilling to accept personal responsibility for errors, problems, and so on.
Shiraz Ram	Electronics	Parts Dept.	Eager worker; quick learner; enthusiastic; punctilious; dealt extremely well with customers; always calm under pressure; sent thank-you notes to his supervisor; stayed in touch with company until graduation. **Hired into Parts Dept.**
Dana Rowam	Automotive	Repair Shop Floor	Good worker; good practical and diagnostic skills; good communicator; likable personality; good sense of responsibility; did not seek employment here.

FIGURE 8.14   (continued)

Methoulios, page 3

Ahmed Sala	Automotive	Repair Shop Floor	Excellent worker; liked and respected by supervisor and mechanics; well above average expertise—had worked as mechanic for three years prior to this experience; did not apply for employment here despite supervisor's encouragement to do so.
Katie Wing	Electronics	Repair Shop Floor	Excellent theoretical knowledge; very conscientious; excellent interpersonal skills; well liked by all; glad she had chance to work here—learned she prefers programming; did not apply for position.

20-- Participation

After discussions with appropriate personnel, I am pleased to inform you that Radisson will have five internship openings for the spring of 20--:

(a) two Automotive Mechanics students in the repair bays
(b) one Electronics student in the automotive service area
(c) one Electronics student in our expanding Parts Department
(d) one Plumbing & Welding student in our Facilities Management area

The placement period will be from January 3, 20--, through April 28, 20--. Our lead contact with Grandstone Technical Institute will be our personnel manager, Ms. Emily Cardinal, who can be reached by phone at 555-0156 and by fax at 555-0143.

Final Remarks

We are pleased that you kept Radisson in mind when planning your Internship Program for the coming year. It is our conviction that partnerships of this kind between post-secondary educational institutions and established businesses are of enormous value. They provide capable students with the practical experience that allows them to enter the workforce better prepared, and they confer on businesses such as ours the opportunity to get to know the people who often become the key to our own continued success. Believing programs such as yours to be essential to the growth of the economy, Radisson remains committed to them.

Thank you again for your interest in Radisson Automobiles. Ms. Cardinal looks forward to receiving your call over the next couple of weeks.

Yours sincerely,

C.R. Chin

Corinne Chin
General Manager

CHAPTER 9

Proposals

A proposal is a CMAPP product that is designed to offer a solution to a problem. Because solving a problem invariably costs time, money, and energy, your proposal must persuade your audience that your solution warrants those expenditures. At the same time, your proposal must clearly and precisely explain the solution and its costs and benefits. Thus, a proposal usually combines persuasion with technical description (see Chapter 6). Proposals can take a variety of forms, including memos and letters.

Classification of Proposals

A common way to classify proposals reflects the CMAPP elements of message and audience. Consider the following four scenarios:

Scenario 1: Solicited Internal Proposal

Griffin Radisson, RAI's president, believes that the morale of senior managers in all seven dealerships has been declining, to the detriment of the company as a whole. He asks the company manager, Celine Roberts, to look into the matter and submit to him a proposal for raising morale.

Since Radisson has requested the proposal, we classify it as **solicited.** Since Radisson and Roberts are part of the same company, Roberts' proposal is termed **internal** and would likely be introduced by means of a transmittal memo.

Scenario 2: Unsolicited Internal Proposal

Jack Lee, the functions coordinator for AAU's Student Association, has thought of a way for AAUSA to make extra money when the new Student Association Building opens. He envisions renting some of the AAUSA space to campus clubs. He decides to write an implementation plan and submit it to the AAUSA president, Dorothy Palliser.

Because Palliser has not been expecting Lee's proposal, we would call it **unsolicited.** Because both individuals are part of the same organization, Lee's proposal is internal. Being relatively short, it would likely take the form of a memo.

Scenario 3: Solicited External Proposal

Cal Sacho, GTI's senior facilities manager, has been charged with studying the geological and geotechnical implications of building an engineering annex. Seeking a competent consulting firm for this major undertaking, he places in the local papers a call for proposals, often referred to as an RFP **(request for proposal).** Always on the lookout for interesting contracts, Mitchell Chung, the AEL senior associate, notices the call and submits AEL's proposal for the study.

In this case, Sacho requested bids; thus, we can label Chung's proposal solicited. Since two separate organizations are involved, the proposal is **external.** Chung would most likely use a letter of transmittal to introduce his proposal.

Scenario 4: Unsolicited External Proposal

Nicolas Pleske, a junior associate with AEL, has experience in marketing and advertising. He has heard through personal contacts that RAI is considering opening a new dealership in his area. Eager to drum up new business, he obtains the name of RAI's president, Griffin Radisson, and creates and submits to him a proposal for bringing RAI's name to the attention of the car-buying public.

Since RAI has not requested anything, we would classify Pleske's proposal as unsolicited. Since AEL and RAI are different organizations, the proposal would be external. Pleske would frame his proposal either as a letter or as a document introduced by a letter of transmittal.

CMAPP Implications

One might assume that insider knowledge and easy access to information would make a solicited internal proposal the easiest to formulate and that, conversely, an unsolicited external proposal would entail the greatest difficulties. For the proposal writer, however, the realities of workplace context and audience can turn the tables.

Scenario 1: Solicited Internal

As the manager of the head office, Celine Roberts knows all the RAI senior managers and has ready access to all relevant information. You would expect that these advantages would make it easier for her to develop her proposal.

Imagine for a moment, though, the reaction of the senior managers when Roberts begins asking questions. Many of them may be suspicious of her motives; some may even feel threatened. Their relationships in RAI are thus likely to be affected, regardless of the eventual proposal she develops. As well, the accuracy of the information the senior managers provide—and thus of Roberts' proposal—may be compromised by their speculations about her need for the information.

Tech Link

Proposalworks.com features a wide variety of resources for proposal writers, including articles on all aspects of the proposal development process. Visit *www.proposalworks.com/ articles_index.html*

Having asked Roberts to propose a solution, Radisson is obviously aware of a problem. Thus, Roberts doesn't need to overcome audience skepticism that a problem in fact exists. What will she do, however, if her research determines that morale has been in decline because of Radisson's own overbearing management style and his unwise operational decisions? In such a case, Roberts' own familiarity with her audience (and the fact that her manager asked for the proposal) might run counter to her desire to be factual and objective.

Scenario 2: Unsolicited Internal

Because his proposal is unsolicited, Jack Lee must first convince Dorothy Palliser that there is a problem to be solved. Thus, his audience's initial skepticism may be high. However, his knowledge of his audience and his own position within AAUSA may well increase his credibility and thus his ability to persuade Palliser.

As a member of the AAUSA and a AAU student, Lee will benefit from specialized knowledge of audience and context. He can use this knowledge to make his proposal more precise, relevant, and convincing. On the other hand, if his relationship with Palliser is not a good one, he will face an uphill battle. Palliser may not be able to react objectively to his proposal and might think that he is making use of his inside knowledge to undermine her position as president of AAUSA.

Scenario 3: Solicited External

Because he is responding to GTI's RFP, Mitchell Chung does not need to convince his audience that a problem exists. He can concentrate instead on finding a workable solution. However, he is likely unaware of—and thus will not be able to respond to—specific GTI in-house concerns. Further, despite the public call for proposals, Cal Sacho's decision may be influenced by internal politics. For example, GTI's board of governors may have decided that small local firms should be given priority, thus leaving AEL (a larger firm) at a hidden disadvantage.

Scenario 4: Unsolicited External

As an outsider, Nicolas Pleske must first persuade his audience that a problem exists. Griffin Radisson, not having requested anything and confident of the strengths of his own business plan, is likely to be highly skeptical and might even take offense. Not being part of RAI, Pleske cannot be certain that RAI is thinking of opening a new dealership. Further, he needs to convince Radisson not only to undertake marketing and advertising but also to hire AEL to develop and implement the program. In fact, he cannot even be sure he has chosen the appropriate audience. Radisson might be annoyed that this promotional proposal was not directed to Celine Roberts.

On the other hand, Radisson, who might regard an unsolicited proposal from one of his own employees as presumptuous, may be intrigued by an outsider's perspective. Unencumbered by RAI's corporate culture, Pleske may be able to offer original ideas that will appeal to his audience.

Alice Reid, University of
Delaware Instructor of
English and Educational
Technology, provides "A
Practical Guide for
Writing Proposals" that
includes a planning sheet
for the proposal and
presentation. Visit
*http://members.dca.net/
areid/proposal.htm*

Informal and Formal Proposals

Internal proposals are sometimes referred to as **informal.** An example of such a proposal is a solution to a supervisor's or colleague's work-related problem. Most informal proposals will run no more than a few pages and will take the form of a memo. If the issue is complex, a longer informal proposal might be framed as a separate document introduced by a transmittal memo.

External proposals may also be termed **formal.** Whether occasioned by a call for proposals or some other stimulus, formal proposals tend to be longer than informal proposals and more complex. Although some may be included within a letter, most will be documents introduced by transmittal letters.

There is no single prescribed structure for a proposal. Its content and organization will be determined by the results of a CMAPP analysis. But informal proposals will typically include the following elements (note the similarity with the deductive approach to persuasion discussed in Chapter 6):

- *Introduction.*   Provide sufficient background for your audience to appreciate the rationale for your proposal.
- *Recommendations.*   Provide a concise list of the proposed steps or actions.
- *Justification.*   Discuss the arguments that support your recommendations. Consider the potential costs and benefits and an implementation timeline.
- *Summary.*   Briefly summarize your proposal. Include a call to action: as in any persuasive communication, specify what you want your audience to do next.

If your informal proposal is more complex or you are preparing a formal proposal, use the following structure (again, note the deductive approach):

- *Introduction.*   Indicate the background. If the proposal is solicited, specify the request to which it is responding. If it is unsolicited, explain your rationale.
- *Proposed Solution.*   Describe precisely the steps or procedures you are suggesting. Indicate the benefits that would result from your solution.
- *Budget.*   If appropriate, you might use heads such as Costs, Staffing, Personnel, or Requirements either instead of the level head Budget or in addition to it. Present the details of the budget clearly and precisely.
- *Benefits.*   Specify the benefits to your audience of implementing your proposal. Use your CMAPP analysis to help define your content.
- *Schedule.*   If your proposal incorporates several sequenced steps, specify when each step should be accomplished. If, as is usually the case, timeliness is important, indicate the deadlines you think are necessary.
- *Authorization/Action Request.*   If it is appropriate for your context and your audience, request approval to begin. In all cases, include a clear call to action.

An informal, unsolicited internal proposal might look like the one shown in **Figure 9.1** on the next two pages. An example of a solicited proposal in letter form is presented in **Figure 9.2** on pages 201 and 202.

FIGURE 9.1 Informal Proposal

AAUSAEx Memo

To: Dorothy Palliser, AAUSAEx President

From: Jack Lee, Functions Coordinator *JL*

Date: Monday, October 18, 20--

Subject: Profitable Utilization of New AAUSAEx Premises

Introduction

As you know, the new Student Association Building (SAB) is scheduled to open in January 20--. Despite its name, the building will not be owned by AAUSAEx but by the university; AAUSAEx has, however, committed to leasing most of the main floor.

AAUSAEx members remain aware of the possibility of financial difficulty in the light of our contracted lease payments, particularly since we have been averse to raising Student Association fees for AAU students.

I would like to propose what I believe is an effective solution, one that I believe would bring social as well as financial benefits.

Proposed Solution

- We obtain permission from AAU administration to sublet part of the premises that we have contracted to lease.
- We subdivide this section into five club rooms and contract with AAU clubs to lease them from AAUSAEx.

Costs

- What has so far been set aside as the general purpose room comprises some 37' × 34' (1,258 square feet). Since we will be leasing space from AAU administration at $.14 per square foot per month, the prorated cost to us of the general purpose room will be approximately $176 per month.
- Robust Construction has given me an informal estimate of approximately $4,000 to convert the general purpose room into five club rooms, each of approximately 76 square feet: divider walls, doors, electrical renovations, and so on. Prorated over one year, this would entail a cost of $333 per month.
- From my informal discussions with the Engineering Club, the Foreign Students Association, and the Athletics Club, I predict that each of the five club rooms could be rented at $85 per month. Since AAU operates on a standard trimester

FIGURE 9.1   (continued)

Dorothy Palliser
October 18, 20--
Page 2

system, the five rooms should be occupied for 11 months per year, providing a total annual income of $4,675 and thus a yearly prorated income of approximately $389 per month.

* The financial implications would thus be:

First Year		Subsequent Years	
Item	Amount	Item	Amount
Monthly Rental to AAU	(176.12)	Monthly Rental to AAU	(176.12)
Monthly Renovation	(333.33)		
Monthly Sublet Income	389.58	Monthly Sublet Income	389.58
Monthly Total	(119.87)	Monthly Total	213.46
First Year Total	**(1,438.44)**	**Yearly Total**	**2,561.52**

* From the above tables, you can see that:
  (a) The first year would show a loss of $1,438.44 that could readily be covered by our "rainy day" fund, which currently stands at $2,000.
  (b) The second year would show a profit of $2,561.52 − $1,438.44 = $1,123.08.
  (c) Subsequent years would show annual profits of $2,561.52.

Benefits
* AAUSAEx will begin to see financial benefits by the end of the third quarter of the second year of operation, by which time the renovation costs will be paid off.
* Subletting the space to campus clubs would foster greater intermingling of both clubs and individual students and would likely result in greater cooperation between AAUSAEx and independent campus clubs.

Schedule
* We should attempt to receive sublet approval from AAU administration before December 1, 20--.
* Immediately upon securing this approval, we should contact the presidents of campus clubs and try to have contracts with them signed by December 15, 20--. Such contracts should be for a minimum of one year.

Authorization
I request that within the next week, you give me your approval to begin implementing this proposal so that I may initiate contact with both AAU administration and AAU club presidents. Please respond by return memo or by e-mail (leej@aau.edu).

FIGURE 9.2   Solicited Proposal

Teletalk   1000 Broadmoor Way Omaha, NE 68116-1844 Telephone: (402) 555-0100 Fax: (402) 555-0130

July 12, 20--

Ms. Gloria Quintero
Director of Consumer Affairs
The Foodworks Market
10 Dunstable Highway
Omaha, NE 68111-6409

Dear Ms. Quintero:

Introduction → As you requested, here is our proposal for conducting a telephone survey to determine consumer interest in the posting of nutritional information in your store's produce department. The objective of the project is to provide the research you need to decide whether to post this information. This proposal describes the need for and the scope of the project and outlines the action plan we would carry out to obtain the customer feedback that will help in your decision.

Background
Consumers are more concerned than ever about their health. Many want to use more fresh fruits and vegetables in the meals they prepare at home. However, because produce is not packaged in containers, consumers cannot check the labels for nutritional value. Thus, they have no source of nutritional information at the point of sale.

Need
Your supermarket has positioned itself as the market leader in customer service. To maintain this position, you want to investigate whether posting detailed nutritional information in the produce department would be valuable to consumers.

Scope of Project
To learn what adult consumers think about the posting of nutritional information, we propose to plan and conduct a comprehensive survey. It would include:
- Identifying potential interviewees.
- Preparing a script for the telephone survey.
- Compiling and analyzing survey results.
- Preparing a final report for Foodworks' management.

FIGURE 9.2   (continued)

Ms. Gloria Quintero
July 12, 20--
Page 2

To get a balanced sampling, we recommend surveying at least 300 adults. We will need the names and telephone numbers of up to 900 adults so that we can be assured of completing 300 interviews.

Action Plan
After you approve the project, Teletalk will require about three working days to pre-pare, test, and revise a script for the telephone survey. After testing the survey on 25 telephone contacts and making any necessary changes, we will proceed to complete 300 telephone interviews during five weekday evenings. One week after completing the survey, we will provide a statistical analysis of the results and a written summary of our findings and recommendations.

Schedule
We can begin this project within a week of receiving your approval. You will receive our analysis and summary about three weeks after we begin.

Cost
Our price for planning, completing, and analyzing this survey is $5,000. Additional costs for telephone charges, postage, and other expenses will be billed at the end of the project.

Qualifications ➤ Teletalk has been privileged to conduct more than one dozen surveys for Foodworks over the past three years. As always, we welcome the opportunity to help you in your goal of identifying and meeting the needs of your consumers. Thank you for asking Teletalk to submit this bid.

Sincerely,

Brad Altman

Brad Altman
Vice President

Qualities of Winning Proposals

To write a winning proposal, you must know your audience. To do this, you may need to research the company to answer the following questions:

- What are the company's goals and objectives?
- Is this a small company with limited resources or a larger company with extensive resources?
- Has the company funded other projects like the one you are proposing?
- Are copies of previously successful proposals available? You may find accepted proposals on public record, on file in libraries, or on the Internet.

Whether your proposal is internal, external, solicited, or unsolicited, you should bear in mind several things.

- Clearly and precisely describe both the problem and your solution to persuade your audience to pay for implementing your solution. Remember, a proposal offers a solution to a problem.
- Demonstrate your strengths and areas of expertise, and support your credentials with examples of your work. Have you completed other projects like this? Do you have professional references you can include? Be sure to include memberships in professional and licensing organizations.
- Highlight the benefits of your proposal to your potential customer. Here you need to go one step beyond listing the features of your product or service. You must show your customer how your recommendations can benefit their work.
- When preparing your proposal, think of ways to counter the inevitable audience skepticism. If your proposal is unsolicited, your audience may question the very existence of the problem you claim to be solving. If your proposal is solicited, you will have to overcome concerns about such things as the cost of your solution. In this case, you will normally have to convince your audience that your solution is superior to those proposed by others.
- Work through your solution in sufficient detail to permit your audience to make an informed decision. Remember that you are targeting your audience's intellect and must provide thorough, cogent arguments. Conversely, you must be brief and concise. Extraneous details may prompt a negative response.
- Ensure that your solution is reasonable and executable. Proposing that a company's CEO be removed to solve an employee morale problem is probably not a reasonable solution.
- Ensure that your solution, particularly your costing, is feasible. A proposal that includes a $5 million dollar marketing and advertising program may be rejected out of hand based simply on financial realities.
- Pay careful attention to the accuracy of your entire message. Numerical errors, faulty terminology, verifiably false assertions, and misspellings will cause loss of credibility for both you and your proposal.

Chapter Review ·

CHAPTER SUMMARY

A proposal offers a solution to a problem, persuades the audience of its validity, and explains its costs and benefits. Proposals can be solicited or unsolicited and internal or external. Each combination (solicited internal, unsolicited internal, solicited external, and unsolicited external) has its own CMAPP implications.

Internal proposals—sometimes referred to as informal—are usually no longer than a few pages and take the form of a memo. Longer internal proposals are documents introduced by a transmittal memo. They typically include an introduction, recommendations, a justification, and a summary.

External proposals—sometimes referred to as formal—tend to be longer and more complex than internal proposals. Most are documents introduced by a transmittal memo. They typically include an introduction, a proposed solution, a budget, a list of benefits, a schedule, and an authorization/action request.

To write successful proposals, research your audience and gauge their reactions to previous proposals. Precisely define both the problem and your solution. Show the audience your areas of expertise, and support your credentials with examples of your work. Provide enough detail to allow your audience to make an informed decision but no so much as to prompt a negative response. Ensure that your solution is reasonable, executable, and feasible. Finally, proofread for numerical errors, faulty terminology, verifiably false assertions, and misspellings.

KEY TERMS

External proposal   Request for proposal
Formal proposal   Solicited proposal
Informal proposal   Unsolicited proposal
Internal proposal

CRITICAL THINKING ACTIVITIES

1. Identify and briefly describe the four types of proposals discussed in this chapter.
2. Using examples, discuss the CMAPP implications for each type of proposal discussed in this chapter.
3. Distinguish between informal and formal proposals. Use examples to help illustrate the differences.
4. Discuss the importance of audience analysis in proposal preparation.

5. What questions should you ask to help determine your potential customer's needs?

6. List and discuss three elements that are important in creating an effective proposal.

7. Do proposals use the direct strategy or the indirect strategy? Explain your answer.

8. Discuss why demonstrating your strengths and areas of expertise is so important when writing proposals. How might an audience react to your proposal if they doubted your credentials?

SKILLS APPLICATIONS

1. Assume that you and several of your classmates believe it would be more beneficial for your education in a particular course to work on a term project rather than take the currently scheduled final exam. Construct a CMAPP analysis and outline for the proposal you would submit to your professor. Prepare your proposal in memo format.

2. Working alone or with a team, select a problem in your school, workplace, or community. Brainstorm possible solutions to the problem; then select the most feasible solution. Construct a CMAPP analysis and outline for your proposed solution. Research your audience using available resources, including the library and the Internet. Select an appropriate format and prepare your proposal. If possible, present your proposal as a team to your audience.

CONTEMPORARY ISSUES CASE

A Moving Proposal.   Miguel's company is moving its offices to a nearby town. The move will result in a one-hour commute for Miguel to and from work each day. Because his job as a writer depends largely on his computer and less so on daily interaction with others, Miguel would like to telecommute. Research telecommuting; then prepare a proposal in memo format for Miguel's supervisor. Be sure to:

1. Propose a specific and feasible solution supported by your research.

2. Highlight the benefits of telecommuting to Miguel's company. Will it benefit financially? Will employee morale improve?

3. Take into account the probable audience skepticism. How will you counter it?

4. Pay attention to the accuracy of your message. Check for numerical errors, faulty terminology, verifiably false assertions, and misspellings.

CASE STUDY

Proposal to AEL from Superlative Design

Situation

In 20--, Leila Berakett, AEL's senior associate in Lansing, Michigan, hired a small local design firm called Superlative Design to remodel the company boardroom. Within months of the job's completion, Berakett began to receive complaints from office personnel about the quality of the workmanship. She conceded that her choice of designer had been a mistake. At the same time, she recognized that Superlative Design had fulfilled the terms of what she now realized had been a vaguely worded contract.

This year, AEL will renovate the consultants' offices. Berakett requested proposals from three design firms. Jessica Greyland, a partner with Superlative Design, learned about the project through an acquaintance; she decided to submit her own proposal, which is shown in **Figure 9.3** on the next page.

Issues to Think About

1. If you were Leila Berakett, what would be your first reaction to this proposal in light of your previous dealings with Superlative Design?
2. Evaluate Greyland's proposal in terms of the following:
    a.   Letterhead
    b.   Inside address
    c.   Salutation
    d.   Grammar and proofreading
3. How would you assess the format of Greyland's proposal? In your answer, consider her use of document visuals and the extent to which she follows (or fails to follow) the business letter conventions discussed in Chapter 7.
4. How might Berakett respond to Greyland's reference to Frank Nabata and Berakett's assistant?
5. Evaluate the proposal in terms of the following:
    a.   Level of discourse
    b.   Level of technicality
6. Which type of proposal organization do you think Greyland was trying to use? How well did she succeed?
7. Greyland has made several assumptions in this proposal. One appears in her first paragraph; another, in the action request. What are the assumptions, and how do you think Berakett would react to them?
8. How would you evaluate the proposal in terms of brevity, precision, and persuasiveness?
9. Is Greyland's proposal solicited or unsolicited? Justify your answer.
10. Create a revised version of the proposal based on your analysis.

FIGURE 9.3   Greyland's Proposal

Superlative Design, Ltd.

Ms. Leila Berakett, Consultant
ACCELERATED ENTERPRISES
342 Center Street West
Lansing, Michigan 48980

201 Madison Road
Lansing, Michigan 48980
Tel: 517/555-0168   Fax: 517/555-0169

April 20, 20--

Dear L. Berakett,

We have heard of your call for proposals of the 3rd inst., this kind of short proposal is our response. Thank you for giving Darrell and I the opportunity to submit this proposals. AEL is a firm we are always happy to have good business relations with.

The quality and excellence of every office facility that we design reflects our commitment to our clients. Our innovations are often cited as excellent. All ready this year we have won an award. We pride ourselves in our ability to quickly and efficiently design well engineered systems. We have yet to miss a deadline in our many years of operation, our ten-year anniversary was celebrated last year.

We are familiar with your staff's needs due to the fact that we worked with you in 20-- on the boardroom project. If you may recall, that interior, which Darrell actually designed, required less changes and cost less than expected. And Darrell is confident he can achieve similar results on current project.

Our Human Factors study report (we did one in absentia so to speak) shows that the absolute best use of your office space is to divide that humungous room into nineteen cubicles, 4 cute private offices, and 2 shared offices. We'll get great affects from the high-res chromatography analysis, the shades and tints and hues will be awesome and Statistics indicate that most workers prefer private spaces that are in close proximity to the people they work with. It is clear that the same principal applies to managers and chief executives. According to our research, the number of Worker Compensation claims among employees who suffer from a form of repetitive motion syndrome is greatly reduced by using high-quality, adjustable chairs and desks.

We have forwarded a copy of this proposal to Frank Nabata in Winnipeg who I remember your secretary said really makes all the big decisions. We will be very interested in what he recommends. If you have any questions, please feel free to contact me whenever. You can either reach me at my office or can call me at my home number, (517)555-0156.

We look forward to starting soon. Thank you for taking the time to review this proposal.

Very sincerely yours,

Jessica Greyland

J. Greyland, Human Factors Consultant
SUPERLATIVE DESIGN
JG/jg

CHAPTER 10

Effective Presentations

*I*nevitably, you will have to speak in public. Whatever your course of studies at your college or university, whatever your career, you will, on occasion, be required to speak to an audience consisting of classmates, colleagues, clients, or strangers. In your personal life, you might be asked to propose a toast at a wedding, act as MC at a social function, or deliver a eulogy at a funeral. At work, you might be required to present reports or projects or demonstrate your company's product or service.

The first group of activities includes examples of **speeches.** Speeches are designed to amuse, console, persuade, or entertain. Their function is primarily social rather than pragmatic, and, though they might be constrained by the rules of etiquette, their approach is fundamentally casual. The second group of activities includes examples of **presentations.** When presenting, you will be concerned with the characteristics of technical communication introduced in Chapter 1: necessity for a specific audience, integration of visual elements, ease of selective access, timeliness, and structure. Further, your effectiveness when giving presentations will derive from your judicious use of the CMAPP approach.

The Development Process

Effective speeches and presentations do not just happen—they take a great deal of planning on your part. Over the years, people have developed various processes for planning speeches and presentations. Deciding which process to use is less important than actually using one. In the context of technical and business communication, the process outlined below is both simple and effective. Note that you will often work on steps 1 through 4 simultaneously, since they tend to be interdependent. Steps 4 through 6 apply the multilevel outlining process you learned in Chapter 3.

1. Conduct your *CMAPP analysis.*
2. Decide on the *specific topic* you wish to cover. If you cannot express your topic in a short phrase, you do not have it firmly fixed in your mind.
3. Formulate your *thesis statement.* A thesis statement is a single sentence that encapsulates your purpose and topic. It will serve as the foundation for your outline in step 6.
4. Conduct your *research.*
5. Determine your goals or objectives—the *main points* of your presentation. These will turn into the level-one heads you create in step 6.
6. Construct a *multilevel outline.* It should contain sufficient detail (e.g., references to quotations and visuals you will use) to permit you to develop a new set of speaking notes months later, should you need to do so. If you are preparing for a manuscript or memorized presentation (discussed later in this chapter), your outline will serve as the skeleton for your text. For an extemporaneous presentation (also discussed later in the chapter), you will "contract" your outline into the speaking notes described in the next step.
7. Develop *speaking notes* (also called *speaker's notes*) for your extemporaneous delivery. Speaking notes are what you actually use while delivering your presentation. Unlike your outline, speaking notes are brief and concise, often to the point of being cryptic. If you were to look at them several months after your presentation, you might well fail to understand them. Because you want your audience to focus on you rather than on your notes, you will want the notes themselves, as well as your use of them, to be as inconspicuous as possible. Here are some suggestions:
   a. Write legibly and in large, clear letters. You should be able to glance quickly at your notes and find your next point without difficulty.
   b. Use single words or very short phrases. Clauses or sentences take longer to "find" when you are trying to glance at your notes without drawing your audience's attention to the fact. You might make use of symbols— for example, a **$** to remind you to discuss financial issues or a 🔒 to prompt you to mention security concerns.
   c. Use white space generously. You will be able to find your points more readily.
   d. On letter-size paper, write on one side only. This will allow you, during your presentation, to move from page to page without making your audience constantly aware that you are doing so. Many presenters put speaking notes on small cards (3" × 5" index cards cut in half, for example) and hold them in the palm of their hand while delivering. If you decide to use cards, you should allow for plenty of white space

(put only three or four items on each card), print on one side only, and number your cards so you can quickly reorder them if you drop them.

8. Prepare your *visual aids*. If visual aids will clarify your message, add interest, or help the audience remember what you say, then they should be added.

9. *Rehearse* your presentation. Practice in front of a video camera and in front of small groups. Critique yourself and ask others to provide specific criticisms and suggestions for improvement. Rehearsal will allow you to test your arguments and your visuals and verify your timing. While rehearsing can feel a bit awkward, most presenters agree that the private discomfort of rehearsal is preferable to the public embarrassment of a flawed presentation.

The CMAPP Approach to Presentations

A CMAPP analysis is the first step in creating your presentation.

Context.   Why are you presenting this information? What expectations does your audience have of you? What expectations do you have of your audience? What relationships exist between you, your audience, and anyone else involved (instructor, classmates, supervisor, colleagues, and so on)? What impact do you think your presentation will have?

Consider the physical conditions, including:

- The size of the room and the distance between you and members of the audience seated farthest from you.
- The size of your audience.
- The necessity for a microphone or sound system.
- The length of time you have been allotted.
- The technology available for integrating visuals.

Message.   Consider the effect of both denotation and connotation when choosing your words. Recall the impact of both information and impression when creating your visuals. Think about the paralinguistic considerations discussed later in the chapter when planning your delivery.

Audience.   What type of audience are you addressing? What is their level of technicality? What biases (positive or negative) might they have toward you before your presentation? Consider the expectations of your audience, including:

- What they likely already know.
- What they likely need to know.
- What they likely want to know.

See the Checklist on the next page for specific issues to consider when analyzing your audience.

Purpose.   What are you trying to achieve by delivering your presentation? How do you want your audience to react to your presentation?

Product.   Which of the four types of presentations (discussed later in the chapter) will you use?

Checklist

Audience Analysis

When considering your audience as part of your CMAPP analysis, you should take into account the following seven factors:

✓ *Age Range.* A group of twenty-somethings will respond differently than a group of seventy-somethings; their interests will be different, as will the cultural referents to which they will likely relate.

✓ *Cultural Background.* Different cultures respond differently to particular stimuli, references, topics, types of humor, presentation approaches, and so on. When developing your presentation, you should take into account the cultural background of your audience.

✓ *Educational Level.* The reactions and expectations of a highly educated audience will likely be different from those of a less well-educated group. Your levels of discourse and technicality should vary accordingly.

✓ *Occupation.* An audience composed of neurosurgeons will be different from an audience composed of loggers. You should be sensitive to the interests and expectations of your specific audience.

✓ *Political and Religious Affiliations.* There are many hot-button issues associated with politics and religion. To be effective, your CMAPP analysis should take into account the potential views and affiliations of your audience.

✓ *Gender.* A group of women is likely to have different interests, preferences, and expectations than a group of men. This general observation refers not to individuals, but rather to commonly observed tendencies within groups.

✓ *Socioeconomic Status.* People from different income groups tend to have different priorities, interests, and expectations. For example, as groups, they are likely to respond quite differently to such issues as taxation, employment insurance, and subsidized housing.

Purpose

You must have a solid idea of what you want your presentation to accomplish and how you want your audience to react. For example, imagine a presentation on an upcoming election. You should choose one of the four purposes described below.

◆ **Descriptive Purpose.** If your primary purpose is to describe, you will want your audience to see (in their mind's eye) something they have not seen before or see something more clearly than before.

◆ **Informative Purpose.** If your main purpose is to inform, you will want your audience to know or understand something they did not know or understand before.

- ***Instructive Purpose.*** If your main purpose is to instruct, you will want your audience to know how to do something that they could not do before.
- ***Persuasive Purpose.*** If your main purpose is to persuade, you must effect a change in your audience, normally in terms of belief, attitude, or behavior.

It is impossible to describe without informing, instruct without persuading, and so on. Although your presentation may incorporate elements of more than one purpose, you should choose a single purpose as the foundation for it to be effective.

Types of Presentations

Broadly speaking, there are four types of presentations. Each has advantages and disadvantages. The type you choose will depend on your CMAPP analysis.

Manuscript Presentation

A **manuscript presentation** is the delivery of a carefully prepared text that you refer to while presenting. The main advantage of this delivery type is that your presentation can be meticulously crafted. You can take pains to ensure that you always have the right word and visual in the right place at the right time. Also, you can deliver the presentation again accurately and with a minimum of effort.

The main drawback of manuscript presentations has to do with the differences between written and spoken language. It's difficult to write a presentation that, upon delivery, does not sound recited—and potentially boring to your audience.

Another disadvantage of a manuscript presentation is that it is more difficult to interact with an audience while referring to a written text. A presenter who never or rarely strays from the written text runs the risk of becoming monotonous.

Memorized Presentation

A **memorized presentation** is the delivery of material that you have composed and memorized. Like manuscript presentations, memorization allows you to craft your presentation carefully. At the same time, you can interact with the audience because the barrier of written text is removed.

It's not an easy task to make memorized text sound spontaneous and natural. Repeating the same presentation can exacerbate the problem. Like actors in a long-running play, presenters may find their delivery becoming stale.

Impromptu Presentation

The least formal of the delivery types is the **impromptu presentation.** You will use it when you are (more or less) unexpectedly called upon to speak. In class or in the workplace, you may be asked for your opinion or your analysis. Although you might have guessed that you would be called upon and your audience will expect you to have some familiarity with the topic, you will not have had the opportunity to thoroughly prepare what you are going to say.

An obvious advantage of the impromptu presentation is that, because you are given little, if any, time to prepare, your audience's expectations are relatively low. In addition, you are free to interact extensively with your audience.

The main disadvantage is the flip side of the first advantage: because you have little time to prepare, your success is much more dependent on your ability to think on your feet. The more complex your arguments, the greater risk that you—and your audience—will become confused. Keep your comments simple!

Extemporaneous Presentation

The **extemporaneous presentation** is the most widely used of the four delivery types. It involves diligent preparation and the delivery of what appears to your audience to be a spontaneous presentation.

The extemporaneous presentation allows you to prepare carefully, tailoring your presentation (including any visuals) to your context, audience, message, and purpose. Moreover, since you will use only speaking notes, you will be able to talk spontaneously and interact extensively with your audience. On the negative side, inadequate preparation will be painfully obvious to both you and your audience. As well, should you lose your focus during the presentation, you will have only the cryptic content of your speaking notes for support.

When preparing your extemporaneous presentation, you should follow the development process outlined earlier in the chapter. Never write out word for word any part of your intended presentation. Doing so will make your presentation as a whole sound uneven and make parts of it sound recited.

Elements of the Presentation

Here is a three-part rule for perfect presentations:

1. Tell them what you're going to tell them.
2. Tell them.
3. Tell them what you told them.

In developing your presentation, you will use the same kind of three-part structure found in all technical communication: an introductory segment, a body, and a concluding segment.

Introductory Segment

The **introductory segment** should normally include all the following elements (except perhaps a self-introduction, which may be unnecessary):

* ***Attention-Getter.***   You'll want to start things off by gaining your audience's full attention. To get it, don't explode firecrackers or do or say anything else that is totally unrelated to your presentation. You might begin with a story or question to pique your listeners' interest.

Tech Link

The Virtual Presentation Assistant, developed by the Communication Studies Department at the University of Kansas, is a comprehensive online tutorial devoted to helping users improve their public speaking skills. Visit *www.ukans.edu/cwis/units/coms2/vpa/vpa.htm*

- ◆ ***Self-Introduction.*** If someone introduces you to your audience, you need not reintroduce yourself. Otherwise, you should clearly state your full name and, if appropriate, your position or title as well.
- ◆ ***Initial Summary.*** Use this summary as a road map to your presentation. You prepare your audience for what is to come by stating your purpose and your main points (typically the level one heads in your multilevel outline).
- ◆ ***Speaker Credibility.*** Tell your audience why you are the right person to talk about the topic. You might mention your experience in the field, your credentials and/or qualifications, or your research on the topic.
- ◆ ***Audience Relevance.*** Based on your CMAPP analysis, indicate why the topic should be of interest to the audience.

Body

The **body** of your presentation is the bulk of your CMAPP message. Its content will depend on your context, audience, purpose, and product (your delivery type). Here are some elements typically found in the body:

- ◆ *Rhetorical Questions.* A **rhetorical question** is a question intended to produce an effect rather than solicit an answer. Within your presentation body, use rhetorical questions to focus your audience's attention on a particular point.
- ◆ *Signposts.* Use **signposts** to indicate where you intend to go and, thus, what listeners can expect. Signposts include such words and phrases as *first, second, on the other hand, however, correspondingly,* and *conversely.*
- ◆ *Transitions.* Related to signposts, **transitions** indicate a change from one point or idea to another. They include such phrases as *Now that we have . . . , let's turn to . . . ,* and *Having looked at . . . , I will now . . . .*
- ◆ *Emphasis Markers.* Use **emphasis markers** to focus an audience's attention on a particular point. Include such phrases as *most important, A key point to consider is . . . ,* and *I'd like to stress that . . . .*
- ◆ *Repetition Markers.* Use **repetition markers** to introduce the reiteration of a point made earlier in the presentation. Include such phrases as *Let me repeat that . . .* and *As I've already mentioned . . . .*
- ◆ *Segment Summaries.* If you are giving a long presentation, provide your audience with brief summaries of the individual segments. A **segment summary** should include a transition into the next segment.

Concluding Segment

Your **concluding segment** should include the following four elements (in the order shown):

1. *Closure.* Use **closure** to let your audience know that you are going to finish soon. However fascinating your presentation may have been, your audience's attention will perk up when you make it clear that you have almost concluded.

You can signal closure by using a phrase such as *in conclusion* or an emphasis marker such as *I'd like to make one final point before I finish.* Never indicate closure prematurely. If your presentation continues for more than a few minutes after you have signaled closure, your audience will likely tune out.

2. *Final Summary.*   At this point, you will sum up the main points of your presentation. A **final summary** is essentially a paraphrase of the initial summary although it does not include a statement of purpose.

3. *Call to Action.*   Most technical communication products conclude with a **call to action** (also known as an action request). If your presentation's main purpose is persuasive, your call to action is likely to be very direct, as in *Cast your ballot for the candidate you know will work hardest for you!* If your purpose is informative, descriptive, or instructive, your call to action will be more subtle. It may be a personal statement or an indication of your hopes.

4. *Close.*   Sometimes your call to action will be sufficient to let your audience know that you have finished. Most of the time, though, it is far better to use a **close,** which indicates explicitly that your presentation is over. You might do so by saying something like, *Thank you for your time today. I've appreciated the opportunity to speak with you.*

Also, be sure to let your audience know at the beginning of your presentation whether or not you will take their questions. Here are some suggestions for dealing with questions from the audience:

◆   If you don't get any questions, don't allow a long and potentially embarrassing silence to develop. Rather, say something like, "Well, since there don't seem to be any questions at this time, I'd just like to thank you again for your attention"—and consider your presentation over.

◆   When an audience member challenges you to clarify or justify a particular point, avoid becoming defensive. Rather, view your answer as an opportunity to reinforce your message.

◆   When an audience member asks you a question that requires a lengthy response, try to organize your answer so that it reflects the three-part rule (introductory segment, body, and concluding segment).

◆   Avoid being drawn into an argument. Whatever the provocation, remain calm.

◆   Don't let any one questioner monopolize the floor. Politely but firmly suggest that someone else be given a chance to speak.

◆   It is often a good idea to repeat or paraphrase a question before answering it. By doing so, you not only ensure that everyone hears the question (especially important if the questioner is soft-spoken), but you also buy yourself time to gather your thoughts and mentally prepare your answer.

Other Factors to Consider

Many experts believe that at least 60 percent of what your audience assimilates and uses to assess you and your presentation has nothing to do with the words you use. Rather, their judgment is based on their perceptions of your appearance, your bearing, and your vocal qualities. Although your audience might not be consciously aware of them, you, as an effective presenter, must be.

Dress

Though it might be wrong, we do judge people by the clothes they wear. Dress appropriately. You wouldn't wear jeans and an old sweatshirt to a formal wedding. Nor would you wear black tie to an auto repair shop. Decide what's appropriate in light of your CMAPP analysis, and consider the kind of image you want to present.

Confidence and Presence

Successful people tend to look successful, and confident people tend to look confident. If you look confident, your audience will likely believe that you are confident, and over time, you will likely become confident, giving you what is often called "presence"—an attribute that is difficult to define, although most of us are quick to recognize it.

Eye Contact

In one-on-one conversations, we naturally make eye contact with each other. When you're presenting, your audience appreciates confirmation that you know that they're there. Making eye contact with your audience is crucial to a successful presentation. Here are some suggestions:

- When dealing with a small audience, try to make eye contact randomly with everyone several times during your presentation. If one or more audience members will not give you the opportunity to do so, don't force the issue.
- If the audience is large, mentally divide the room into segments and look at each segment several times in the course of your presentation.
- Limit eye contact to a second or two; otherwise, people may think you're staring and become uncomfortable and/or resentful.

Posture and Movement

Don't slump—good posture is an indication of self-confidence. Stimulate your audience's interest (at least on an unconscious level) by moving around a bit. You don't need a choreographed routine; just avoid remaining motionless.

Facial Expressions and Gestures

Your presentation will be more effective if you show some facial animation and use natural gestures. If you use a pointing gesture, make sure you're not pointing at someone in your audience. Most people don't like even the appearance of being singled out.

 Tech Link

Presentations.com offers an excellent selection of practical articles on creating and delivering effective presentations. Visit **www.presentations.com**

Volume

Vary the volume of your voice for effect. Some highly competent presenters use everything from a stage whisper to a shout. Even if you avoid extremes, you should also avoid the monotony of unchanging volume.

Speed

A metronome keeps time by ticking at unvarying speed. A lack of variety in the speed with which you speak causes the same monotony and a loss of audience interest.

Tone, Pitch, and Intonation

In face-to-face conversations, you automatically vary your tone, pitch, and intonation. When you ask a question, for example, you tend to end on a rising tone. When surprised, you tend to use a higher pitch. As you converse, your intonation changes to show emotion, emphasis, and so on.

Natural variations in tone, pitch, and intonation add interest to your presentation and help keep your audience attentive. If you speak with little or no variety of tone, pitch, and intonation, you will sound as though you are reciting something of no interest to you. Computer-generated voices might do that, but effective presenters should not.

Enunciation and Pronunciation

Ensure that you speak clearly and that you have mastered the pronunciation of whatever terms or names you intend to use. If you slur or mumble or if you falter over or mispronounce words you yourself have chosen, your audience is unlikely to request a repetition. They will, however, judge you.

Hesitation Particles

You may have noticed that some inexperienced speakers seem to say *um* or *uh* quite frequently. Just as unconsciously, others may say *you know* or *like* with irritating regularity. Such "fillers," as they are sometimes called, eventually draw your audience's attention away from your message. For most of us, avoiding fillers is difficult. Doing so requires a conscious awareness of our words while we are speaking. Gaining that facility, however, will make you a more effective presenter.

Time Management

Pacing your presentation takes practice and experience. Ensuring that you have left enough time for all of your points is just as important as making certain that you do not run out of content halfway through your allotted time. Your audience expects you to take the time you have—not much less and certainly not much more. Probably the best way to test your time management is to rehearse.

Visuals and Visual Aids

Visuals are playing an increasingly important role in effective presentations. As you discovered in Chapter 5, visuals should:

- Illustrate, not overpower.
- Explain, not confuse.
- Enhance, not detract.
- Simplify, not complicate.
- Fulfill a CMAPP purpose, not merely decorate.
- Be visible to all.
- Be intelligible to all.

Types of Visual Aids

Compare the advantages and disadvantages of the following types of visual aids with the needs of your presentation to determine which type to use.

Computer Presentations, Transparencies, and Slides. Generally, these types of visual aids have similar content and are created with software such as Microsoft PowerPoint. The difference lies in how they are presented.

- *Computer Presentation.* The computer is connected to projection equipment that displays the slides you have prepared with presentation software. As the slides appear on your computer monitor, your audience sees the images projected on a screen.
- *Transparencies.* Presentation visuals are printed on clear acetate film and then projected on a screen with an overhead projector.
- *Slides.* Images are transferred to 35mm slides, placed in a slide carousel, and projected on a screen with a slide projector.

Many computer presentation software programs allow you to create a **multimedia presentation,** incorporating sound, **animation** (movement of text or images on a slide), and video clips (brief video features that usually include sound). Adding these special features results in a more visually stimulating presentation than can be achieved with transparencies and slides.

Handouts. **Handouts** are one of the most popular forms of presentation visuals. They allow your audience to take a more active part in the communication; they also give your audience information to take with them for future reference.

You can distribute handouts before, during, or after your presentation. Here are some advantages and disadvantages of each strategy:

- *Before.* Distribution will not interfere with your presentation, and you can refer to any part of the handout at any time. Your audience can also use handouts as note-taking guides. But your audience will likely continue to examine (and perhaps rifle through) the material until their curiosity has been satisfied—not just until you want to begin.

Tech Link

The 3M Meeting Network web site, in partnership with Presentations Magazine, features a variety of helpful articles on creating effective presentation visuals. Visit *www.3m.com/ meetingnetwork/ presentations/creating.html*

◆   *During.*   You can retain your audience's attention until you distribute the material, and you can refer to your handouts from the moment you distribute them. But the distribution will be an interruption: people will search for their copies and will begin to examine what they have received.

◆   *After.*   You have your audience's attention throughout your presentation. But you cannot effectively refer to material in your handout because your audience does not yet have it.

How you design your handouts and time their distribution should be determined by the results of your CMAPP analysis.

Props.   **Props,** or three-dimensional objects, can be presented from the front of the room or passed among audience members. Be sure, however, that the object is large enough and the crowd is small enough for your prop to be visible. Your props might include models, samples, or even people.

Posters and Flip Charts.   **Posters** and **flip charts** are similar in size, and both generally are displayed on an easel. For posters, prepare your visuals ahead of time. For flip charts, you can either prepare your visuals ahead of time and flip through them as you speak or you can write your key points as you speak.

Choosing the Appropriate Visual Aid

As you consider which type of aids to use in your presentation, answer the questions provided in the Checklist for Choosing Visual Aids below.

 Checklist

Choosing Visual Aids

✓   Which options are available in the location where you will be making your presentation? Some of the options require access to specific electronic equipment.

✓   Which option will be best in helping your audience understand and remember your message?

✓   How large is your audience, and how large is the room? A poster or flip chart would be appropriate for a small group, but not appropriate for a larger group.

✓   How much detail do you have to give your audience? Slides or computer presentations may not work well when you have many numbers or detailed information to present.

✓   How much time do you have to prepare your visual aids? Preparing transparencies or a multimedia presentation will take more time than using a flip chart.

✓   Should you use more than one type of visual aid? All of the visual aids can be used alone or in combination.

Presenting Your Visual Aids

As you present your visual aids, keep in mind some basic guidelines for using your visual aids in a professional manner.

- *Display your visual aids at the right time.*   Visual aids can become a distraction if you display them before you are ready to discuss their content.
- *Display the points on your visual aids at the right time.*   A visual aid can also become a distraction if you display all the points before you're ready to talk about them. Reveal only the point you are talking about, and cover remaining points until you're ready to discuss them. In computer presentations, you can use a feature called **building** that allows you to program a slide easily so that bulleted points come into view one at a time.
- *Practice using your visual aids before the audience arrives.*   You need to have a dress rehearsal for your presentation, particularly if you are using visual aids. Go to the presentation room, and practice with your visual aids. Make sure you test the equipment ahead of time.
- *Face the audience when using your visual aids.*   Audience members prefer to see the front of you. When you speak, they can hear you better if you are facing them rather than the screen behind you.

Conquering Stage Fright

In popular surveys, people often rank fear of speaking in public above fear of dying. (There are no documented cases of anyone actually dying of stage fright!) Dealing with that fear is important. Your presentation will not be effective if you don't appear calm and confident. Note the word *appear*. In the context of a presentation, what counts is not how you actually feel but rather how you appear to feel. Your heart may be thudding, but your audience can't hear it; nor can they see the perspiration on your sweaty palms or feel the dryness in your throat. As far as your audience is concerned, if you appear to be in control of yourself and your presentation, you are in control.

There's some truth to the old saying "Fake it till you make it!" Each time you "fool" an audience by *appearing* confident, you fool yourself a little too. Do this often enough, and you will find that you are actually becoming more confident. Remember another cliché: Nothing succeeds like success.

Here are some tips for dealing with stage fright:

- *Avoid stimulants.*   A high dose of caffeine may make you feel better, but it won't make your audience feel better if your performance inevitably suffers as a result.
- *Practice breathing and visualization techniques.*   Get into the habit of taking several slow, deep breaths just before you walk up to deliver your presentation. Long before you reach that point, you can also use a technique known

as **visualization,** or positive imaging. Follow the tips in the Visualization Checklist below to imagine yourself delivering a successful presentation and reaping the rewards of having done so.

♦   *Imagine the worst-case scenario.*   Accept the fact that, despite your best efforts, you are occasionally going to flop. Think of the worst possible result, consider how you'll deal with it, and—almost always—watch it not happen. And if the worst does happen? Those who have had that experience have somehow managed to survive. So will you.

♦   *Be prepared.*   As with most things in life, proper preparation pays off. Take or make the time to prepare thoroughly. Conduct a CMAPP analysis, and apply its results long before you stand before an audience.

♦   *Maintain a positive attitude.*   If you believe that you're going to do poorly, you just may. On the other hand, if you can convince yourself that you're going to do well, that your audience wants you to succeed (which is usually the case), that the experience will be rewarding for both you and your audience, and that success is within your grasp, your convictions will likely come true.

✔ Checklist

Visualization

✓   *Relax.*   Close your eyes, take some deep breaths, and try to clear your mind.

✓   *Draw a mental picture (or create a mental video).*   Show yourself delivering a successful presentation. Visualize yourself projecting a positive and competent image—speaking with confidence, maintaining excellent posture, and projecting dignity.

✓   *Add details to your picture and visualize success.*   Banish all negative visions and thoughts (fear, failure, anxiety, error). See yourself as already having delivered a successful presentation.

✓   *Incorporate words, actions, and senses into your picture.*   Mentally "practice" exactly how you plan to deliver your presentation. This "mental rehearsal" will strengthen your actual performance.

✓   *Dwell on your picture, and be able to recall it instantly.*   Repeat the visual picture as often as possible before the actual event to boost your confidence and calm your nerves.

Chapter Review

CHAPTER SUMMARY

The first step in planning a presentation is conducting a CMAPP analysis. Second, decide on a specific topic and formulate your thesis statement. Research your topic. Determine your main points, and use them as level-one heads to construct an outline. Next, develop your speaking notes. Prepare visual aids to add to your message. Finally, rehearse your presentation.

To conduct a CMAPP analysis, consider the physical conditions and your relationship with the audience, the obvious and underlying meanings of your message, your audience's level of technicality and expectations, how you want your audience to react, and which of the four types of presentations you will use.

Use a descriptive purpose to show your audience something they have not seen before. Use an informative purpose to teach or explain something new to your audience. Use an instructive purpose to teach your audience how to do something they could not do before. Use a persuasive purpose to effect a change in belief, attitude, or behavior in your audience.

A manuscript presentation is the delivery of a prepared text that you refer to while presenting. A memorized presentation is the delivery of material that you have composed and memorized. An impromptu presentation is an unexpected presentation. An extemporaneous presentation is the delivery of a prepared speech using only speaking notes, not memorization or a manuscript.

In your introductory segment, get the audience's attention, introduce yourself (if you haven't already been introduced), give an initial summary, display your credibility, and indicate your topic's relevance to the audience. In your body, use rhetorical questions, signposts, transitions, emphasis and repetition markers, and segment summaries. In your concluding segment, signal closure, provide a final summary, a call to action, and a close. You may decide to accept questions after your presentation.

Dress appropriately. Display confidence even if you don't feel it. Make eye contact with your audience. Don't slump. Move around and use facial expressions and natural gestures. Vary your speaking volume, speed, tone, pitch, and intonation. Enunciate and use correct pronunciation. Avoid hesitation particles. Pace yourself so that you use no more and no less than your allotted time.

Common visual aids are computer presentations, transparencies, slides, handouts, props, posters, and flip charts. Consider the physical and technical limitations of your location, the size of your audience, and how much time you have to prepare visual aids.

To appear calm and confident during your presentation even if you aren't, avoid caffeine, practice breathing and visualization techniques, imagine the worst-case scenario, be prepared, and maintain a positive attitude.

KEY TERMS

Animation

Attention-getter

Audience relevance

Body

Building

Call to action

Close

Closure

Computer presentations

Concluding segment

Descriptive purpose

Emphasis markers

Extemporaneous presentation

Final summary

Flip charts

Handouts

Impromptu presentation

Informative purpose

Initial summary

Instructive purpose

Introductory segment

Manuscript presentation

Memorized presentation

Multimedia presentation

Persuasive purpose

Posters

Presentation

Props

Repetition markers

Rhetorical question

Segment summaries

Self-introduction

Signposts

Slides

Speaker credibility

Speech

Transitions

Transparencies

Visualization

CRITICAL THINKING ACTIVITIES

1. Distinguish between a presentation and a speech.
2. Briefly explain how each of the five CMAPP components applies to presentations.
3. Will oral presentations be important to you in your probable career? If so, how?
4. Identify and describe five factors to consider in audience analysis.
5. Identify the four main types of presentations, and indicate the principal advantages and disadvantages of each.
6. Identify and describe at least three strategies for dealing with stage fright.
7. Identify and describe the four types of purpose discussed in this chapter.
8. Describe the purpose and physical makeup of speaking notes, and explain the relationship of those notes to the multilevel outline.
9. Identify and describe at least three elements found in each of the following:
    a.   Introductory segment
    b.   Body
    c.   Concluding segment
10. Identify five aspects of a presentation that are not based on the speaker's words. Briefly explain the importance of each to an effective presentation.

11. Briefly describe three types of visual aids available to you as a presenter. Using the criteria for choosing visual aids, give a scenario in which each of those aids would be appropriate.

12. As an audience participant, which of the guidelines for presenting visual aids have you seen presenters overlook most frequently? Why do you think the guideline is violated so frequently? What are the results?

13. Explain the advantages and disadvantages of distributing handouts:
    a. Before the presentation.
    b. During the presentation.
    c. After the presentation.

SKILLS APPLICATIONS

1. Listen to a presentation and prepare a written evaluation of the speaker's effectiveness. Comment on the delivery of the presentation as well as the effectiveness of any visual aids.

2. Assume that you work for the recruitment office of the school or college you attend(ed). Outline a presentation for student recruitment. Visit or call the appropriate office to obtain pamphlets, brochures, and so on, to locate information for the presentation. Visit the school's web site if it has one. Develop an outline and visual aids for your presentation.

3. Develop an introduction to a speech designed to persuade people to buy a product of your choice. Your introduction should include an attention-getter, an initial summary, and audience relevance.

CONTEMPORARY ISSUES CASE

Presentation Technology.   During your first year as a life insurance and securities consultant, you have helped many clients set up investment and savings programs. One thing about the job that has surprised you, though, is the amount of time you have spent educating your clients, many of whom were unaware of basic financial principles about saving and investing. During your sales calls, you have used educational materials published by the companies whose products you sell. Recently, you've begun to consider how you might update and liven your presentations by using your laptop computer for the informational portion of your sales presentations.

1. What basic issues should you consider as you begin preparing your computer sales presentation?

2. What guidelines should you follow regarding the use of a laptop computer as a presentation tool?

CASE STUDY

AEL Presentation to Students

Situation

AEL's senior partners, Sarah Cohen and Frank Nabata, have for some years had a social relationship with Carole Schusterman, RAI's general manager, and her husband, Ben. Over supper one evening, Carole mentions Radisson's highly positive assessment of its participation in Grandstone Technical Institute's Internship Program. Intrigued, Cohen and Nabata consider how AEL might benefit from a similar involvement with GTI. They conclude that while AEL would not be able to accommodate GTI students in the context of an internship or co-op program, the company would have much to gain from an organized effort to attract bright young people into the business. With this in mind, they arrange for Noah Avigdor, a senior AEL associate, to deliver presentations to students in each of the cities in which AEL maintains offices.

Avigdor has his office contact the universities and arrange for him to deliver 30-minute presentations to groups of fourth-year students in the areas of particular interest to AEL: chemical, civil, and geological engineering and software design and development. The preparatory work Avigdor does for his presentations can be seen in **Figures 10.1, 10.2, 10.3,** and **10.4** on the next five pages.

Issues to Think About

1. What is your overall impression of Avigdor's CMAPP analysis (**Figure 10.1** on the next page)?
2. Which important element is missing from each component of the analysis?
3. How well do you think Avigdor has planned for his presentations? Justify your point of view with examples.
4. How would you deal with the problem of multiple audiences that Avigdor faces?
5. How accurately do you think Avigdor's topic and thesis statement (**Figure 10.2** on page 228) represent his ideas? How might you rephrase both?
6. Look at Avigdor's multilevel presentation outline in **Figure 10.3** on pages 229 and 230. How might you explain the absence of visuals to illustrate sections III and IV?
7. Has Avigdor adhered to the principles of subordination, division, and parallelism in his outline? What changes would you suggest?
8. What can you say about the relationship between Avigdor's outline and his speaking notes (**Figure 10.4** on page 231)? What changes might you make to the speaking notes?

FIGURE 10.1   Avigdor's CMAPP Analysis

Recruitment Presentation: CMAPP Analysis

Context:

- Students likely interested in available employment after graduation
- Many may not have heard of AEL: probably necessary to establish relationship
- Top students likely to hear several recruiters and have several options
- Others likely there because of few possibilities: important for me to present AEL as top firm looking only for best students
- Presentations likely to be in classrooms, small conference rooms, and so on; will probably vary from university to university
- Technology available: data projector only a possibility; therefore, prepare visuals for overhead projector—almost certainly available
- Probably groups of 10–50 students; will vary according to institution and how well recruitment presentation is publicized
- Length of presentations: about 30 minutes, including question period at end
- Some students may expect me to sign recruitment offers; if so, I must try to maintain their enthusiasm but temper it with patience
- AEL hopes to receive applications from at least 50 students

Message:

- AEL's reputation
- Outline of AEL's organization and activities
- Opportunities for postgraduation placement in the various fields: What? Where? When? Starting salaries?
- Typical career advancement opportunities at AEL
- Means to indicate interest: statement of interest forms
- "AEL is interested in you"

Audience:

- Education: impending graduation in technical specialty areas (at least a bachelor's degree)
- Age range: 21–24
- Attitude: Most likely to be enthusiastic; some skeptical and/or unmotivated
- Sex: Likely even M/F split, although possible preponderance of males
- Cultural background: extremely varied
- Economic status: most likely to be from middle- to upper-middle-class backgrounds; as students, a significant number may be experiencing financial difficulties

FIGURE 10.1   (continued)

- Political bias: most likely to be sympathetic to conservative platform
- Know: most likely aware of current entry-level job market in their fields; likely have idea of type of position/company they are looking for
- Need to know: what opportunities are available, how to contact us, how to apply
- Want to know: whether AEL's opportunities are really of interest to them (type of work, benefits, corporate culture, cost of living in respective cities, travel opportunities, and so on); how to find out more

Purpose:

Persuasive—I want to:

- Obtain a sense of numbers and types of potential employees.
- Present AEL as modern, energetic, ethical, profitable, exciting, etc.
- Stimulate interest of the best students.
- Convince students to follow up with AEL offices in respective cities.

Product: extemporaneous presentation with overheads as visuals.

FIGURE 10.2   Avigdor's Topic, Thesis Statement, and Objective

Topic: Working with AEL

Thesis Statement: If you are a qualified, ambitious graduate in a relevant field, you should apply to AEL for excellent entry-level opportunities.

Objectives:

1. Description of AEL
2. What we are looking for
3. Who we are looking for
4. Next steps

FIGURE 10.3   Avigdor's Multilevel Presentation Outline

I. **Introduction**

   (A) "Career success won't come by itself!"   *Visual #1: AEL logo/building photo*

   (B) My position

   (C) Relevance to you as impending graduates

   (D) Why AEL is interested in you

II. **Description of AEL**

   (A) History

      (1) Engineers in Lansing   *Visual #2: photos of Cohen & Nabata*

      (2) Growth of consulting activities

      (3) Opening of offices   *Visual #3: Map showing location of offices*

   (B) Organization   *Visual #4: Organizational Chart*

      (1) Senior partners and partners

      (2) Senior associates and associates

      (3) Senior consultants and consultants

      (4) Junior consultants

      (5) Staff associates

   (C) Locations   *Reprise Visual #3: Map*

   (D) Areas of endeavor

      (1) Civil engineering   *Visual #5: Vanier Place project Ann Arbor U.*

      (2) Chemical engineering   *Visual #6: MicroGen Test Labs*

      (3) Geological engineering   *Visual #7: Dam Project*

      (4) Software design   *Visual #8: HelioTech "Vivacious" brochure cover*

      (5) Software development   *Visual #9: HelioTech Software Test Lab*

      (6) Now investigating

         (a) Environmental engineering

         (b) Industrial safety

         (c) Urban planning

III. **What we are looking for**

   (A) Demonstrated attitudes

      (1) Cooperation

      (2) Team spirit

      (3) Enthusiasm

      (4) Desire to succeed

      (5) Client satisfaction

   (B) Qualifications

      (1) Only the best of the best!

      (2) Appropriate degree (see II, D above for list)

FIGURE 10.3   (continued)

(3) Grades
    (a) At least 3.4 GPA in relevant subjects AND
    (b) At least 3.2 GPA each term throughout degree program
(C) Experience
    (1) Not mandatory but an advantage
    (2) Internship/co-op is desirable in appropriate field
    (3) Extracurricular if relevant

IV. Who we're looking for

(A) Entry-level candidates for all offices

(B) People willing to relocate

(C) People willing to travel

(D) People looking for self-motivated work
    (1) Senior firm members seek contracts
    (2) Other consulting staff often work independently

(E) People able to work under little or no supervision

(F) People who take pride in their own work and want the company's name to be
    recognized for quality and integrity
    (1) You represent the company
    (2) The company represents you

V. Next Steps

(A) Take brochures   *Visual #10: Show sample brochure*

(B) Think over what I've said

(C) Send letter of application to senior associate   *Visual #11: List of senior associates*
    in city of interest according to handout

(D) If no word within three weeks, follow up with phone call

VI. Conclusion

(A) Brief summation of points

(B) Recommendation to act immediately: competition becomes stiffer

(C) Question period

(D) Thanks and hope to see you again   *Reprise Visual #1: AEL logo/building photo*

FIGURE 10.4   Avigdor's Speaking Notes

CHAPTER 11

Seeking Employment

Seeking employment is the subject of a vast number of books and web sites. Enter the keyword *resumes* in a search engine and you may be presented with thousands of resources! So, what can you expect to learn from this short chapter? You will find recommendations and tips designed to point you in the right direction. Your progress will be up to you. There is no sure-fire recipe for success; rather, you need determination, hard work, and tenacity.

Despite what the self-help gurus might say, you also need a certain amount of luck. Admittedly, the more you know about the subject, the better your chances of winning. But the element of chance still plays an inevitable role.

The good news is that knowledge and skills will invariably help you land that dream job. At the very least, they will help you to create a winning employment application package. The five elements of this all-important package are:

1. Preparation—doing your homework before you send out your application
2. Cover letter—using an effective CMAPP analysis to compose the best application for the occasion
3. Resume—tailoring your content, form, and format as needed
4. Interview—saying the right things at the right time
5. Follow-up—remembering that you're probably not the only player in the game

Preparation

Unless your sole employment goal is wealth, don't get into a field and then try to find a way to like it. Rather, determine what you enjoy and are good at, and then find a way to make a living at it. Therefore, your first step in seeking employment should be preparation. Assess yourself: What are your personal goals? What are your career goals? What qualifications do you have to help you meet these goals? This assessment will give you a better understanding of what you enjoy and what you are good at and will help you focus as you begin your job search.

Assess Your Goals

The first step in any job search is to analyze your personal and career goals. This process will help you clarify what is important to you and what isn't. The Checklist below will help you determine what characteristics to look for when seeking employment.

 Checklist

Personal Goals

✓   What do I most enjoy doing?

✓   What are my interests?

✓   How important is material success?

✓   How important is recognition?

✓   Where do I want to live?

✓   Do I want to work inside or outside?

✓   Do I want to work mainly with people? With machines? With ideas?

✓   How frequently do I want to travel for the job?

Career Goals

✓   What kind of work do I enjoy?

✓   What do I want to be doing five years from now?

✓   How much do I want to earn next year? Five years from now?

✓   Where do I want to work?

✓   How far do I want to advance? What position do I want to hold five years from now? Ten years from now?

✓   What is my ideal balance between personal and work obligations?

✓   Do I prefer steady, predictable work hours or a varied, flexible work schedule?

Add any questions that help you clarify what you want from a career. List the more important goals before the less important goals. Revisit these goals and use them as your guide through the job search process.

Analyze Your Qualifications

Analyzing your qualifications, skills, abilities, and accomplishments gives you the information you need to prepare a resume and sell yourself during an interview.

You might begin by creating a file, or **portfolio,** to hold information about your skills, abilities, and accomplishments. Your portfolio might take the shape of a file folder, computer files, a notebook, or a small briefcase containing samples of your work, transcripts, letters of recommendation, and related items. Items you might include in your portfolio are as follows:

- Academic transcripts
- Letters of recommendation
- Copies of job application forms
- Awards
- Test scores
- Certificates, diplomas, or other evidence of course work completed
- Samples of work or projects completed

As you continue to analyze your qualifications, think about the skills, abilities, and accomplishments that have given you satisfaction or fulfillment and that make you marketable. Think about accomplishments that reflect your creativity, initiative, and ability to work well with others. You should include in your portfolio details about qualifications such as education, work experience, achievements, activities, special skills (such as leadership, time management, and so on), and personal traits.

A Reality Check

Once you've identified your dream job, you should rid yourself of any illusions you might have about how easy it will be to land it.

- Don't believe that your credentials, qualifications, experience, and enthusiasm make you unique. However good you are at what you want to be paid to do, you can count on there being a great many others of equal or better merit, trying to make sure that they, rather than you, get the position.
- Don't believe the fairy tale that if you want a job badly enough, it will drop into your lap. Doing, not wanting, brings results.
- Unless you are graduating at the top of your class from a prestigious institution or unless you are in a field that is currently in extremely high demand, don't believe that employers are desperately seeking you. They are more likely to be searching for ways to keep their businesses profitable—with or without you.

◆   Many employers have indicated that their hiring is based 90 percent on aptitude and their firing based 90 percent on attitude. The moral of that story is that if you look for employment on the assumption that you can always "take the course again" or submit a "rewrite" for better grades or that a potential employer has a responsibility to help you obtain what you want, you are likely to be cast aside before you are even hired.

Beginning Your Job Search

Having dismissed your illusions, you can take action. Here are some suggestions for beginning your job search:

◆   *Network.*   Probably the majority of career positions are filled through **networking.** People know people who know people who know people; therefore, get to know people. Use personal contacts, libraries, and Internet resources to obtain the names of people who work in companies that operate in the area that interests you. Ask for a bit of their time, stressing that you are not trying to obtain a job, just trying to find out more about the industry and what it values. Most people will be quite accommodating if you specify that you want no more than half an hour—and then stick to it. Thus, when you do apply for a job, you are likely to have—and be able to demonstrate— greater familiarity with the field. That knowledge gives you an added edge over other applicants.

◆   *Read ads carefully.*   Notwithstanding the previous point, it is likely that you will at times respond to an advertised position. If so, treat the text of that advertisement as a combination of explicit and encoded information. Pay attention to what the ad says and to what it likely implies. For example, if it says, "No phone calls, please," deciding to call anyway will likely be treated as an unwillingness to accept direction rather than as initiative. Similarly, if the ad asks for specific remuneration expectations, the employer may be trying to find out whether you are already sufficiently familiar with the field to know typical pay and benefits.

◆   *Judge yourself.*   If you aren't thoroughly familiar with all the terminology in the ad, perhaps you shouldn't apply. If an ad mentions Java and Active X programming or Monte Carlo simulation for molecular modeling, the potential employer presumes that qualified candidates know and use the jargon.

◆   *Research your field.*   Research the fields that you think might interest you. Although you're unlikely to really know what's involved until you begin working, you can at least form a preliminary opinion by investigating the literature, researching the field on the Web, and talking to people who are already in the field. You can also look at texts on seeking employment, although you should remember that their authors were also seeking to sell their books.

Tech Link

JobStar Central offers career information such as guides for specific careers and online assessment tests. It also provides tips and advice for writing successful resumes and cover letters. Visit **http://jobstar.org**

- *Use a variety of sources to identify job openings.* To locate actual job openings, look beyond your local newspaper. Check with school placement offices, personal contacts, professional publications, employment agencies, temp agencies, internships, and libraries. Additionally, you can connect with thousands of jobs from all over the country through web sites that list job openings. You might begin by checking a few of the following:

  - ***www.hotbot.com***
  - ***www.careerpath.com***
  - ***www.monster.com***
  - ***www.jobtrak.com***
  - ***www.headhunter.net***

- *Don't procrastinate.* A job search is not an easy process—it involves a lot of time and effort. So, several months before you expect to begin your search, start investigating the job market in the fields that interest you.

Cover Letters

Why bother sending a cover letter? After all, isn't the resume the important thing? The rationale for taking the trouble to create an effective cover letter is as follows:

- Analogous to a report's transmittal letter, a cover letter introduces both you and your resume.
- You can use the cover letter's content, form, and format to your advantage in selling your resume and yourself.
- Sending a cover letter is an expected convention. Its absence would appear unprofessional to potential employers.

Content

An effective cover letter should incorporate well-reasoned points to press your case.

- Address the letter to a specific person. If you do not know the name of the person in charge of the department you are applying to (or the person in charge of employment), call the company and ask.
- Refer precisely to what you are applying for. If you are responding to an advertisement, be specific. For example, referring to "your recent ad in the local paper" is vague. Specifying "Software Programmer, described on page F8 of the Careers Section in the April 8, 20--, edition of the *Tribune*" does two things: it tells the reader what you are talking about, and it suggests to the potential employer that you will be specific and precise in your work.

- Avoid superfluous information. For example, beginning with "Let me intro-duce myself. My name is [your name], and I would like to apply for . . . ," leaves your reader thinking, "I know that from the letterhead; don't waste my time." Putting serious effort into your initial CMAPP analysis for your cover letter will help you ensure it is precise, concise, and tailored to the audience.

- Focus explicitly on what you can do for the company, not on what the company can do for you. Remember, they are understandably looking to *their own benefit,* not yours.

- Reiterate any specific points in your resume that you believe are of particular interest.

- Include a clear call to action. Again, think of your CMAPP analysis, and consider the language you are using. A very weak (though unfortunately common) action request is "If you have any questions, please don't hesitate to call me at . . . ." In effect, you are telling your reader not to call you unless he or she has questions—even, for example, if the person were considering offering you an interview. A much stronger closing is "I would appreciate the opportunity to discuss my qualifications with you. Please call me at 555-0192 between 8:30 A.M. and 4:30 P.M. any weekday."

Tech Link

CareerLab's Cover Letter Library features an extensive sampling of letters for the job search. Visit **www.careerlab.com/letters**

Form

If you can obtain next-to-no information about your specific audience, how can you determine the appropriate levels of discourse and technicality? Your CMAPP analysis will help you decide. For example, if the context is that of a specialized, technical position, you should probably assume that your audience has certain technical expectations. If the context is more general, that factor too should influence the construction of your letter. In all cases, you should be careful to keep your writing as clear, concise, and precise as possible.

Format

Beyond a requirement for professional appearance, there is no single prescribed format for cover letters. You should, however, follow certain guidelines.

- Do not exceed a single page.
- Use letterhead stationery. (All good word processors now enable you to produce your own.)
- Include in your letterhead your full name, your address, any phone numbers you think would be useful to your audience, and (if you have one) your e-mail address. If you maintain a web site, include it only if its existence would be relevant to the employer.
- As much as possible, follow the business letter conventions discussed in Chapter 7. If you cannot identify your audience appropriately, you might consider the simplified block format since it requires neither an honorific nor a salutation.

Resumes

A resume (spelled with or without the accents) is often called a **curriculum vitae** (abbreviated as c.v.), Latin for *life's path.* You can also consider your resume:

- A short analytical summary of your salable credentials and qualifications.
- A short analytical report on the relevant aspects of your background.
- A short persuasive document functioning as a complementary attachment to your cover letter.
- Introduced by its cover letter, a short, external, probably solicited proposal for assisting the organization to which you are applying.

Your resume is, in effect, all of the above. Furthermore, it is one of the most important documents you will ever create. It is a reflection of you that you want examined by people from whom you hope to obtain substantial, long-term benefit.

Message

A common mistake many people looking for employment make is to construct a resume carefully and then use it when applying for a variety of positions. Doing so violates the principles of good CMAPP analysis. Each application necessarily involves a different context and a different audience. The individual resume's message, therefore, must be specific to that context and audience. Although your background, of course, remains the same (as might the basic elements of your product—your resume), you must tailor your document. This means you may need to create a "new" resume each time you make an application. You will want to highlight certain experience, stress particular accomplishments, use your format to convey specific impressions, and so on.

Very common at the beginning of a resume is an elliptical clause or a single sentence indicating your **professional objective.** Following is an example.

Example of a Professional Objective

To apply my accounting skills and experience in a large, well-respected firm that offers the potential for career advancement to senior management ranks.

Should you include a professional objective in your resume? One school of thought advocates including a professional objective, maintaining that it demonstrates forethought and long-term commitment. Another advises against including one, pointing out, first, that if you are interviewed, a manager will prefer to discuss the issue directly and, second, that if your stated objective does not match that of the employer (to you, a poorly known audience), it will likely work against your candidacy. Conduct the most accurate CMAPP analysis you can, and decide whether to include an objective.

⬛Tech Link

This site from Accent Resume Writing features practical guidance for resume writing as well as examples and critiques of resumes. Visit **www.accent-resume-writing.com**

Audience

Although the situation may well vary, you are likely to have both a primary and a secondary audience when you submit a resume to an organization.

Primary.   Your primary audience is probably an employee in the personnel or human resources department. Remember that this person's customary role is not to choose your application from the numerous applications the company has likely received. Rather, it is to find reasons (indicated within your resume and/or your cover letter) to eliminate your application from the running. Thus, your resume and letter must be persuasive enough to convince this primary audience not to exclude you.

Secondary.   Your secondary audience will probably be a manager—one who has authority over the position in question. That individual's role may include reviewing the applications selected by the primary audience and deciding which few candidates are most suitable for interviews. Thus, your resume must persuade your secondary audience as well.

Purpose

Another frequent but mistaken assumption is that your resume's purpose is to get you a job. It isn't. Its purpose is to get you an interview, your opportunity to convince your audience to offer you the position.

Product

You should consider several CMAPP issues in particular.

Form.   Brevity, precision, and concision are crucial. Avoid wasting words and space. For example, using the headings *Name* and *Address* to introduce your name and address is counterproductive: your audience recognizes the information. Also keep the following points in mind:

- Choose action verbs over weaker, roundabout constructions: *apply,* not *make application; ensure,* not *make certain that; guided,* not *looked to the guidance of; created,* not *established the creation of;* and so on.
- Use phrases or elliptical clauses rather than complete sentences. Remember, however, to observe the principle of parallelism rigorously; otherwise, your text is liable to lose cohesion, coherence, and consistency.
- Use levels of discourse and technicality according to your context and your audience; your choice should derive from your CMAPP analysis.
- Proofread carefully. Even a single error lessens your credibility.

Format.   The appearance of your resume reflects your abilities. Use level heads effectively. Commonly, these appear as though in the left-hand column of a table, where they introduce the information that appears in a wider right-hand column. (See **Figure 11.1** on the next page for an example.) Your goal should be accessibility: you want your audience to extract important items without having to read every word.

> **FIGURE 11.1**   A One-Page Reverse Chronological Resume

Rick Vanderluin, a senior employee with the marketing firm of Avery and San Angelo, heard through the grapevine that RAI might be looking to create a marketing department. He decided to apply to Celine Roberts, RAI's company manager. Here is the one-page resume he attached.

Richard (Rick) Vanderluin

1151 St. James Court Hartford, CT 06101
(860) 555-0138 Fax: 555-0118 E-mail: vanderl@aol.com

Academic	MBA (1990)	University of Connecticut
	BA (1988)	University of Connecticut

Career

2000 to Present **Senior Associate**: Avery and San Angelo (Hartford, CT)
- Report to senior partner.
- Supervise staff of six.
- Develop promotional strategies for several large clients, including Loblaws, Steinberg, and CIBC.
- Assess and recommend new target opportunities: generated $2.5 million in new business in 20--.

1997–2000 **Director of Marketing**: Rawlings Hotel (Hartford, CT)
- Reporting to general manager, set up hotel's marketing department.
- Supervised marketing staff of two.
- Developed new marketing strategies: hotel revenue increased by 27%.
- Secured profitable linkages with out-of-town business and government, including Chamber of Commerce, American Dentistry Association, and American Medical Association.
- Actively pursued convention and meeting business: from 1998–2000, secured a minimum of five association annual conventions.

1993–1997 **Sales Director**: FastService Hotels Ltd. (Hartford, CT)
- Exercised full line responsibility for all company sales staff.
- Coordinated corporate-sponsored functions for all four FastService Hotels.
- Actively solicited tourism business: received FastService's "Most Successful Manager" award in 1994 and 1995.

1990–1993 **Sales Associate**: Hartford Motors (Hartford, CT)
- Reported to sales director.
- Recommended and developed marketing campaigns, increasing sales by 13% in 1992.
- Sold new and used Cadillacs and Lincolns.

References Available on request.

Length.   How long should your resume be? Again, there are two schools of thought.

- As a general rule, your resume should be limited to one page. The rationale is that the audience will not be inclined to take the time or trouble to read more than one page. After all, resumes merely identify candidates for the next step in the selection process.
- Regardless of the number of pages, your resume should include everything relevant to the application. The rationale is that the audience is trying to exclude applications and is likely to do so if the sparse content of a single page does not provide enough information to permit a confident decision. Your audience will inevitably exclude a resume of uncertain value rather than take the trouble to contact you for further information.

Here is further evidence of the uncertain nature of submitting applications. Unless you know your audience well enough to decide which of the two points of view they favor, you are gambling. You can try to boost your odds by using a third option. Create a one-page "summary" resume; indicate *Details Attached* at the bottom; and include a more comprehensive version, perhaps titled *[Your name]— Detailed Resume.*

Do the best CMAPP analysis you can, decide which approach to take, and create the most professional document possible.

Type.   Broadly speaking, you can organize your resume in one of two ways. A **chronological resume** groups information according to when it occurred, while a **functional resume** groups information according to its function.

Chronological Resumes

Since the ordering of employment information is typically from most to least recent, the chronological resume is often referred to as being in reverse chronological order. (An example is Rick Vanderluin's resume in **Figure 11.1.**) Skills and accomplishments are integrated within each employment segment. This is viewed as a traditional format and is probably the most common—and thus the most commonly expected on the part of your likely audience.

The chronological resume is particularly effective for illustrating an improving career path. On the other hand, it tends to draw attention to any lack of career progress (if you are just beginning, for example) and to any chronological gaps (if you were unemployed for a protracted period while caring for a family, for example).

Functional Resumes

The functional resume focuses on your skills and accomplishments. You organize your background information around the practical benefits you can offer your potential employer. Functional resumes are very effective for highlighting *what you can do* rather than *when you did it.*

Note, however, that functional resumes are less common than chronological resumes. Consequently, some audiences question them, suspecting that they are designed to obscure unflattering information. In making your choice, therefore, you must perform as accurate a CMAPP analysis as possible. **Figure 11.2** on the next page shows Vanderluin's resume reworked as a functional resume.

Relevant Information

There are no certainties in choosing the information to incorporate in a resume. Obviously, the better you know your context and your audience, the more effectively you can decide what to include or exclude. Here are a few general guidelines.

- Include only relevant employment experience. If you are applying for a job as a research technician and have paid experience as a technical assistant and as a nightclub bouncer, the former is pertinent—the latter is not.

- Remember that you may have acquired relevant, transferable employment skills even though you were not being paid at the time. A potential employer is primarily interested in the assets you can bring, not in how much you were paid to acquire them.

- Under a separate heading in a chronological resume (and within the appropriate "function" in a functional resume), include hobbies from which you gained expertise useful to the potential employer. If, for example, you have gained a high standing in one of the martial arts, your accomplishment could be relevant to an application with a police force or a security firm. Your valuable baseball card collection would not be.

- If you are looking for a summer job or just starting out in your career or if a position has a particular academic requirement, your grades, degrees, diplomas, scholarships, or academic awards will probably be taken as evidence of commitment and accomplishment. Otherwise, they are likely superfluous.

- Job awards such as salesperson of the month or highest record of accuracy in test results are likely to be worthwhile inclusions.

- Use your CMAPP analysis to decide how far back to go. Again, if you have a very short employment history, you may even want to include relevant summer jobs held during high school. If you have been working for several years, include only what is of particular relevance to the position for which you are applying.

- If you have been led to understand that you should include references or letters of reference, do so. Otherwise, it's usually sufficient to include the phrase "References available on request." Note, however, that if you receive an interview, you must make sure to have the information with you. Interviewers may become impatient with candidates who apologize and offer to forward reference details later.

FIGURE 11.2   A Functional Resume

Richard (Rick) Vanderluin

1151 St. James Court Hartford, CT 06101
(860) 555-0138 Fax: 555-0118 E-mail: vanderl@aol.com

Academic	MBA (1990)	University of Connecticut
	BA (1988)	University of Connecticut

Marketing Skills

- Developed promotional strategies for several large clients of the marketing firm of Avery and San Angelo, including Loblaws, Steinberg, and CIBC.
- Assessed and recommended new target opportunities: generated $2.5 million in new business for the marketing firm of Avery and San Angelo.
- Developed new marketing strategies that increased Rawlings Hotel revenue by 27%.
- Secured profitable linkages with out-of-town business and government, including Chamber of Commerce, American Dentistry Association, and American Medical Association.
- Recommended and developed marketing campaign for Hartford Motors, increasing sales by 13% in 1992.

Sales Skills

- For Rawlings Hotel, secured a minimum of five association annual conventions in each of two years.
- Actively solicited tourism business for FastService Hotels, receiving the "Most Successful Manager" award in 1994 and 1995.
- Sold new and used Cadillacs and Lincolns.

Administrative Skills

- Set up and managed Rawlings Hotel's marketing department.
- Coordinated corporate-sponsored functions for all FastService Hotels.
- Exercised full line responsibility for staff of up to six sales and marketing professionals.

References   Available on request.

Electronic Resumes

More and more organizations are permitting—and, in some cases, encouraging or even requiring—**electronic resumes.** The two types of electronic resumes are **scannable resumes** and **online resumes.**

Scannable Resumes.   To economize their search for employees, many companies are using scanners and specialized software programs to screen employees. Other companies are relying more and more on Internet resume data-banks, such as monster.com. What implications does this technology have for your resume? Companies scan the resumes they receive and store the information using **keywords.** When a position opens in the company, a computer looks up all the resumes that include their targeted keywords. For example, a company looking for an accountant might search for the keywords *accounts receivable, accounts payable, payroll, journals,* and so on.

A **keyword summary** can be included in your resume to highlight keywords. Keywords should be nouns rather than verbs or adjectives and should include roughly 25 words that can include job titles, skills, software programs, and selected jargon for your field. Your list of keyword descriptors should appear immediately following your name and address on your resume. After your keyword summary, your resume should continue with the standard parts and sections.

When submitting a scannable resume, follow these guidelines:

- Send only originals on white paper with black ink.
- Submit as many pages as you want (the computer doesn't tire of reading).
- Limit visual effects to capitalization and bold headings. Avoid italics, underlining, boxes, columns, or shaded areas because they sometimes confuse the computer.
- Use only 10- to 14-point font sizes.
- Mail resumes flat. Do not fold or staple pages. Creases can cause scanner problems, and staples have to be removed.

Figure 11.3 on the next page shows Rick Vanderluin's resume prepared in a scannable format.

Online Resumes.   An online, or hypertext, resume is an HTML document that can be viewed on the Internet. This type of resume generally uses links to other screens, which expand on information that might be omitted in a one-page resume. For example, as part of work experience, the prospective employee could provide a link to detailed job descriptions, drawings or blueprints, or other items from a portfolio. Online resumes can have distinct advantages for candidates in technical fields.

Resume Ethics

Undeniably, some people have submitted successful applications that contain deliberate and inaccurate exaggeration. While your resume must be persuasive and while you should try to word it in a way that casts a favorable light on you and on

⊠ Tech Link

Quintessential Careers features Scannable Resume Fundamentals, including samples and actual guidelines from Johnson & Johnson. Visit *www.quintcareers.com/ scannable_resumes.html*

FIGURE 11.3   Scannable Resume

Richard (Rick) Vanderluin
1151 St. James Court Hartford, CT 06101
(860) 555-0138 Fax: 555-0118 E-mail: vanderl@aol.com

KEYWORDS

Senior Associate, Director of Marketing, Sales Director, Supervisor, Promotional Strategy Development, New Business Development, Revenue Growth, Advertising Industry, Hotel Industry, Automotive Industry, Leadership, Project Management, Team Building, MBA, University of Connecticut

EXPERIENCE

Marketing Skills, Avery and San Angelo (Hartford, CT)

2000 to Present

Report to senior partner.

Supervise staff of six.

Develop promotional strategies for several large clients, including Loblaws, Steinberg, and CIBC.

Assess and recommend new target opportunities: generated $2.5 million in new business in 20--.

Director of Marketing, Rawlings Hotel (Hartford, CT)

1997–2000

Reporting to general manager, set up hotel's marketing department.

Supervised marketing staff of two.

Developed new marketing strategies: increased hotel revenue by 27%.

Secured profitable linkages with out-of-town business and government, including Chamber of Commerce, American Dentistry Association, and American Medical Association.

Actively pursued convention and meeting business: from 1998–2000, secured a minimum of five association annual conventions.

Sales Director, FastService Hotels Ltd. (Hartford, CT)

1993–1997

Exercised full line responsibility for all company sales staff.

Coordinated corporate-sponsored functions for all four FastService Hotels.

Actively solicited tourism business: received FastService's "Most Successful Manager" award in 1994 and 1995.

Sales Associate, Hartford Motors (Hartford, CT)

1990–1993

Recommended and developed marketing campaigns, increasing sales by 13% in 1992.

Sold new and used Cadillacs and Lincolns.

EDUCATION

MBA, 1990, University of Connecticut

BA, 1988, University of Connecticut

your activities, do not cross the bounds of truth. You will recall the earlier comment regarding aptitude and attitude. Consider how you would be viewed if, for example, your resume specified that you were an expert user of the UNIX operating system, and, after a few weeks' employment, your lack of expertise became obvious. Don't compromise your integrity by exaggerating your worth.

Interviews

A profitable way to look at an employment interview is as a series of rapid, impromptu presentations. Interviews may last anywhere from 20 minutes to several hours, and they may take place on a single day or over several days. During the interview process, you may be interviewed by one person or by several persons. How you present yourself is crucial—first impressions count. An interviewer often makes a decision not to hire during the first 15 seconds of an interview.

As a job applicant, you can use the interview as an opportunity to determine if you want to work for a particular company. Use the interview to present yourself and to evaluate the organization and the job in light of the personal and career goals you've defined for yourself.

Interview Tips

Your success in the interview depends largely on your preparation. Review your research on the company and position, and consider the following:

- Use the CMAPP analysis you performed before submitting your application.
- Your overall purpose at this stage is to convince your audience to hire you rather than someone else.
- Anticipate which questions your prospective employer may ask, and practice your responses. A list of commonly asked interview questions is presented in **Figure 11.4** on the next two pages.
- Each time the interviewer asks a question or asks you to play a role in a scenario, you can benefit from the impromptu presentation skills you have learned.
- Take advantage of the effective use of the paralinguistic factors and of the three-part rule introduced in Chapter 10.
- Your audience will likely want to see how well you can think on your feet.
- Before you submitted your application, you had the luxury of broad preparation; you should now have at least a basic understanding of the company's main functions.

This preparation, coupled with on-the-spot audience analysis, will allow you to ask intelligent, relevant questions of your own—an opportunity commonly afforded applicants. What you ask will depend on your context and audience. Nonetheless, as you prepare questions, keep the following points in mind:

- Although you may consider a comment humorous, your audience may find it disrespectful.

- There is a fine line between laudable self-assurance and arrogance. Unless you are negotiating for a senior position, concluding your interview by asking about stock options is not likely to sit well with your audience.

- It is acceptable to ask how long it might be—in ballpark terms—before a decision is made and whether there is anything else you can offer that might help your audience reach its decision. Be careful of connotation here. You should not ask whether you can now correct something you think you expressed poorly during the interview.

- If you have been successful in doing your homework about the organization, and if you're sure your information is accurate, you can ask about company operations. Make sure, however, that what you mention is public knowledge. This is not the time to try to impress the audience with your ability to ferret out confidential information about them! Similarly, name-dropping is unlikely to impress your audience. In both cases, you're courting the consequences of the aptitude/attitude issue mentioned earlier.

FIGURE 11.4   Commonly Asked Interview Questions

Educational Experiences

1. What did you major in? Why?

2. Which courses did you like best? Least? Why?

3. What motivated you to seek a college education?

Work Experiences

4. Why do you want to work for this company?

5. What kind of work did you do in your last job? What were your responsibilities?

6. Describe a typical day on your last (or present) job.

7. What was the most difficult problem you encountered on your last (or present) job, and how did you handle it?

8. What did you like best about your previous position(s)? What did you like least?

9. Why did you leave (or why do you want to leave) your job?

10. What do you know about our company?

11. What aspects of this job appeal to you most?

(Figure continued on next page.)

FIGURE 11.4   (continued)

Human Relations

12.   What kind of people do you enjoy working with? What kind of people do you find difficult to work with?

13.   How do you get along with others in work situations?

14.   Have you worked previously in teams? How do you get along with others in a team environment?

Goals

15.   What are your career goals?

16.   Why did you choose this particular field of work?

Self-Concept

17.   What are your greatest strengths? Weaknesses?

18.   What qualities do you need to strengthen?

19.   Tell me about yourself.

20.   Why do you think you are qualified for this job?

21.   How do you spend your leisure time?

22.   What do you consider to be your chief accomplishment in each position you've held?

23.   What have your supervisors complimented you on? Criticized you for?

Questions, Answers, and Legal Issues

Your audience is there to assess you—not only to find out about your likely ability to do the job, but probably to decide if they would like to work with you. Thus, thinking back to Chapter 1's discussion of ethics in technical communication, you should be honest and forthright.

With certain exceptions, employment law prohibits questions about your sex, age, religion, or ethnic background. **Figure 11.5** on the next page lists examples of illegal interview questions. If your interviewer asks similar questions, consider politely indicating that you believe the question is inappropriate, tactfully avoiding it, or diplomatically stating that you might be agreeable to answering it if your interviewer can demonstrate how the information is relevant to the job.

If you believe that you are being unfairly pressed, consider whether you are seeing a reflection of the working environment. Ask yourself if you would really like to be a part of such an organization. Remember that unethical interview questions may reflect how the employer treats employees.

FIGURE 11.5   Illegal Interview Questions

1.   Are you married (single, divorced, widowed)?

2.   Do you have small children? Do you plan to have children?

3.   What is your date of birth?

4.   Have you ever been arrested?

5.   Where were you born?

6.   Where does your husband (wife, father, mother) work?

7.   Are you pregnant?

8.   Do you belong to a religious organization? Which one?

9.   Do you rent or own your home?

10. What is your maiden name?

11. Do you have a girlfriend (boyfriend)?

Follow-up

Some authorities specify a standard **follow-up** to your interview: a short letter expressing your appreciation for the interviewer's time and reiterating your interest in the position. A follow-up letter is often an excellent strategy. It shows your continued involvement, stresses your interest, and may well be what distinguishes you from other candidates.

Unfortunately, however, some audiences react to such letters negatively. They see them as meddling or as an inappropriate attempt to influence their decision. While you may think this perspective unproductive, it is not one you should ignore. You may even wish to conclude your interview by asking whether you could take the liberty of following up within the next few days. Unless the response is a clear and definitive "no," writing the follow-up letter is probably to your advantage.

Make sure you do not allow reasonable follow-up to become pestering. Unless your interviewers have clearly indicated otherwise, they are unlikely to welcome repeated queries about their decision. Remember that your peace of mind, however important to you, is probably not the first priority in their working lives.

Chapter Review

CHAPTER SUMMARY

Begin seeking employment by assessing your personal and career goals and analyzing your qualifications. You may want to create a portfolio with transcripts, letters of recommendation, copies of job application forms, awards, test scores, certificates or diplomas, and samples of work or projects completed. Remember that finding a job is a difficult and time-consuming process. It will take a lot of planning and initiative on your part. Use a variety of sources to find job openings, including networking contacts, school placement offices, professional publications, employment agencies, internships, libraries, and the Internet. Don't apply for jobs for which you aren't qualified.

Always send a cover letter with your resume. Address it to a specific person. Be specific about what position you are applying for. Avoid superfluous information. Focus on what you can do for the company, not on what the company can do for you. Conclude with a clear call to action. Limit your cover letter to one page, and use letterhead stationery.

Tailor your resume for each position you're applying for. Research your audience to determine whether or not to include a professional objective. Consider both your primary and secondary audiences, especially when determining whether to limit your resume to one page. Chronological resumes organize information according to when it happened. Functional resumes are less common. They organize information by the benefits it can offer a potential employer. Limit visual effects and use a standard type size for your scannable resume. Consider including a keyword summary. Online resumes can be viewed on the Internet. They use links to provide detailed information that cannot fit on a one-page resume.

Before an interview, think of possible questions the interviewer might ask and practice answering them. Use your CMAPP analysis to prepare questions of your own. Certain questions about sex, age, religion, or ethnic background should not be asked in an interview. In most cases, you should follow up with a short letter.

KEY TERMS

Chronological resume	Keyword summary
Curriculum vitae	Networking
Electronic resume	Online resume
Follow-up	Portfolio
Functional resume	Professional objective
Keywords	Scannable resume

CRITICAL THINKING ACTIVITIES

1. What are the five elements of the employment application package discussed in this chapter?
2. On what attributes do many employers seem to base their hiring and firing decisions? Why do you think this is the case?
3. Briefly explain how networking can help you find job openings.
4. What are the principal reasons for sending a cover letter with your resume?
5. How should you decide on the level of technicality for your cover letter?
6. Which format issues should you consider for your cover letter?
7. What is another term for a resume?
8. A resume could be considered a combination of which four CMAPP products?
9. How long should a resume be and why?
10. What is the principal advantage and what is the main possible disadvantage of including a professional objective?
11. What are the two basic types of resumes? How do they differ? What are the principal advantages and disadvantages of each?
12. What are the unique features of a scannable resume? When might you prepare and use a scannable resume?
13. What are the unique features of an online, or hypertext, resume? When might you prepare and use an online resume?
14. How is a job interview like an impromptu presentation?
15. List and explain three key factors in the success of a job interview.

SKILLS APPLICATIONS

1. Select a help-wanted advertisement from the newspaper or from a job search web site. Research the company and position, and then create a resume and cover letter for the position.
2. Contact at least two people from different companies or organizations who are authoritatively involved in the hiring process. Ask them for a few minutes of their time to help you with your project. Ask them what they look for in a cover letter, a resume, and an interview. In a short oral or written analytical report (perhaps to your class), compare and contrast the answers you received and draw conclusions from them.
3. Research a company that interests you and a position within that company for which you might interview. Prepare a list of five to eight interview questions you might ask in an interview with that company. Keeping that company and position in mind, prepare answers to the commonly asked interview questions listed in **Figure 11.4.**
4. Begin building a job search portfolio by gathering as many of the documents described in this chapter as you can. Include a list of your skills, abilities, and accomplishments as well as an assessment of your personal and career goals.

CONTEMPORARY ISSUES CASE

Ethical Interviewing.   After months of networking, you've finally landed an interview for the job of your dreams. The interview is going extremely well, and you have every indication that you'll receive an offer for the job. As the interview draws to a close, the interviewer asks if you're married and whether family commitments might affect your availability to work long hours. You indicate that you understand long hours will be required on occasion, which isn't a problem for you. But the interviewer presses for specific information about your personal life.

1. How would you respond to the interviewer?
2. What might this interview tell you about the company in general? Would the interviewer's questioning affect your interest in the company?

CASE STUDY

Cover Letters from AAU Students to AEL

Situation

Wally Strong, a fourth-year electrical engineering student at AAU, and George Nagmara, an AAU civil engineering student, heard Noah Avigdor's presentation on employment with AEL. (See Chapter 9's case study.) Both men decide to apply and prepare cover letters, which appear in **Figures 11.6** and **11.7** on the next two pages.

Issues to Think About

1. Strong and Nagmara attended the same presentation and created cover letters addressed to the same company. What can you say about the two letters in terms of the following CMAPP components?
    (a) Audience: Examination of sources to determine a specific audience and response to what the audience knows, needs to know, and wants to know
    (b) Message: Content of the letter to fit the context and the audience
    (c) Form: Language appropriate to the context and the audience
    (d) Purpose: Clear indication to the audience of the purpose of the letter
    (e) Product: Credibility deriving from the quality of the product, impression of the author as a potential employee, and specific format issues
2. What do you think may have been Strong's principal error or errors?
3. Why do you think that Strong did not attach a resume? Why do you think Nagmara did?
4. How would you describe Strong's action request? How would you formulate it? How does it differ from Nagmara's?
5. How would you account for the differences between the two letters?
6. How do you think Frank Nabata and Leila Berakett (AEL's senior associate) are likely to respond to both letters?

FIGURE 11.6   Strong's Cover Letter

1225 Davenport Road Ann Arbor, MI 48103
555-0126 Cell: 555-0188
03/03/20--
Employment Manager, AEL
342 Center Street West
Lansing, MI 48980

Dear Employment Manager,

Hello. My name is Wally Strong and I have been going to Ann Arbor U for a while in engineering. I'd like to apply for any of the positions that your person talked about when he visited where I was at school.

My studies were completed after I finished my forth year at AAU. I took a lot of different courses but really majored in engineering, most of my grades were pretty good but I did get a couple of not so good ones too, but I'm sure what I learned in engineering can be applied practically to whatever kind of engineering you do there in Lansing, where I've always wanted to live. That's the reason why I'm applying to you rather than trying to get a good offer closer to home here.

I'm sure you'll be able to make really good use of all my engineering and communication skills because I know you do a lot of consulting and my specialty is in electrical engineering, I hear in the papers that Lansing is looking to lay some new electrical grids with Labrador. Yes I do try to keep up with the news, that's another reason why you'll probably want me.

I'm not married and don't have any responsibility which would make it easy for me to move whenever you'd need me to start. (Actually, I have a camper van and don't have a lot of stuff, so I can move myself pretty easily and save you the money.)

I sure hope you'll at least interview me for this job because I'm sure that when you see my credentials and background in detail (I can send a copy right away if you want to see them before you speak to me) you'll think I'm worth it.

Thanks for taking the time to read this and think of me. If you have any questions at all just call me anytime, even on my cell at 555-0188, though that's probably long distance, hope you don't mind.

Thanks again, it'll be really great to meet you!

Wally Strong
Wallace (Wally) Strong

FIGURE 11.7   Nagmara's Cover Letter

George Nagmara

March 6, 20--

Mr. Frank Nabata
Senior Partner
Accelerated Enterprises Ltd.
342 Center Street West
Lansing, MI 48980

Dear Mr. Nabata:

I am writing in light of Mr. Noah Avigdor's February 23, 20--, presentation to students at Ann Arbor University (AAU).

You will note from my enclosed resume that I am currently completing my M.Sc. degree in Civil Engineering here at AAU, for which I expect to maintain my current GPA of 4.00. You will likewise note that I returned to AAU to undertake my graduate degree after a hiatus of three years, during which time I was employed as an Engineer Trainee at the firm of Lather and Brown in Detroit, my hometown. Mr. William Brown has agreed to offer me a reference, should you wish to speak to him. He can be reached at his office at 555-0151.

I would be keenly interested in the possibility of a civil engineering career with Accelerated Enterprises. I expect to be in Lansing from May 2 through May 12, following my thesis defense here in Ann Arbor. Therefore, I would be grateful if you could spare me an hour of your time during that period so that we might discuss how my education and experience could be of benefit to Accelerated Enterprises.

Could you please have your office contact me as soon as possible at the address, phone, fax, or e-mail shown below so that we might arrange a time convenient to you.

Thank you for your consideration. I look forward to meeting with you.

Yours truly,

George Nagmara

George Nagmara

Enclosure

478 Blair Drive Ann Arbor, MI 48103
Tel: (734) 555-0142 Fax: (734) 555-0177 E-mail: nagmara@aau.edu

APPENDIX

Grammar and Style Guide

Section 1: Parts of Speech

Every word in a message has a use. Understanding word usage will help you communicate more clearly and effectively. Familiarity with the parts of speech will help you choose the best word at the right time.

Nouns

A **noun** is a word used to name people, places, or things. Nouns are the largest group of words in the language, and they are used more frequently than any other part of speech. Almost every sentence you read, write, speak, or hear contains at least one noun. Most sentences contain more than one noun.

Categories of Nouns

It is helpful to sort all nouns into one of two very broad categories: proper nouns and common nouns.

Proper Nouns. A proper noun names a specific person, place, or thing. Proper nouns are always distinguished by capital letters.

SPECIFIC PEOPLE	SPECIFIC PLACES	SPECIFIC THINGS
Meera	Seattle	Bic pens
Mr. Yukimura	Tibet	Canon copiers

Common Nouns. A common noun is a word that identifies a person, place, or thing in a general way.

baseball fan	moviegoer	assets	goodwill
boy	table	joy	team

Common nouns can be compound (*editor in chief, vice president, son-in-law, board of directors*).

Noun Plurals

Most noun plurals are formed by using one of three rules.

Rule 1. Add *s* to the end of most nouns.

	SINGULAR	PLURAL
Common Nouns	pamphlet	pamphlets
	song	songs
Proper Nouns	Chang	the Changs
	Corvette	Corvettes
	New Yorker	New Yorkers
Abbreviations	CPA	CPAs
Numbers	1800	the 1800s

Rule 2. Add *es* to any singular noun that ends in *s, x, z, sh,* or *ch.*

SINGULAR	PLURAL	SINGULAR	PLURAL
lens	lenses	tax	taxes
Lopez	the Lopezes	bush	bushes
Lynch	the Lynches	wrench	wrenches

Rule 3. Add an *s* to form the plural of any noun ending in *y* when the *y* follows a **vowel** (*a, e, i, o,* or *u*). With the exception of proper nouns, to form the plural of nouns that have a **consonant** (all letters except vowels) before the final *y,* change the final *y* to *i* and then add *es.*

	SINGULAR	PLURAL
Nouns ending in a vowel + *y*	delay	delays
	key	keys
	relay	relays
Nouns ending in a consonant + *y*	city	cities
	territory	territories

Foreign Words.   Because the *s* ending is standard for English plurals, plurals that do not end in *s* may sound odd. English claims a considerable number of such words, mostly borrowed from Latin and Greek.

SINGULAR	PLURAL	SINGULAR	PLURAL
medium	media or mediums	alumnus	alumni
crisis	crises	matrix	matrices

Nouns Ending in o.   Nouns that end in *o* form their plurals in one of two ways. Many simply add *s* to form their plurals. Others add *es* to form their plurals.

SINGULAR	PLURAL	SINGULAR	PLURAL
ratio	ratios	radio	radios
potato	potatoes	veto	vetoes

Compound Nouns.   Compound nouns may be spelled as separate words; in this case, the most important word is made plural.

SINGULAR	PLURAL
editor in chief	editors in chief
vice president	vice presidents

Compound nouns may be joined by hyphens; in this case, the base form is made plural.

SINGULAR	PLURAL
brother-in-law	brothers-in-law

Compound nouns may be spelled as one word; in this case, the plural is formed by adding *s* or *es* or changing the *y* to *i* and adding *es* (depending on the word ending).

SINGULAR	PLURAL
letterhead	letterheads
textbook	textbooks

Proper Names.   When forming plurals, treat a proper name like any other noun with this exception: Add only *s* to all proper nouns that end in *y;* ignore the "change *y* to *i* . . ." rule with proper names. In the examples shown below, the word *the* is inserted before the plurals to simulate real-life use.

SINGULAR	PLURAL
John Haggerty	the Haggertys
Rosemary Portera	the Porteras

One-Form Nouns.   Some nouns have only one form. Depending on the noun, that one form may be either always plural or always singular.

ALWAYS PLURAL	ALWAYS SINGULAR
thanks	news
belongings	headquarters

A **collective noun,** such as *tribe* or *jury,* represents a group that usually acts as a single unit.

The *jury* eats in the cafeteria at noon.

Possessive Nouns

Possessive nouns show possession. To form the possessive, add an apostrophe plus *s* to all singular nouns, both common and proper.

man	+	's	=	one man's opinion
Mr. Ross	+	's	=	Mr. Ross's district

Add only an apostrophe to any plural noun if it ends in *s*.

executives	+	'	=	three executives' goals
district attorneys	+	'	=	the district attorneys' ideas

Irregular plural nouns (such as *men, women, children,* and *alumni*) and some compound nouns are examples of plural forms that do not end in *s*. For these exceptions, add an apostrophe plus *s* to form their possessives; in other words, apply the rule for singular nouns.

women	+	's	=	both women's investments
brothers-in-law	+	's	=	my two brothers-in-law's kitchens

Pronouns

Pronouns are convenient substitutes for nouns, and they help to communicate the nominative, objective, and possessive forms to listeners and readers.

Personal Pronouns

A **personal pronoun** substitutes for a noun that refers to a specific person or thing.

Nominative Case.   A **nominative case pronoun** *(I, we, you, he, she, it, they, who, whoever),* sometimes referred to as a subjective case pronoun, may be used as a subject or a predicate nominative. A predicate nominative is a noun or pronoun that refers to the subject and follows a form of the verb *to be (am, is, are).*

Carla and *I* voted for him.

It is *she* who received all the attention. (predicate nominative)

Objective Case.   An **objective case pronoun** *(me, us, you, him, her, it, them, whom, whomever)* may be used as a direct or indirect object of a transitive verb, which is a verb that denotes action and needs an object. A **direct object** is a noun or pronoun directly affected by the action of the verb. (They chose *me*.) An **indirect object** is a noun or pronoun that receives the verb's action. (They gave *me* a gift.) An objective case pronoun may also be used as the object of a preposition.

Please send *them* by express mail.

Ned bought *her* a burrito.

Give it to *whomever* you see first.

Possessive Case.   A pronoun that indicates ownership or possession is a **possessive case pronoun** *(my, mine, our, ours, your, yours, his, her, hers, its, their, theirs, whose)*. Unlike nouns, pronouns do not need an apostrophe to signal possession.

These are *our* folders.

The fancy clothes are *hers.*

My going to the party surprised Jose.

Reflexive Pronouns

A **reflexive pronoun,** which ends in *self* or *selves,* refers to a noun or pronoun that appears earlier in a sentence.

We found *ourselves* reminiscing at the reunion. (The reflexive pronoun *ourselves* refers to *we.*)

Interrogative Pronouns

An **interrogative pronoun** begins a question that leads to a noun response. Interrogative pronouns are *who, whose, whom, which,* and *what.*

Who is in your office?   *Whom* do you want to call?

Whose are these?   *Which* of those are important?

Demonstrative Pronouns

A **demonstrative pronoun** is used to "point to" a specific person, place, or thing. The four demonstrative pronouns are *this, that, these,* and *those.*

Do you prefer *this* monitor or *that* one?

These books should be moved next to *those* shelves.

Verbs

The most important part of speech in a sentence is probably the **verb,** which expresses action, a state of being, or a condition of the subject of the sentence. No sentence is complete without a verb, and some sentences have more than one verb.

Types of Verbs

Every sentence must have a verb in order to be complete. Verbs are either action or linking verbs. Linking verbs include state-of-being verbs and condition verbs.

 Action Verbs. **Action verbs** help to create strong, effective sentences. Action verbs may take direct and indirect objects.

Mr. Gomez *teaches* me Finance 102.

Gabrielle *wrote* legibly.

 State-of-Being Linking Verbs. **State-of-being verbs,** sometimes called *to be* verbs, do not have direct or indirect objects; instead, these verbs have predicate nominatives and predicate adjectives. The verb *to be* has many different forms to denote the present, past, or future state of being.

The new president *is* Mr. Jongg. (The predicate nominative is *Mr. Jongg.*)

The old software programs *were* expensive and inefficient. (The predicate adjectives are *expensive* and *inefficient.*)

 Condition Linking Verbs. A **condition verb** does not have an object or an indirect object. Instead, it connects an adjective to the subject. Condition linking verbs either refer to a condition or appeal to the senses.

The assistant *appears* cooperative.

The health food *tastes* delicious.

Transitive and Intransitive Verbs

A **transitive verb** is a verb that must have an object to complete the meaning of a sentence.

Clark *suggested.* (Incomplete—What did he suggest?)

Clark *suggested* a profitable method. (Complete)

An **intransitive verb** is a verb that does not need an object to complete the meaning of a sentence.

The recruits *laughed.*

The merchandise *is* here.

He *will be* treasurer. (*Treasurer* is a predicate nominative, not an object.)

Verb Tenses

There are six verb tenses in English; they indicate the time an action takes place. These six tenses are categorized into two groups, simple and perfect.

Simple Tenses.   The simple tenses are called present, past, and future. A **present tense verb** expresses present occurrences (what is happening now).

Computer services *sell* information.

Georgia *is teaching* a course in merchandising.

A **past tense verb** expresses action recently completed.

Restless, the commander *paced* all night.

Tammy *was visiting* her bedridden father.

A **future tense verb** expresses action or condition yet to come. Future tense is formed by placing the helping verb *will* before the main verb.

I *will vote* on election day.

The accountants *will be consulting* with their clients.

Perfect Tenses.   A **perfect tense verb** describes the action of the main verb in relation to a specific time period in the past, from the past to the present, or in the future. The three perfect tenses are present perfect, past perfect, and future perfect. Form the perfect tense by preceding the past participle form of the main verb with either *have, has,* or *had.*

A **present perfect tense verb** indicates continuous action from the past to the present. *Has* or *have* precedes the past participle form of the main verb.

Francois *has voted* in every election since 1986.

They *have been jogging* every day since the beginning of the month.

A **past perfect tense verb** indicates action that began in the past and continued to the more recent past when it was completed. *Had* precedes the past participle form of the main verb.

Francois *had voted* in every election until last week.

They *had been jogging* every day until this past Monday.

A **future perfect tense verb** indicates action that will be completed at a specific point in the future. *Will have* precedes the past participle form of the main verb.

Including next year, Francois *will have voted* in every election since 1986.

By next Tuesday, they *will have been jogging* for a month.

Active and Passive Voice

Voice indicates whether the subject is doing the action or receiving the action of a verb. **Active voice** means that the subject of a sentence is doing the action.

Gianni *completed* his report using his computer.

Alberta *rode* her bike to work and back.

The young sprinter *won* the race.

Passive voice means that the subject of a sentence is receiving the action. The passive voice is formed with the past participle and a form of the verb *to be.*

The report *was completed* by Gianni.

The bike *was ridden* to work and back by Alberta.

The race *was won* by the young sprinter.

Verbals

A **verbal** is a verb form used as a noun, an adjective, or an adverb. The three verbals are infinitives, gerunds, and participles.

Infinitive.   An **infinitive** is a verb form that functions as a noun, an adjective, or an adverb, but not as a verb. An infinitive is formed by placing the word *to* in front of a present tense verb.

To run like the wind is Jaime's dream. (noun)

Her desire *to become* principal is noble. (adjective)

Racine International was founded *to promote* world peace, and its mission remains the same today. (adverb)

Gerund.   A **gerund** is an *–ing* verb form that functions as a noun. Gerunds may be used in a phrase that contains the gerund, an object, and its modifiers.

Avoiding the awful truth was her tendency. (subject)

Su Yung's career is *refurbishing* boats. (predicate nominative)

Every Friday they love *swimming* at the YMCA. (direct object)

Telly's habit, *falling* off to sleep, gets him into trouble in class, especially on test days. (appositive)

His talent for *guessing* someone's age is uncanny. (object of preposition)

Participle.   A **participle** is a verb form that can be used either as an adjective or as part of a verb phrase. The present participle is always formed by adding *ing.* The past participle is usually formed by adding *d* or *ed* to the present tense of a regular verb, or it may have an irregular form. The perfect participle always functions as an adjective and always is formed by combining *having* with the past participle of the verb.

Casey has a *snoring* dog on her front porch. (present participle)

There were six *launched* satellites that summer. (past participle)

This is a *broken* arrow. (irregular past participle)

Adjectives

An **adjective** is a word that describes or limits nouns or noun substitutes (pronouns, gerund phrases, and infinitive phrases). Adjectives answer the following questions about nouns:

- Which one? *this* proposal, *those* appointments
- How many? *six* calls, *few* tourists
- What kind? *ambitious* student, *creative* teacher

She is reading a *suspenseful* book. (The adjective *suspenseful* describes *book.*)

Casey's stylish suit was perfect for *Dot's* wedding. (The adjectives *Casey's* and *stylish* describe *suit; Dot's* describes *wedding.*)

Articles

Although classified as adjectives, the words *the, a,* and *an* are also called **articles.** *The* denotes a specific noun or pronoun. *A* or *an* denotes a nonspecific noun or pronoun.

Place the article *the* before a noun to designate that the noun is specific, not general.

the person (a specific person)   the toy (a specific toy)

Place the article *a* before a noun that begins with a consonant sound to designate that the noun is general, not specific.

a person (a nonspecific person)	a toy (a nonspecific toy)

Place the article *an* before a noun that begins with the sound of a vowel.

an honorable leader	an attractive child

Nouns and Pronouns Used as Adjectives

Nouns or pronouns that precede and modify other nouns and answer questions such as *which one* or *what kind* are used as adjectives.

Luis had four *theater* tickets. (Usually a noun, *theater* serves as an adjective describing the kind of tickets.)

Did you see *my mathematics assignment?* (The pronoun *my* and the noun *mathematics* are used as adjectives to identify which assignment.)

Proper Adjectives

Proper nouns that precede and modify other nouns serve as **proper adjectives.** Begin proper adjectives with capitals.

Burton is proud of his *New York* accent.

Our family thoroughly enjoys *Thanksgiving* dinner.

Marta has lost her favorite *Ann Arbor University* sweatshirt.

Compound Adjectives

A **compound adjective** is two or more hyphenated words that precede and modify nouns.

The *well-known* mystery writer is signing copies of his book.

Vivian is selling *long-term* insurance policies.

This *fast-acting* medicine will lessen your pain very quickly.

Comparison of Regular Adjectives

Adjectives have three degrees for comparison: the positive degree, the comparative degree, and the superlative degree.

To create the comparative degree of regular adjectives, either add *er* or *more* or add *er* or *less* to the positive degree form. To create the superlative degree of regular adjectives, either add *est* or *most* or add *less* or *least* to the positive degree form. Use the **positive degree** to describe one item.

Ryan is an *efficient* worker.

The box is a *big* carton.

Also use the positive degree to express equality.

He is as *big* as you.

Use the **comparative degree** to describe two items.

The box is a *bigger* carton than the first one.

Ryan is *less efficient* than Hsinchen.

Use the **superlative degree** to describe three or more items.

The box is the *biggest* carton of the three.

Ryan is the *least efficient* of the new employees.

Comparison of Irregular Adjectives

A few frequently used adjectives do not form their comparisons in the usual manner (adding *er* or *more* or *est* or *most*).

POSITIVE	COMPARATIVE	SUPERLATIVE
good book	better book	best book
bad result	worse result	worst result
little amount	less amount	least amount
many reports	more reports	most reports
much laughter	more laughter	most laughter

Absolute Adjectives

Some adjectives cannot be compared because they do not have degrees; they are already at the maximum level of their potential. These adjectives are referred to as **absolute adjectives.** Some examples are *immaculate, perfect, square, round, complete, excellent,* and *unique.* When you use these words in your sentences, use them alone or precede them with the terms *more nearly* or *most nearly.*

The food at Tim's restaurant is *excellent.*

Your yard is *more nearly square* than your neighbor's.

This typeface is *unique* to the economics textbook.

Adverbs

An **adverb** is a word that modifies an action verb, an adjective, or another adverb. Most adverbs end in *ly.* An adverb answers the questions *how, when, where, how often,* or *to what extent.*

He wrote the paper *correctly.* (how)

He wrote the report *yesterday.* (when)

He wrote the report *here.* (where)

He wrote the report *twice.* (how often)

He wrote the report *very* quickly. (to what extent)

Modifying Action Verbs

Adverbs modify action verbs but not linking verbs. Linking verbs are modified by adjectives, as in "She *appears* **happy.**" or "George *is* **intelligent.**" Action verbs, on the other hand, require adverbs.

She gave it to me *gladly.*

The dog sat up and begged *just once.*

Modifying Adjectives

An adverb that modifies an adjective usually answers the question *to what extent.*

The cookies are *very* good. (The adverb *very* modifies the adjective *good.*)

That new project is *tremendously* complex. (The adverb *tremendously* modifies the adjective *complex.*)

Modifying Other Adverbs

An adverb also can answer the question *to what extent* about another adverb in a sentence.

The grammar school pupil did her work *too* quickly. (The adverb *too* modifies the adverb *quickly.*)

We purchased the printer *very* recently. (The adverb *very* modifies the adverb *recently.*)

Accompanying Verb Phrases

Because adverbs modify action verbs and verb phrases that include action verbs, adverbs such as *never* or *always* frequently appear in the middle of verb phrases.

Ned is *always* writing e-mail messages.

I have *never* seen such an amazing use of cinematography before.

That has *already* been ordered.

Conjunctive Adverbs

A special group of adverbs called conjunctive adverbs includes words such as *therefore, moreover, however, nevertheless,* and *furthermore.* A **conjunctive adverb** is a transitional word that joins two independent but related sentences.

They remained at work late; *therefore,* they were able to complete the project.

She works after school as a docent; *moreover,* she waits tables on the weekend.

Comparison of Adverbs

Like adjectives, adverbs have three degrees of comparison: positive, comparative, and superlative. Adverbs usually show their comparative form by adding *er* or *more* or *less* to the simple form (positive degree). They show their superlative form by adding *est* or *most* or *least* to the simple form.

POSITIVE	COMPARATIVE	SUPERLATIVE
arrived late	arrived later than she	arrived latest of all
clearly written	more clearly written	most clearly written

Prepositions

A **preposition** is a word that usually indicates direction, position, or time. A preposition is linked to a noun or noun substitute to form a phrase.

She walked *into* the classroom. (direction)

She stood *behind* the open gate. (position)

She left work *before* lunch. (time)

The examples below are some of the most commonly used prepositions.

about	at	by	like	toward
above	before	concerning	of	under
across	behind	during	off	until
after	below	except	on	up
against	beneath	for	out	upon
along	beside	from	over	with
around	beyond	into	to	without

The Role of the Preposition

Prepositions introduce phrases called **prepositional phrases.** A prepositional phrase begins with a preposition and ends with a noun or noun substitute that functions as the object of the preposition. In addition, one or more adjectives that modify the object may appear in a prepositional phrase.

Place the carton *behind the tall cabinet.* (The preposition is *behind;* the object is the noun *cabinet; the* and *tall* are modifiers.)

Gary believes that learning a spreadsheet software program is *beyond him.* (The preposition is *beyond;* the object is the pronoun *him.*)

Prepositional Phrases Used as Adjectives. Prepositional phrases may be used to modify nouns and noun substitutes in sentences. They can have the same function as adjectives and answer questions such as *what kind* or *which one* about the words they modify.

Robert is *among those here.* (The prepositional phrase *among those here* modifies the noun *Robert.*)

They, *without a doubt,* are the most considerate people I have ever met. (The prepositional phrase *without a doubt* modifies the pronoun *they.*)

Prepositional Phrases Used as Adverbs. Prepositional phrases may be used to modify action verbs, adjectives, or adverbs. Prepositional phrases can have the same function as adverbs and answer questions such as *when, where, why, how,* or *to what extent* about the words they modify.

After lunch, Maria filed the papers. (when)

Ms. Torres is very knowledgeable *about the subject.* (how)

Conjunctions

A **conjunction** is a word that joins two or more words, phrases, or clauses. There are three types of conjunctions: coordinate conjunctions, correlative conjunctions, and subordinate conjunctions.

Coordinate Conjunctions

A **coordinate conjunction** joins words, phrases, and clauses of equal grammatical rank. **Equal grammatical rank** means that the connected elements are the same part of speech. For example, the connected elements may be nouns, verbs, prepositional phrases, or independent clauses. The coordinate conjunctions are *for, and, nor, but, so, or,* and *yet.*

Leo is studying computer science, *for* he plans to be a systems analyst. (The conjunction *for* joins two independent clauses.)

The teacher *and* the principal spoke. (The conjunction *and* joins two nouns.)

Tien wanted to attend the workshop, *but* she couldn't spare the time. (The conjunction *but* joins two clauses.)

Philippa says she loves to travel, *yet* she has never been on an airplane. (The conjunction *yet* joins two clauses.)

Correlative Conjunctions

A **correlative conjunction,** like a coordinate conjunction, is a word that connects words, phrases, and clauses of equal grammatical rank. Correlative conjunctions differ from coordinate conjunctions because they are always used in pairs for emphasis.

Both Greg *and* Barbara applied for the teaching position.

Neither Greg *nor* Barbara applied for the teaching position.

Not only Greg *but also* Barbara applied for the teaching position.

Subordinate Conjunctions

A **subordinate conjunction** joins elements of unequal grammatical rank. It is primarily used to connect dependent clauses with independent clauses.

Although we couldn't attend, we sent a donation.

Jules and Beth will visit *provided* they are allowed.

Interjections

An **interjection** is a word or an expression that has no grammatical relationship with other words in a sentence. An interjection is primarily used to express strong emotion; therefore, it is often followed by an exclamation point.

Hey, get your coffee cup off my monitor!

Your idea is sure to work. *Super!*

Section 2: Sentence Parts and Sentence Structure

A **sentence** is a group of related words that contains a subject and a predicate and expresses a complete thought. The sentence is the core of all communication. When forming sentences, the parts of speech are arranged into subjects and predicates.

The Subject in a Sentence

A **subject** is either the person who is speaking; the person who is spoken to; or the person, place, or thing that is spoken about.

Simple Subject

The **simple subject** is the main word in the complete subject that specifically names the topic of the sentence. The simple subject of a sentence is never in a prepositional phrase.

John writes articles.

John, the young journalist, has written articles.

Complete Subject

The **complete subject** includes the simple subject plus all of the sentence that is not part of the complete predicate.

John writes articles.

John, the young journalist, has written articles.

Compound Subject

A **compound subject** is two or more simple subjects joined by conjunctions such as *and, or, nor, not only/but also,* and *both/and.*

John and Sally work for our company.

Not only Jorge but also Svetlana will attend the career fair tomorrow.

When two nouns in a subject refer to one person, place, or thing, the article *the* (or *a*) is omitted before the second noun.

The *teacher* and *counselor* is my friend.

When two nouns in a subject refer to two people, places, or things, the article *the* (or *a*) is placed before each noun.

The teacher and *the counselor* are my friends.

The Predicate in a Sentence

The discussion of a predicate is divided into three brief parts: the simple predicate, the complete predicate, and a compound predicate.

Simple Predicate

The **simple predicate** is the verb in the complete predicate.

John *writes* articles.

John, the young journalist, *has written* articles.

Marisol *walked* the dog around the block.

Complete Predicate

The **complete predicate** is everything in the sentence said by, to, or about the subject; it always includes the main verb of the sentence. Whatever is not included in the complete subject of a sentence belongs in the complete predicate.

John *writes articles.*

John, the young journalist, *has written articles.*

Marisol *walked the dog around the block.*

Compound Predicate

A **compound predicate** consists of two or more verbs with the same subject. The verbs are connected by conjunctions such as *and, or, nor, not only/but also,* and *both/and.*

John and Sally *discussed* the matter and *concluded* that our actions were incorrect.

The engineer not only *complained* but also *refused* to finish the project.

Objects and Subject Complements

Objects and **subject complements** help complete the thought expressed by a subject and simple predicate.

Objects

An **object** is a noun, pronoun, clause, or phrase that functions as a noun. It may be direct or indirect.

A **direct object** helps complete the meaning of a sentence by receiving the action of the verb. In fact, only action verbs can take direct objects. Direct objects answer the questions *what* or *whom* raised by the subject and its predicate.

Louis closed the *door.* (Louis closed what?)

The boy lost his *mother.* (The boy lost whom?)

An **indirect object** receives the action that the verb makes on the direct object; you cannot have an indirect object without a direct object. Neither the direct object nor the indirect object can be part of a prepositional phrase.

The indirect object usually answers the question *to whom is this action being directed.* You can locate the indirect object by inverting the sentence and adding *to.*

Michiko gave *Thomas* the candy bar. (The candy bar was given by Michiko to Thomas.)

Nancy brought the *twins* broccoli with cheese. (Broccoli with cheese was brought to the twins by Nancy.)

Subject Complements

A **subject complement** is either a noun or pronoun that renames the subject or an adjective that describes the subject. In either case, it always follows a state-of-being or linking verb (such as *am, is, are, was, were, has been, seems, appears, feels, smells, sounds, looks,* and *tastes*).

Petersmeyer is an honest *banker.* (The noun *banker* renames *Petersmeyer.*)

Her writing appears *magical.* (The adjective *magical* describes *writing.*)

Clauses, Phrases, and Fragments

A **clause** is a group of words with a subject and a predicate; a **phrase** is a group of words with no subject or predicate.

Clauses

A clause is labeled **independent** if it can stand alone as a complete sentence.

One of our sales managers has developed an excellent training manual, which we plan to use in all future training sessions.

A clause is labeled **dependent** if it cannot stand alone as a complete sentence.

One of our sales managers has developed an excellent training manual, *which we plan to use in all future training sessions.*

Phrases

A **phrase** is a group of related words that does not contain both a subject and a predicate.

A **verb phrase** is a group of words that functions as one verb.

Frederico *will be finished* when we call him.

The IBC Corporation *has been supplying* us with these products.

A **prepositional phrase** is a group of words that begins with a preposition and ends with a noun or a noun substitute.

Place both cartons *on the desk.*

The boxes *in the office* belong *to him.*

Phrases add detail, interest, variety, and power to your writing. Compare the examples below.

Horace writes.

An avid storyteller, Horace writes shocking turn-of-the-century ghost tales for impressionable teenagers.

Fragments

A **fragment** is an incomplete sentence that may or may not have meaning. Fragments that have meaning in context *(Good luck on your trip.)* can be used in business messages. However, do not use fragments that have no meaning.

Fragment: Sam, the vice president's brother.

Sentence: Sam, the vice president's brother, got a hefty raise.

Fragment: Because the beds were uncomfortable.

Sentence: Because the beds were uncomfortable, Goldilocks slept on the floor.

Fragment: As soon as I receive a raise.

Sentence: I will plan my vacation as soon as I receive a raise.

Sentence Structures

Your communications will be more stimulating if you vary the types of sentences you write. There are four basic **sentence structures,** which are classified by the number and type of clauses they have.

Recall that the two types of clauses are independent (main) and dependent (subordinate). As an effective business communicator, you can emphasize an idea by placing it in an independent clause or you can de-emphasize an idea by placing it in a dependent clause.

The Simple Sentence

A **simple sentence** contains one independent clause and no dependent clauses. There may be any number of phrases in a simple sentence. Especially in business writing, a simple sentence can clearly and directly present an idea because there are no distracting dependent clauses. However, if overused, too many simple sentences can sound monotone or abrupt.

Pavarotti sings. (simple sentence)

Pavarotti and Domingo sing. (simple sentence with compound subject)

Pavarotti sings and acts. (simple sentence with compound predicate)

Luciano Pavarotti, the exquisite Italian tenor, sings like an angel. (simple sentence with various phrases)

The Compound Sentence

A **compound sentence** contains two or more independent clauses and no dependent clauses. In other words, two main ideas share equal importance. Note in these examples that the two independent clauses are joined by a coordinating conjunction, a conjunctive adverb, or a semicolon.

Mr. Feinstein is the founder, and he was the first president of FSI. (coordinating conjunction)

Are you going to the farmer's market, or are you going to the grocery store? (coordinating conjunction)

It's getting late; however, I am glad to stay here and finish this project. (conjunctive adverb)

Erin loves to ride horses; Connor loves to draw horses. (semicolon)

The Complex Sentence

A **complex sentence** contains one independent clause and one or more dependent clauses. In this structure, one or more ideas are dependent upon the main idea. Use dependent clauses to de-emphasive less important or negative ideas or to provide detail and support to the main clause.

Although it is important to proofread, many people do not take the time.

Dan, who cannot swim, hates wading in Lake Waldo because it appears polluted.

You should understand that Karen and Tim are happily married.

The Compound-Complex Sentence

A **compound-complex sentence** contains two or more independent clauses and one or more dependent clauses. This structure offers the business writer a variety of ways to present ideas and emphasize or de-emphasize details. Because this structure can become long and complicated, be careful how you use it in business communications. In the examples below, the independent clauses are in **bold** and the dependent clauses are in *italics*.

Since Noni left the folders on the desk, **her assistant decided to finish up,** and **he did a good job** *even though he was tired.*

Sierra and Casey, *who are cousins,* **play together often;** however, **their fathers,** *who are brothers,* **don't see enough of each other** *because they both travel so much.*

Subject-Verb Agreement

Good communicators make sure that their subjects and verbs always agree *(he walks, they walk)*. Grammatical errors in subject-verb agreement offend the receiver and label the person who erred as a careless writer or speaker.

Number

Third-person singular pronouns and singular nouns require a singular verb that ends in *s* when the present tense is used. Third-person plural pronouns and plural nouns require a plural verb that does not end in *s* when the present tense is used.

Joy telephones her parents daily. (singular)

Ari drives to his client's warehouse every Monday. (singular)

Joy's *parents telephone* her daily. (plural)

The *musicians record* their music when they have a chance. (plural)

Inverted Sentences

If a sentence is **inverted** (predicate precedes subject), putting the sentence in normal order will help you check subject-verb agreement.

Inverted Order: In the recruit's many strengths *lies* her *admiration.*

Normal Order: Her *admiration lies* in the recruit's many strengths.

Inverted Order: In the box *are* two *bags* of apples.

Normal Order: Two *bags* of apples *are* in the box.

Intervening Phrases

Intervening words do not affect subject-verb agreement and should be ignored. Note these examples with the intervening words in **bold** and the subjects and verbs in *italics*.

The *manager* **of the sports teams** *is traveling* to New Orleans.

A *professor,* **rather than the college administrators,** *represents* the institution at the convention.

My *assistants,* **along with the company comptroller,** *work* overtime on this project.

A Number, The Number

When used as a subject, the expression *a number* is considered to be plural and needs a plural verb.

A number of inquiries *come* to our office each day.

There *are a number* of tourists at our concert.

When used as a subject, the expression *the number* is considered to be singular and needs a singular verb.

The number of attorneys in Philadelphia *is* on the rise.

Names of Companies

Names of companies are usually considered singular. Although a firm's name may end in *s* or include more than one individual's name, it is still one business.

Gordon, Rodriguez, and Ramirez is representing the plaintiff.

Amounts

An amount that is plural in form takes a singular verb if the amount is considered to be one item.

One hundred dollars is a generous wedding gift.

An amount that is plural in form takes a plural verb if the amount is considered to be more than one item.

Fifty-one dollar bills are in my wallet.

Compound Subjects Joined by *And*

Because errors in subject-verb agreement commonly occur with compound subjects, take a careful look at some special guidelines. Usually, a compound subject joined by *and* is plural and requires a plural verb.

Mei-ling and Yuan are visiting their parents in Wuxi.

Sometimes compound subjects are treated as one item and require a singular verb.

Peanut butter and jelly is a popular sandwich in the grammar school.

If *each, every,* or *many a* precedes a compound noun, always use a singular verb.

Many a homeowner and investor *has supported* this tax increase.

Compound Subjects Joined by *Or/Nor*

When a compound subject is joined by *or, nor, either/or,* or *neither/nor,* the verb agrees with the subject that is closest to the verb.

Tracey or *Hal seems* to be well qualified for the position.

Either George or *his sisters are* catering the buffet.

Neither the supervisors nor *the security guard has seen* the criminal.

Pronoun-Antecedent Agreement

The noun or noun phrase that is replaced by the pronoun is called the **antecedent** of the pronoun. The pronoun must agree with its antecedent in person, number, and gender.

- **Person.**   Use a first-person pronoun to represent the persons speaking *(I, we)*. Use a second-person pronoun to represent the persons spoken to *(you)*. Use a third-person pronoun to represent the persons spoken about *(he, she, it, they)*.
- **Number.**   Use a singular pronoun *(he, she)* to refer to an antecedent that is a singular noun. Use a plural pronoun *(they)* to refer to an antecedent that is a plural noun.
- **Gender.**   Use a masculine pronoun *(his)* to refer to an antecedent that is a masculine noun. Use a feminine pronoun *(her)* to refer to an antecedent that is a feminine noun. Use a gender-neutral pronoun (such as *it*) to refer to an antecedent that is a gender-neutral noun (such as *table*).

John encouraged *his* staff.

Teri will be pleased when *she* sees *her* bonus.

Third-Person Pronoun Agreement

While writers do not have many problems matching first- and second-person pronouns with their antecedents, they do, on occasion, find that third-person pronouns present problems in gender and number.

The gender of the antecedent in a sentence is not always obvious. For example, nouns such as *manager, nurse, astronaut, president, systems analyst,* or *worker* could apply to either gender. Here are two alternative solutions:

1. Use both masculine and feminine pronouns to agree with an antecedent if its gender is unknown.
2. Change the antecedent to a plural form, and use the gender-neutral plural pronoun *their*.

A *doctor* tends to *his or her* patients without favoritism.

The *astronauts* cooperate 100 percent with *their* peers at NASA.

A problem may arise when applying the number-agreement principle to a collective noun *(jury, panel, committee)*. You must first determine whether the group is acting as a unit or individually.

The *committee* submitted *its* report. (acting as a single unit)

The *police* were given *their* assignments. (acting as individuals)

Compound Antecedents

A **compound antecedent** is an antecedent that consists of two or more elements. Agreement in number may present a problem if an antecedent is compound. To eliminate errors when this occurs, follow these three principles:

1. When two or more elements are connected by *and,* use a plural pronoun to refer to the antecedent.
2. If two or more elements of a compound antecedent are joined by *or/nor, either/or,* or *neither/nor,* (a) use a singular pronoun if all elements are singular or (b) use a plural pronoun if all elements are plural.
3. If elements are connected by *or/nor, either/or,* or *neither/nor* and one part of the antecedent is singular and the other is plural, the pronoun must agree with the part that is closest to the verb. If applicable, place the plural item last and use a plural verb and pronoun.

The manager and the word processor planned *their* itinerary.

Faye or Tom can work on *her or his* papers now.

Neither Lars nor Hal has completed *his* book report.

The trainees or their supervisors will finish *their* statistical computations.

Neither the men nor the women plan to share *their* profits on the sale.

Neither the boxers nor the manager expressed *his* (or *her*) opinion.

Either the engineers or the architect gave *her* (or *him*) suggestions for renovation.

Either the architect or the engineers gave *their* suggestions for renovation.

Indefinite Pronoun Agreement

An **indefinite pronoun** refers in general terms to people, places, and things. Some pronouns in this category are always singular, such as *one, each, every, anybody,* and *anything.*

Every auditor had an opportunity to ask *his or her* questions.

Each of the data operators is concerned about *his* or *her* job.

Other indefinite pronouns are always plural, such as *many, few, both,* and *several.*

Many will hand in *their* questionnaires.

Few accountants receive *their* CPAs.

Some indefinite pronouns, such as *all, any, some, more,* and *most,* can be either singular or plural depending on the noun or object of the preposition that follows them.

Singular: *Most of the report* had *its* spelling checked.

Plural: *Most of the reports* have *their* spelling checked.

Parallel Construction

Another kind of agreement is parallel construction. A construction that is not parallel will have a conjunction that joins unmatched elements. An adverb may be joined to a prepositional phrase, or a verb phrase may be joined to a noun. Constructions that are not parallel are grammatically incorrect.

Incorrect: Customers want *not only* good service *but also* to be treated with courtesy. (A correlative conjunction joins a noun with an infinitive verb phrase, which is an unparallel construction.)

Correct: Customers want *not only* good service *but also* courtesy.
OR Customers want *not only* to receive good service *but also* to be treated with courtesy.

Incorrect: The expert works cleverly *and* with speed. (A coordinate conjunction joins an adverb with a prepositional phrase, which is not a parallel construction.)

Correct: The expert works cleverly *and* speedily.

Incorrect: Jack is responsible for washing, ironing, and to fold the clothes. (an unparallel series)

Correct: Jack is responsible for washing, ironing, and folding the clothes.

Incorrect: His territory is larger than the Brainerd Realty Company. (confusing comparison)

Correct: His territory is larger than the Brainerd Realty Company's territory.

Section 3: Punctuation

For readers to interpret your ideas and inquiries precisely as you intend, you need to use correct punctuation in every message you write. Punctuation tells your readers where one thought ends and the next begins; punctuation clarifies and adds emphasis.

Punctuation includes external marks such as periods, question marks, and exclamation points. Punctuation also includes internal marks such as commas, semicolons, colons, quotation marks, parentheses, dashes, apostrophes, and hyphens.

The Period

A **period** can be used to indicate the end of a sentence, to indicate the end of an abbreviation, and to accompany an enumeration.

Periods at the End of Sentences

A period is used at the end of a declarative sentence, a mild command, an indirect question, and a courteous request. A **declarative sentence** makes a statement.

Gloria and Ralph are upgrading their software programs.

The choir members will sing in Italy during the holiday season.

A **mild command** is a stern request from the writer to the reader.

You should watch your step or you will fall.

Return the defective hard disk to the plant today.

Please pay attention to this section.

An **indirect question** is a statement that contains a reference to a question.

They inquired how your parents are feeling since their accident.

The judge asked if the prosecutor had any more questions for the witness.

A **courteous request** is a polite way to ask for action on the part of the reader; it does not ask for a *yes* or *no* answer.

May I have an interview when convenient.

Would you be kind enough to revise the proposal and return the corrected copy.

Periods with Abbreviations

Periods are placed after many commonly used abbreviations to indicate that the words are shortened forms of longer words.

Mr. (Mister)	Jr. (Junior)	Dr. (Doctor)
Ltd. (Limited)	Inc. (Incorporated)	Sr. (Senior)

Periods in Enumerations

When numbers or letters are used in a vertical list, periods are placed after each number or letter.

Your child will need the following items for the outing:

1. One change of clothing

2. Bathing suit, swim cap, sandals, and towel

3. Snack money

4. Sunscreen lotion and bug repellant

The Question Mark

A **question mark** is used after a direct question and after each part in a series of questions. The response may be a single word, or it may be one or more sentences.

Question Marks after Direct Questions

Use a question mark after a complete or incomplete sentence that asks a direct question.

Do you agree that summer seems to pass more quickly than winter?

Have you considered relocating to find suitable employment?

Question Marks in a Series

Occasionally a series of questions may help your writing. For emphasis, follow each segment in the series with a question mark.

Were all the votes counted? all the winners notified? all the losers contacted?

Did she apply to Temple University? to Boston College? to the University of Miami?

The Exclamation Point

An **exclamation point** is a mark of punctuation that follows a word, a group of words, or a sentence that shows strong emotion. When an expression shows excitement, urgency, or anger, the exclamation point, together with the words, conveys the strong emotion intended by the writer. In business writing, use exclamation marks sparingly.

Quick! Here's an opportunity to make money!

I'll never do that again!

The Comma

External punctuation marks tell the reader whether a sentence is a statement, a question, or an exclamation. Internal punctuation marks clarify the message intended by the writer. Of all the internal punctuation marks discussed here, the comma is, without a doubt, the most frequently used and misused.

Commas are used with introductory elements, independent clauses, nonessential elements, direct addresses, numbers, abbreviations, and repeated words. Commas also are inserted in a series and between adjectives. In addition, commas can indicate the omission of words and promote clarity in sentences.

With Introductory Elements in Sentences

Insert a comma after an introductory word, phrase, or clause.

Meanwhile, I will begin the next phase of the project. (introductory word)

Therefore, I wish to announce my candidacy. (introductory word)

In the long run, the cutback will be beneficial. (introductory phrase)

Because we have no record of the sale, we cannot help you. (introductory clause)

Although he was not present, his influence was evident. (introductory clause)

With Independent Clauses in Compound Sentences

When independent clauses in a compound sentence are joined by a coordinate conjunction (such as *for, and, nor, but, or,* or *yet*), precede the conjunction with a comma.

I will go to the hockey game on Friday, or I will babysit for my niece.

We thought he was guilty at first, but now we have changed our minds.

When each independent clause in a compound sentence has fewer than four words, no comma is needed.

Yoshi spoke and they responded.

I rode but he walked.

With Nonessential Elements

Nonessential elements are set off from the rest of a sentence with commas. Examples of **nonessential elements** are interrupting expressions, nonrestrictive elements, and appositives. Nonessential elements include information that may be interesting but is not necessary to the meaning or structure of a sentence.

To determine if the information is essential, temporarily omit it. If the meaning of the sentence stays the same, set off the nonessential word, phrase, or clause with commas.

Interrupting Expression.   Any expression that is nonessential and interrupts the flow of a sentence is set off with commas.

The most interesting part of the movie, *I believe,* is the ex-wife's entrance.

He should, *on the other hand,* separate the items in the box.

Nonrestrictive Element.   A nonrestrictive phrase or clause adds information that is not essential to the meaning of the sentence.

Jeffrey Chang, *who graduated from Loyola,* is my neighbor.

We plan to order Part 643, *which Steve recommended.*

A phrase or clause that is essential to the meaning of a sentence is called a **restrictive phrase,** or a **restrictive clause,** and is not set off with commas.

Ask the nurse *who was on duty that night.*

The man *who was just hired* is part of my team.

Appositive.   An **appositive** is a noun or noun substitute that renames and refers to a preceding noun. Appositives provide additional information that is not necessary to the meaning of a sentence. They are set off from the rest of the sentence with commas.

The paper contained the forecasts for the next quarter, *July through September.*

Ruby Muñoz, *the councilwoman,* is soliciting suggestions to bring up in council.

With Direct Address

To personalize a message, a writer may use **direct address** by mentioning the reader's first or last name in the beginning, middle, or end of a sentence. Because the name is not needed to convey the meaning of the sentence, it is set off with commas.

Dr. Oakes, you have been exceedingly helpful to my family.

Have I told you, *Gwen,* that we appreciate your purchase?

In a Series

Use a comma to separate three or more items in a series of words, phrases, or clauses. Although some experts omit the comma before a conjunction in a series, you may include the comma to avoid confusion.

Evan's college essay was *thoughtful, humorous, and brief.*

I will be going *to the movies, to the mall, or to my grandparents' home* Saturday evening.

Wake up early, prepare and serve breakfast, and take the children to the school bus.

Between Adjectives

Use a comma between two adjectives that modify the same noun when the coordinate conjunction *and* is omitted. If the word *and* wouldn't make sense between the adjectives, do not insert a comma.

The *short, thin* teenager envied the *tall, husky* football players.

Janet's *royal blue* suit is inappropriate attire for a job interview.

With Omission of Words

Occasionally, a writer may omit words that are understood by the reader. Inserting a comma at the point of omission provides clarity.

The treasurer is Johnetta; the *secretary, Garth;* and the *vice president, Warren.*
(The word *is* is omitted twice in the sentence; commas are inserted at the points of omission.)

In Numbers

Use commas to indicate a whole number in units of three whether in money or items.

$2,468   34,235 hot dogs   526,230 pins

For Clarity

Occasionally, a sentence requires a comma solely to ensure clarity.

Not Clear: Shortly after the teacher left the classroom.

Clear: Shortly after, the teacher left the classroom.

With Abbreviations

Writers who use abbreviations such as *etc., Jr., Sr.,* and *Inc.* should be familiar with the following comma rules concerning these abbreviations.

   Rule 1.   In a series, insert a comma before *etc.* Insert a comma after *etc.* when it appears in the middle of a sentence.

We will be taking camping clothes: shorts, boots, swimwear, *etc.*

The computer setup consisted of a CPU, a monitor, a printer, *etc.,* and cost $1,500.

Rule 2.   Generally, place a comma before *Jr.*, *Sr.*, and *Inc.* when the abbreviations appear in a name. Also insert commas after the abbreviations in the middle of a sentence.

Harry Larkin, *Jr.,* was elected to the presidency.

Able, *Inc.,* is owned by a conglomerate in New York.

The Semicolon

A **semicolon** is a form of punctuation used to denote a pause. Semicolons are stronger than commas but weaker than periods.

Between Independent Clauses

Use a semicolon between two related independent clauses instead of using a comma and a coordinate conjunction.

George is studying economics; his brother Dave is majoring in accounting.

Elaine will attend the July convention; she then will vacation in Lofton.

Before Conjunctive Adverbs

Use a semicolon before a conjunctive adverb *(moreover, nevertheless, however, consequently)* that joins two independent clauses. Conjunctive adverbs, which function as transitional expressions, introduce the second clause.

His report is too long; *therefore,* he cannot submit it until he revises it.

The voice-mail system can be easy to use; *however,* it tends to confuse some callers.

In a Series

Use a semicolon before expressions such as *for example (e.g.), that is (i.e.),* and *for instance* when they introduce a list of examples.

You can attend some interesting functions; *for example,* art shows, dance performances, or special film screenings.

They must follow smart money management principles; *that is,* save part of their income, make purchases they can afford, and avoid buying inferior goods.

In Compound Sentences

Use a semicolon before a coordinate conjunction in a compound sentence when either or both of the clauses have internal commas and the sentence might be misread if a comma is inserted before the conjunction.

I requested a return call, information about a particular check, and a phone number; instead, I received a reference to the wrong check and an incorrect phone number.

On Wednesday, March 12, 20--, the group will meet; but Flora will not officiate unless she has recovered from her illness.

In a Series Containing Commas

Use semicolons to separate items in a series when an item or items contain commas.

The mortgage company has branches in Newport, Rhode Island; Atlanta, Georgia; and Chicago, Illinois.

Acklin, the chairperson; Ikuko, the secretary; and Maria, the treasurer, were there.

The Colon

A **colon** is a form of punctuation that directs the reader's attention to the material that follows it. The material that follows the colon completes or explains the information that precedes the colon.

Before a Series

Use a colon when the words *the following, as follows,* or *are these* are near the end or at the end of a sentence that introduces a series of items.

Each person will need the following at the meeting: a computer, a printer, a set of instructions, and a writing tablet.

Before a List

Use a colon before a vertical itemized list. As with a series, the words *the following, as follows,* or *are these* may precede the colon.

Your instructions for Sunday are these:

1. Open the office at 9 A.M.

2. Check Saturday's mail, and call me if Pinder's check arrived.

3. Answer the telephone until noon.

Before a Long Quotation

Use a colon to introduce a long quotation of more than two lines.

Chien remarked: "When I think of my home in Beijing, I can just picture the people riding their bicycles to work early in the morning and returning from work late in the evening."

Between Special Independent Clauses

Use a colon instead of a semicolon to separate two independent clauses when the second clause explains the first.

Lucia is a skilled artist: She won an award for sketching animals.

Here is one way to improve your sense of humor: Recall experiences that seemed serious at the time, and realize how funny they actually were.

After a Salutation

When using mixed punctuation in a letter, use a colon after a salutation.

Dear Sir: Dear Dr. Santiago: Dear Ms. Linden:

In Time Designations

Use a colon between the hour and the minutes when the time is expressed in numerals.

Let's meet at 11:30 A.M. in the lobby of the office building.

The Dash

A **dash,** formed by keying two unspaced hyphens, is an informal punctuation mark. A dash is used with appositives or other nonessential elements that contain commas, before a summarizing statement, with a sudden change of thought, or before a detailed listing.

With Nonessential Elements

For emphasis, use a dash to set off appositives and other nonessential elements from the rest of the sentence. Some of the nonessential elements may have internal commas.

The stockbroker's office—newly equipped, nicely decorated, and spacious—is perfect for the hospitality reception.

Paolo's new car—a Toyota—is equipped with power locks and a sunroof.

Before a Summarizing Statement

Use a dash after a listing at the beginning of a sentence that is followed by a summarizing statement. Summarizing statements usually begin with the words *all* or *these*.

A nurturing manner, a love of people, and an unselfish attitude—these are three traits school counselors need.

Precision in grammar and facts—both are necessary for effective writing and speaking.

With a Sudden Change of Thought

Use a dash to indicate a sudden change of thought or a sudden break in a sentence.

Here is the perfect suit for work—and it's on sale too!

"Then we both agree that—oh no, now what's wrong?" asked Amy with a troubled look on her face.

Before a Detailed Listing

Use a dash to set off a listing or an explanation that provides details or examples.

The restaurant features exotic desserts—Polynesian pudding, Hawaiian coconut sherbet, and Samoan almond supreme cake.

Do your graduates have employable skills—excellent oral communications, a keyboarding speed of at least 70 wpm, and desktop publishing experience?

The Hyphen

A **hyphen** is a punctuation mark used after some prefixes and in forming some compound words.

After Prefixes

Use a hyphen after prefixes in some words. If you are unsure whether a word needs a hyphen, consult a dictionary.

ex-president	pro-American
de-emphasize	co-coordinator

In Compound Words

Use a hyphen in some compound words. In the English language, some compound words are written as one word, others are written as two words, and still others are hyphenated.

up-to-date reports	self-confident speaker
well-informed reporter	two-year-old child
Abe's mother-in-law	one-half the members

Some compound adjectives, such as *up to date, well informed,* and *two year old,* are hyphenated if they precede the noun they modify, but they are not hyphenated if they follow the noun.

The schedule is up to date.

Our up-to-date equipment improves productivity.

Quotation Marks

Quotation marks indicate a direct quotation, a definition, nonstandard English, a word or phrase used in an unusual way, or a title.

With Direct Quotations

When stating someone's exact words, enclose the words within opening and closing quotation marks.

Betty exclaimed, "It's getting late; let's go!"

"We'll leave now," answered Jeff. "We don't want to miss the train."

Within Quotations

Use single quotation marks to enclose a quotation within a quotation.

Amanda stated, "They listened to the president when he said, 'Our competition is getting ahead of us.'"

With Other Punctuation Marks

When placing ending quotation marks, follow these guidelines.

   Rule 1.   Place periods and commas within ending quotation marks.

"I concur," said the investor, "with your suggestion."

   Rule 2.   Place semicolons and colons outside ending quotation marks.

His best lecture is called "Psychoanalysis in the 1990s"; have you heard it?

This is the "beauty of San Diego": ideal temperatures and clear skies.

Rule 3. Place question marks and exclamation points inside the ending quotation marks when the quoted material is a question or an exclamation.

She shouted, "Watch out!"

He replied, "What's happening?"

Rule 4. Place question marks and exclamation points outside the ending quotation marks when the sentence, but not the quoted material, is a question or an exclamation.

Did Lydia actually say, "I will attend the seminar"?

I told you to label the package "Fragile"!

With Definitions and Nonstandard English

Use quotation marks to designate a term that is defined in the same sentence in which the term appears.

A "couch potato" is someone who watches television all day and all evening.

Use quotation marks to enclose slang words or expressions.

He referred to his car as a "dumb bunny."

With Titles

Use quotation marks to enclose the titles of parts of whole works, such as magazine articles and chapters. Also use quotation marks to enclose titles of lectures, songs, sermons, and short poems.

I read the article "The New Subcompact Cars" in *Consumers Digest.*

Parentheses

A **parenthesis** is used in pairs to set off nonessential words, phrases, or clauses. The pair is called **parentheses.** Parentheses also are used with monetary designations, abbreviations that follow names, references and directions, and numerals and letters accompanying a list.

With Nonessential Elements

De-emphasize nonessential elements by placing them in parentheses. When the items in parentheses appear at the end of a sentence, place the external punctuation mark after the ending parenthesis.

A high percentage of the alumni (73 percent of those surveyed) opposed changing the name of the college.

We received a visit from our ex-president (1997–1998).

When an item in parentheses is a complete sentence, capitalize the first word and end the item with an internal punctuation mark.

Luis and Ramona relocated to Brooklyn last month. (Didn't you meet them in San Juan?)

When a dependent clause is followed by an item or items within parentheses, place the comma after the ending parenthesis.

When they arrive at the airport (around 6 P.M.), George will meet them and drive them to their hotel.

With Monetary Designations and Abbreviations

Used primarily in legal documents, parentheses enclose a numerical designation ($500) following a verbal designation of money.

Compensation is not to exceed five hundred dollars ($500) for services rendered.

In addition, parentheses are used with abbreviations that follow names.

The Association for Business Communication (ABC) had selected Clifford Chung as its interim executive director.

With References and Directions

Use parentheses to set off both references and directions to minimize their importance in a sentence.

You may consult the appendix (page 345) for the correct format.

This trip (see the enclosed brochure) is a once-in-a-lifetime opportunity.

With Numerals and Letters Accompanying a List

When numerals or letters are used to list items in a sentence, parentheses may be used to enclose the numerals or letters.

Please include (a) your date of birth, (b) your social security number, and (c) your password.

The Apostrophe

The **apostrophe** is used primarily to indicate the omission of one or more letters or numbers in a contraction, to indicate possession in nouns and indefinite pronouns, and to denote time and money.

In Contractions

Although sometimes considered overly informal, contractions are accepted in today's business world by many communicators. However, use contractions sparingly. To indicate a contraction, insert an apostrophe in the space where the missing letter or letters belong.

don't (do not)	didn't (did not)	we'll (we will)
won't (will not)	doesn't (does not)	I'm (I am)
you're (you are)	aren't (are not)	hasn't (has not)
haven't (have not)	I'd (I had or I would)	shouldn't (should not)

To indicate an omission in a number, insert an apostrophe in the space where the missing number or numbers belong.

Martin graduated in '99. (1999)

The reunion had been planned for this year but was rescheduled for '02. (2002)

In Possession

Apostrophes are used in the possessive case in nouns.

The *boy's* suit needs pressing. (singular possessive)

The *boys'* suits need pressing. (plural possessive)

Add an apostrophe plus *s* to an indefinite pronoun, such as *someone* or *everyone,* to show possession. In compound words, add the apostrophe to the last word to indicate possession.

Someone's monitor has been left on.

The server came with the water pitcher and refilled *everyone's* glass.

My *brother-in-law's* education prepared him for his career as a lawyer.

In Time and Money

Add an apostrophe or apostrophe plus *s* to *dollar, day, week, month,* and *year* to indicate each word's relationship with the noun that follows it.

A *week's* salary is needed to pay the rent, but two *weeks'* salary is needed for the car payment and the insurance bill.

Buy ten *dollars'* worth of produce at the farmer's market.

Phoenix is only an *hour's* drive from here.

In Plurals

Add an apostrophe plus *s* to lowercase letters and to some abbreviations to form the plural.

We sometimes find it difficult to distinguish her *a's* from her *o's.*

Do not include so many *etc.'s* in your listings.

Section 4: Style

The basic rules for abbreviation, capitalization, and number usage may be called elements of writing style. Writers who are concerned about these three aspects of their business and personal writing will minimize the number of distractions in a message and bring consistency to their writing.

Abbreviations

An abbreviation is a shortened form of a word or a group of words. Shortened forms should be used sparingly in business letters because they sometimes obscure the writer's meaning and they present an informality that may offend the reader.

Shortened forms that apply to business writing include courtesy titles, *Jr.* and *Sr.* designations, and initials; professional titles and academic degrees; addresses and states; and names of companies, organizations, and government departments. In addition, abbreviations such as *A.M., P.M., Co., Inc., Corp.,* and *Ltd.* appear in business communications. Although many abbreviations are followed by periods, some abbreviations are not.

Courtesy Titles and Family Designations

Abbreviate a personal title that precedes a person's name.

Messrs. White and Rome represent our firm at the negotiations. (The title *Messrs.* is the plural of the title *Mr.*)

We will interview *Ms.* Violeta Ruiz. (*Ms.* is a title for a woman that omits reference to marital status; it does not have a full-length form. *Ms.* is not an abbreviation for *Miss* or *Mrs.*)

Abbreviate family designations, such as *Jr.* and *Sr.,* that appear after a person's name. Commas usually set off the family designations.

Carl Brockman, *Jr.,* is the first speaker on the program.

Sometimes people use an initial to indicate the first letter of their first name or middle name.

I. H. Roth uses his first and middle initials, not his first name.

Gladys *S.* Blackwood insists that her middle initial appear on all correspondence.

Professional Titles

Some professional titles are abbreviated in business writing.

Dr. Sergio Silva is an internist in private practice.

The company lawyer, Sonia Ramos, *Esq.,* has an office on the eleventh floor. (The title *Esq.* is set off with commas.)

Academic and Professional Degrees

Abbreviate academic and professional degrees that follow a person's name.

Luisa Barnes, *Ed.D.*   Letitia Anderson, *M.D.*

Steven Joffe, *Ph.D.*   Edwin Jeifreys, *D.D.S.*

Addresses

In business correspondence, do not abbreviate words such as *street, avenue, boulevard, road, north, south, east,* and *west.* However, do abbreviate compass designations after street names.

Our new address is 123 South Main Street.

The meeting will take place at 4 Spring Boulevard.

Our president lives at 1605 Bird Lane *NW.*

States

Two-letter postal abbreviations appear in all capital letters without punctuation. Use these abbreviations with the appropriate five- or nine-digit ZIP Codes in your correspondence.

Two-letter postal abbreviations are used in full addresses within the text of a letter but are not used when a state name appears in a sentence by itself.

Please send the information to Ms. Lucy Sands, 1004 Clemens Avenue, Roslyn, *PA* 19001-4356.

The cellular phone will have to be shipped directly to Pennsylvania.

Companies, Organizations, and Government Departments

You may abbreviate the names of some well-known companies and organizations if the institutions themselves use the abbreviations. This policy also applies to U.S. government departments.

ABC (American Broadcasting Company)	AMA (American Medical Association)
FBI (Federal Bureau of Investigation)	IBM (International Business Machines)

Company, Incorporated, Corporation, Limited

The abbreviations *Co., Inc., Corp.,* or *Ltd.* may be used in a company name if the company uses it as part of its official name.

Our accountant previously worked for Mobil Oil *Corp.*

The British firm Lourdes, *Ltd.,* distributes this product.

Do not abbreviate *company, incorporated, corporation,* or *limited* when it appears in lowercase letters in a sentence.

One firm has *incorporated* into the other.

She now owns her own software development *company.*

Expressions of Time

The abbreviations A.M. and P.M. may be used to designate time when they accompany numerals.

The next meeting is called for 8 *A.M.* on Tuesday, but I don't think I can make it at that time.

I stayed late at work—I was there until 8:30 *P.M.*

Familiar Business Abbreviations

Here are more examples of abbreviations, some of which tend to be used in informal business communications such as memos.

ASAP (as soon as possible)	CEO (chief executive officer)
C.O.D., c.o.d., COD (cash on delivery)	EST (Eastern standard time)
FYI (for your information)	GNP (gross national product)
P.O. Box (Post Office Box)	vs. (versus)

Miscellaneous Abbreviations

Some abbreviations used in statistical documents should not be used in business letters.

mfg. (manufacturing)	reg. (registered)
pd. (paid)	whlse. (wholesale)

Other abbreviations such as *No.* (number) and *Acct.* (account) may be used in technical documents and also in business correspondence when they are followed by numerals.

Please refer to check *No.* 654.

This information pertains to *Acct.* 6J843.

Units of Measure

The following abbreviations, though not acceptable in standard business correspondence, are widely used in technical documents.

mph (miles per hour)	in. (inches)
oz (ounce)	ft (feet)
lb (pound)	kg (kilogram)
cm (centimeter)	yd (yard)

Days and Months

In lists and business forms, the abbreviations for days and months are acceptable. They are not acceptable in general business correspondence.

Mon. (Monday)	Tues. (Tuesday)
Wed. (Wednesday)	Thurs. (Thursday)
Fri. (Friday)	Sat. (Saturday)
Sun. (Sunday)	Jan. (January)
Feb. (February)	Mar. (March)
Apr. (April)	Aug. (August)
Sept. (September)	Oct. (October)
Nov. (November)	Dec. (December)

Capitalization

A **capital letter** is used in the first word of a sentence, quotation, salutation, complimentary close, and outline. Further, capitalize titles of persons, written works, and proper nouns.

To Begin a Sentence and to Begin a Quotation

To indicate the beginning of a sentence, capitalize the first letter of the first word.

The tax collector is at the door.

When did this problem begin?

When a complete sentence that states a rule or emphasizes a statement is preceded by a colon, capitalize the first letter of the first word.

It is a perfect beach day: *The* sun is out, the breeze is warm, and the temperature is balmy.

Capitalize the first word of a direct quotation.

He said, *"Let* me help you perform the end-of-month audit."

Do not capitalize the second part of an interrupted direct quotation.

"We should congratulate Gail," James stated, *"on* her recent promotion."

In a Salutation and Complimentary Close

In a business letter, capitalize the first letter of the first word, the person's title, and the proper name in a salutation. Also capitalize the first word in a complimentary close.

Dear Ms. Morales	Yours truly	Sincerely

Titles of Persons

Capitalize professional titles that precede proper names.

Dr. Nancy Musi	*Governor* Louis Ramos

Capitalize professional titles that do not precede proper names but that refer to specific, well-known individuals.

The *President* is concerned with the uprising in Europe. (refers to the President of the United States)

Generally, do not capitalize a job title that follows a name.

Tanya Blank is the *marketing manager* for our company.

Titles of Written Works

Capitalize all words in report headings and the titles of books, magazines, newspapers, articles, movies, television programs, songs, poems, reports, and chapters except for the following:

- The articles *the, a,* or *an*
- Short conjunctions (three or fewer letters)
- Short prepositions—including the word *to* in an infinitive

U.S. News and World Report (magazine)

How to Succeed in Business Without Really Trying (movie)

Capitalize an article, a short conjunction, or a short preposition when it is the first or last word in a heading or title.

The Far Pavilions

As You Like it

Proper Nouns and *I*

Capitalize the names of specific people, places, and things. Also, always capitalize the pronoun *I* wherever it appears in a sentence.

Names of People.   Capitalize all proper names and nicknames.

Yoko Tanaka is a professor at the university.

Capitalize all titles of family members when the titles are used as proper nouns and are not preceded by a possessive noun or pronoun. Do not capitalize titles for family members, however, if they are preceded by a possessive noun or pronoun.

Let's visit *Grandmother* this morning.

Are you accompanying *Mother* and *Father* on the trip?

My *grandfather* started this business.

Names of Places.   Capitalize the names of streets, parks, buildings, bodies of water, cities, states, and countries.

He lives at 106 *Green Street.* (street)

I have not visited *Jackson, Mississippi.* (city and state)

Names of Things. Capitalize the proper names of historical events, companies, documents, organizations, institutions, government departments, periods in history, course titles, and automobiles.

She is a veteran of *World War II.* (historical event)

Walt is a systems analyst for the *General Electric Company.* (company)

Have you studied the *Constitution* of the United States? (document)

I graduate from *Furness Junior High School* in 1995. (institution)

Glenda enrolled in *Physics 103.* (course title)

Suzanne's new car is a *Ford Taurus.* (automobile)

Capitalize some adjectives that are derived from proper nouns.

Several excellent *Spanish* students are enrolled in my class.

Do I detect a *Bostonian* accent?

Capitalize most nouns that precede numbers or letters.

Flight 643	Chapter VI	Vitamin C
Chart 6J	Invoice 1675	Check 563

Exceptions to this guideline include *line, paragraph, verse, size, page,* and *note* when they precede numbers or letters.

---

line 4	paragraph b	verse 16-5
size 10	page 24	note 14

Commercial Products

Do not capitalize common nouns that refer to but are not part of a proper noun.

Bic pen	Maytag dishwasher	Breyers ice cream

Points of the Compass

Capitalize compass points (*north, south, east,* and *west*) when they refer to a geographical area or a definite region. Do not capitalize compass points, however, when they indicate a direction or a nonspecific location.

The corporate office is in the *South.*

Travel *east* to the river; then drive *south* to the farm.

Months, Days, and Holidays

Capitalize the months of the year, the days of the week, and the names of holidays.

In *December,* we are having a company party on a *Monday* or *Tuesday.*

Where are you having your *Thanksgiving* dinner—at your house or at your aunt's house?

Seasons of the Year

Do not capitalize *summer, fall (autumn), winter,* or *spring* unless a specific designation accompanies the season.

Our *Spring* Blockbuster Sale begins March 21.

Old Man *Winter* is just around the corner.

After this icy *winter,* we are looking forward to *spring.*

The leaves turn beautiful colors in the *fall.*

Nationalities, Races, Religions, and Languages

Capitalize the names of nationalities, races, religions, and languages.

Many *Mexican* tourists visit San Diego.

Black History Month attracts noted *African-American* speakers.

Students learned about *Judaism, Christianity,* and *Buddhism* in Comparative Religion 101.

Her job at the World Bank requires her to learn *French, German, Italian,* and *Russian.*

Deities

Capitalize nouns that refer to a deity.

God	Allah	Vishnu	Jehovah	Christ

Academic Degrees

Because academic degrees such as *Doctor of Philosophy* and *Doctor of Education* are capitalized, also capitalize their abbreviations.

Leonard, a consultant, has *Ed.D.* printed on his business stationery and business cards.

Number Expression

Because numbers are used in most business communications, writers must present them accurately and clearly to the reader. In correspondence, writers commonly refer to quantities, dollar amounts, percentages, dates, addresses, time, invoice numbers, and similar items. In reports and proposals, tables, charts, and graphs frequently accompany statistics. Numbers generally are written in word style in more formal and literary communications. Numeral style generally is used for routine business and personal writing.

Ten-and-Under / 11-and-Over Rule

Write quantities of ten and under in words.

Mail *three* copies of the proposal to us.

We rented a *four*-bedroom house in the mountains.

Write quantities of 11 and over in numerals.

Would you buy *25* yellow-lined writing tablets for them?

Charles received *16* inquiries the first day of the session.

One exception to the ten-and-under/11-and-over rule involves indefinite or approximate numbers. Use words to express these numbers in a sentence.

Several *thousand* people attended the concert.

Use words for numbers in a sentence that includes two or more related numbers all ten and under. If the numbers are all 11 and over, use numerals.

Daniel has written *five* articles, *one* anthology, and *three* textbook chapters.

Bring *15* copies of the report, *12* copies of the names, and *25* copies of the newsletter.

When two or more related numbers are included in a sentence—some of which are ten and under and some of which are 11 and over—use numerals for all numbers.

Our inventory list of paint shows *18* cans of white, *24* cans of eggshell, and *9* cans of light blue.

Consecutive Numbers

When two related numbers appear next to each other in a sentence, write the shorter number in words and the other in numerals.

Ms. Chan received *160 two*-inch samples.

Oscar brought *twelve 36*-inch pieces of wood to the classroom.

Consecutive Unrelated Numbers

If two unrelated numbers appear next to each other in a sentence, separate them with a comma to avoid confusion.

In *1997, 18* of the girls made the All-State Team.

Numbers to Begin Sentences

Use words to express a number at the beginning of a sentence. If a number is very long, rewrite the sentence.

Eighty-one questionnaires were returned.

A total of *5,243* employees applied for the new health-care benefit. (Rewrite the sentence to avoid spelling out *5,243* at the beginning of a sentence.)

Numbers in Dates

When the day follows the month, express the day in numerals.

Kim's presentation is March *26*.

Use ordinals *(rd* or *th)* with the day when the day precedes the month and when the month and the year are omitted. Write out the ordinal *(first)* or use numerals *(1st)* if the month is omitted.

Your letter of the *26th* arrived today.

Numbers in Addresses

In ordinary text, use numerals to express house and building numbers except for the number *one.*

One East Grayson Place   *6743* North Market Road

Use words for streets numbered first through tenth and numerals with ordinals for streets numbered 11th and over.

---

210 West *Fifth* Avenue   634 South *21st* Street

Numbers with Money

Write sums of one dollar or more in numerals preceded by a dollar sign ($).

Our total expenses are *$5.00* for the program and *$3.50* for a soda and a snack.

For sums less than one dollar, use numerals followed by the word *cents.*

The small tablet costs *75 cents.*

In a series of amounts in the same sentence, use a consistent format.

Budget *$57.00* for the book, *$3.50* for the pens, and *$0.99* for the paper clips.

Write approximate amounts in words.

A *few hundred* dollars should cover the cost of the trip.

Use a combination of words and numerals to express very large amounts of money.

They won a *$20 million* state lottery last Tuesday.

Numbers with Percentages, Decimals, and Fractions

Use numerals followed by the word *percent* to express percentages.

The department store is offering a *40 percent* discount.

Always express decimals in numerals. A zero placed at the left of a decimal point helps prevent the reader from overlooking the decimal point.

0.364   0.457   0.064

Express simple fractions in words.

We will need *three-quarters* of an hour to travel.

Express mixed numbers in either a fraction or a decimal unless they begin a sentence.

The job will take *2.5* hours to complete.

Two and one-half pounds of coffee are enough for the group.

Numbers with Time

Use numerals before *A.M.* and *P.M.*, but use words before *o'clock*. To express the time on the hour, omit the colon and two zeros.

One session begins at *9 A.M.;* the other begins at *1 P.M.*

A *ten o'clock* meeting could extend past noon.

Section 5: Documentation Styles

Whenever you use someone else's material, you must document your sources. Sources should be documented in a manner that makes it easy for readers to locate additional information about the material and in an acceptable citation style.

Types of Citations

Most source documentation falls within two categories: that which appears within the text and that which appears at the end of a document. The **in-text reference** provides immediate identification of the source of the material and makes it easy for the reader to locate more detailed information at the end of the report.

Reference lists, works cited lists, and **bibliographies** appear at the end of a document. All three lists contain the information necessary for the reader to locate the original source material. Reference lists include only information used to support the material discussed in the document. Works cited lists must include all the works cited within the report. They are sometimes labeled as Literature Cited, Works Consulted, or Bibliography. A bibliography is not as limited as a reference list. A bibliography may include related material, background information, and additional readings. It is also acceptable to annotate a bibliography.

Citation Styles

Three of the most widely used documentation styles are from the University of Chicago Press's *The Chicago Manual of Style,* the American Psychological Association (APA), and the Modern Language Association of America (MLA).

The Chicago Manual of Style

The Chicago Manual of Style is the reference guide for most publishers and editors. *The Chicago Manual of Style* supports both a documentary-note style and an author-date style. **Figure 1** on the next page shows examples of both styles. In the documentary-note system (see the Newspaper reference in **Figure 1**), the writer provides notes and retrieval information about the source information in a parenthetical note. This style can eliminate the need for a comprehensive bibliography.

FIGURE 1   References Using *The Chicago Manual of Style*

Book, one author

Logan, P. *Small Winners*. New York: Stallings Publishing Co., 1998.

Book, two authors

Parker, Erica M., and T. M. Gauge. *Winning Is Not the Only Thing*. Phoenix, AZ: McDougle Press. 1998.

Journal article

Jiang, J. J. "Systems success and communication." *The Journal of Computer Intelligence* 9 (1998): 112–117.

Magazine article

Johnson, K. "Losing and the loser psychology." *Successful Challenging,* 10 April 1998, 43–45.

Newspaper

This type of citation is commonly incorporated into the text of the report; for example,

An article in the *Modesto Daily Times* of December 21, 1998, describes recent weddings in the Modesto area. Common elements in these weddings included . . . .

Unpublished interview

Susanboy, Martha. Interview by author. Clever City, UT, 12 January 1996.

APA

The APA style is the style most often used in reports produced by individuals in the social and physical sciences. For in-text citations, the APA style calls for a simple author-date format *(Henson & Means, 2000).* An APA-style bibliography or reference list is alphabetized by the author's last name. **Figure 2** on the next page shows the correct presentation of references using the APA style.

MLA

The MLA style is the standard for many writers in business, industry, government, and the media. In the MLA style, in-text citations refer the reader to a comprehensive works cited list at the end of the document. The format of the in-text citation is author-page *(Henson 365).* **Figure 3** on page 319 shows acceptable reference format using the MLA style.

FIGURE 2   References Using the APA Style

Reference Type	Reference Format
Annual Report	Willamette Company, Incorporated. (2000). *2000 Annual Report.* Seattle, WA: The Willamette Company, Incorporated.
Book, one author	Logan, P. (1998). *Small Winners.* New York: Stallings Publishing Co.
Book, two authors	Parker, Erica M., and T. M. Gauge. (1998). *Winning Is Not the Only Thing.* Phoenix, AZ: McDougle Press.
Book, edited	David, Gill A. (Ed.). (1999). *The Horse that Won the World.* Kansas City, MO: Lopes and Kinner Publishing.
Brochure	Collision Center. (2000). *Accidents Do Happen.* [Brochure]. Ruston, LA: Louisiana's Collision Center.
CD-ROM encyclopedia article, one author	Lee, Tyler (1996). Filing Systems. *Fileproof '99* [CD-ROM]. Silicon Valley, CA: FoolProof Systems, Inc.
Encyclopedia article, one author	Callens, Elizabeth. (1999). Database systems. *The Computer's Users Encyclopedia.* Dallas, TX: Automated Press.
Film, videotape, or audiotape	*Successful Computer System Projects.* (1999). [Film]. Atlanta, GA: Systems Development Resource Center.
Government publication	U.S. Department of Defense. (2000). *The Cost of the B-1 Bomber.* Washington, DC: National Press, Inc.
Internet, Web	Combining ethics and your travel. (1999). *Ethnic-o-Travel.* [Online]. Available: (http://www.travelsites.com/dogood.htm). Cited 1999 May 13.
Interview	Susanboy, Martha, professor, Clever City State. (1996, January 12). Interview by author. Clever City, UT.
Journal article	Jiang, J. J. (1998). Systems success and communication. *The Journal of Computer Intelligence, 9,* 112–117.
Magazine article	Johnson, K. (1998, April 10). Losing and the loser psychology. *Successful Challenging 45,* 43–45.
Newspaper article, no author	"Is the weather really cyclical?" (1998, December 28). *Ruston Daily Journal,* B-7.
Newspaper article, one author	Marks, Amy. (1998, December 21). "Successful Weddings in Modesto." *Modesto Daily Times,* C-12.
Online newspaper	Adams, B. M. (1999, February 10). "The exciting international lawyer." [Online]. *Lawyers Journal 34,* 23–26. Available: (http: www.alajournal.com/realworld.htm).

FIGURE 3   References Using the MLA Style

Reference Type	Reference Format
Annual Report	Willamette Company, Incorporated. *2000 Annual Report*. Seattle, WA: The Willamette Company, Incorporated.
Book, one author	Logan, P. *Small Winners*. New York: Stallings Publishing Co., 1998.
Book, two authors	Parker, Erica M., and T. M. Gauge. *Winning Is Not the Only Thing*. Phoenix, AZ: McDougle Press, 1998.
Book, edited	David, Gill A., ed. *The Horse that Won the World*. Kansas City, MO: Lopes and Kinner Publishing, 1999.
Brochure	Collision Center. *Accidents Do Happen*. Ruston, LA: Louisiana's Collision Center, 2000.
Encyclopedia article, one author	Callens, Elizabeth. "Database systems." *The Computer's Users Encyclopedia*. 1999 ed.
Film, videotape, or audiotape	*Successful Computer System Projects*. Film. Atlanta, GA: Systems Development Resource Center, 1999.
Government publication	U.S. Department of Defense. *The Cost of the B-1 Bomber*. Washington, DC: National Press, Inc.
Internet, Web	"Combining Ethics and Your Travel." *Ethnic-o-Travel*. 1999. 4 Mar. 1999. <http://www.travelsites.com/dogood.htm>.
Interview	Susanboy, Martha. Personal Interview. 12 Jan. 1999.
Journal article	"Systems Success and Communication." *The Journal of Computer Intelligence* 9 (1998): 112–117.
Magazine article	Johnson, K. "Losing and the loser psychology." *Successful Challenging* 15 Aug. 1999: 43–45.
Newspaper article, no author	"Is the Weather Really Cyclical?" *Ruston Daily Journal* 28 Dec. 1998: B-7.
Newspaper article, one author	Marks, Amy. "Successful Weddings in Modesto." *Modesto Daily Times* 21 Dec. 1998: C-12.

INDEX